HELD
HOSTAGE

NEGOTIATING LIFE AND DEATH FOR THE LAS VEGAS POLICE DEPARTMENT

DENNIS FLYNN

WILDBLUE
PRESS

WildBluePress.com

HELD HOSTAGE published by:
WILDBLUE PRESS
P.O. Box 102440
Denver, Colorado 80250

WILDBLUE PRESS is registered at the U.S. Patent and Trademark Offices.

ISBN 978-1-942266-08-2 Trade Paperback

ISBN 978-1-947290-07-5 eBook

Interior Formatting/Book Cover Design by Elijah Toten
www.totencreative.com

HELD HOSTAGE TESTIMONIALS

"A riveting true life account of his work as a police crisis negotiator in rough and tumble Las Vegas. This book takes the reader into a specialized world that few will ever experience; a world of immense pressure, critical decision making, and uncertain outcomes."

Gary W. Noesner

Chief, FBI Crisis Negotiation Unit

Author of *Stalling For Time: My Life as an FBI Hostage Negotiator*

"From a negotiator with a heart as big as the city he served, Flynn tells compelling yet humble stories of Sin City's most harrowing police standoffs. His refreshingly candid revelations of the lessons learned remind us all of the complex, emotional and sometimes heartbreaking nature of this business. The analyses alone are worth the price of the book and should be mandatory reading for every crisis negotiation and tactical team leader."

Deb McMahon, owner, Crisis Systems Management, a crisis/hostage negotiation training and consulting company as well as author of *Into the Chaos: Crisis Negotiation Field Manual*

HELD HOSTAGE

CONTENTS

Case photos can be found at the end of each chapter.

PROLOGUE

I started my career with the Las Vegas Metropolitan Police Department in September, 1985. I chose LVMPD as they are the seventh largest police department in the United States and, with over 4,000 employees, offered plenty of room for advancement. Las Vegas is home to over two million people and is host to 43 million visitors every year. There is a lot of work to keep us busy, just as there was back then.

As with nearly all other police agencies, we were assigned to patrol after graduation from the academy and completion of field training. Working patrol offered a wide variety of calls which we were dispatched to every day. It also allowed us to hone our policing skills, to find out what works for us and what does not. Not being a very big guy, I had to learn quickly how to talk with people. I mistakenly thought all the defensive tactics they taught us in the police academy would surely allow me to take down any person I could encounter on the street. Wrong. After getting my butt handed to me more than a few times, learning to defuse situations through talking became much easier than always trying to go hands on with someone.

I found when I watched not only what I said, but even more importantly how I said it, I had more success talking with suspects. I built on those skills and started listening to what the suspect was saying, not just talking over them. While I thought I had discovered something new, one of the more senior officers laughed at my discovery and explained the art of active listening to me. Using some of the skills of active listening he showed me, coupled with being cognizant of my body language when I was both listening and talking with suspects, I found the suspects that I used to try and force into submission would willingly go with me. Because of this approach, not only would they go willingly, it became easier for suspects to talk with me which lead to them making more admissions during my interrogations.

I soon found out what many of the senior guys already knew; treat people, regardless of who they are, fairly and with dignity, and the job becomes much easier. I guess it was a bit of a "rite of passage", to get out of the police academy and wear a badge that felt like it weighed ten pounds. I believed I was "Johnny Law" and thought people would have to do whatever we tell them to do just because we have that big old badge on our chest which forces them to submit to our authority. It took me getting a few raps in the face to learn how wrong I was.

As I became better at defusing situations verbally and increased the amount of confessions I was able to obtain, I became drawn towards the investigative side of police work. In 1990, I was fortunate to be selected for my first plain clothes assignment, working on a street-crime type squad, which allowed me to continue working on my interview and interrogation skills, yet still work in the field so as not to miss the excitement of "in progress" type calls.

I truly loved my job! Not only did we go to some of the most "hot" calls, but we helped track down the suspect, build our case on them, and try to get them to confess. It didn't seem like it could get any better. That was until I paid attention to the guys who rolled on the calls where we located an armed suspect who barricaded in a structure and refused to come out. This team of cops and SWAT officers as I would later learn, would respond with cool guns and equipment, and later they would hand over the suspect to us. Many of these men were large in stature and the ones who were not had incredible talent. It looked like the only position available to me might be "Doggy Door Entryman". But as I watched more, I saw there was another group assigned to them, a team that seemed to work a little bit behind the scenes.

In the early 1990s, our agency called this group the Hostage Negotiation Team (HNT). Although I only had about seven years on the job, I knew there were not that many "hostage" incidents every year so how could they have an entire team dedicated to this? I became curious and wanted to see what went on behind the scenes and learn more.

Although they were called the HNT, I learned they only responded to approximately one or two "true" hostage situations each year. The more I inquired, the more my eyes were opened on not only what this team did, but how many lives they helped save every year.

During the early 1990s, the LVMPD HNT was actually made up of two teams with four people on each team. One team would be on-call during the even numbered months and the other during the odd numbered months. And although they only responded to one or two hostage incidents per year, which I learned was about average nationwide, they actually responded to 30-40 events each year involving barricaded subjects or suicidal individuals. Used in conjunction with the SWAT team, the HNT would try and make contact and convince the person to come out.

I learned that the makeup on each of the HNT teams consisted of a primary negotiator, a secondary negotiator, a third person who gathered intelligence on the subject, and the fourth person who acted as the team leader. I saw what they did and I wanted in.

LVMPD's Hostage Negotiation Team was then and remains today a part-time team. It is an ancillary assignment, done in conjunction with a team member's primary assignment. The team members, including the team leaders, are assigned to various places throughout the agency, and work their normal jobs. When an incident occurs requiring an HNT response, the on-call team is requested and they fall under the SWAT umbrella, reporting to the SWAT Commander, and responding to the incident. And for LVMPD, HNT only responds with SWAT, never by themselves. Interestingly, the HNT is rank neutral. Aside from each team's designated team leader, the team members can be officers, detectives, sergeants, and lieutenants but when they arrive on an HNT incident, with the exception of the team leader, each team member's voice is equal. Their rank plays no role.

In 1992, I sought out the SWAT Commander who, along with the two Team Leaders, had a say as to who was allowed to attend the HNT school, and explained my desire to attend the next school. Because the turnover on the team is exceptionally low the HNT school was only taught once every 2-3 years. I explained to the SWAT Commander all that I had achieved and my ability to talk with people.

The SWAT Commander seemed less impressed with my talking abilities and more concerned with my age and what life experiences I had. As I awkwardly tried to fill in pauses in the conversation with all I had accomplished in my relatively short police experience, the SWAT Commander began to tout the tenure of some of the current team members. Surely, I explained, they all had to have started somewhere and all I needed was my chance to show what a great talker I was. Probably because he took some pity on me, and maybe to teach me a valuable lesson, the SWAT Commander said he would let me attend the next HNT course, but I would not be considered for selection for the team. I wondered why he would make such a decision, but I would soon learn.

I attended my first HNT school in 1994. I showed up for the first day of the week-long class, ready to impress everyone, especially the SWAT Commander, with all my abilities. He had no idea how many people I had interviewed and got to confess. Surely after he witnessed me spin my yarn, he would reconsider his decision. As the class introductions began, it was clear I was the youngest in the class. I had barely a lick of the experience others in the class had. But I remained committed. After the opening class on the first day, it was like being hit with a brick. A good negotiator was not a good talker; the real skill set was being a good listener. Someone who could empathize with the position the person in crisis was in. I suddenly understood the wisdom of the SWAT Commander.

I sat in class and applied myself the very best I could but it was extremely evident I was in over my head. Others in the class, who had more tenure and were more mature, grasped the concepts being taught better and could relate with many of the situations people in crisis would go through. I was in my mid-20s, not married, no kids. What the hell did I know about the stress of divorce? I struggled as I tried to talk my way through exercises, failing to apply the active listening concepts we had just been taught. The class ended horribly for me. I was embarrassed at how poorly I had done. I had no one else to blame but myself as I thought I knew better and was eager to show everyone how well I would do.

A few weeks later, the SWAT Commander reached out to me and invited me to lunch. I knew I had to accept his invitation but I was worried about the "I told you so" tongue lashing I would get. When I arrived for the lunch date, I got anything but. I sat with a kind man who said he was worried about even letting me attend the class as he knew I was not ready. As the old saying goes, "When the student is ready, the teacher will appear". Here he was again in front of me, giving me guidance that I was too ignorant to previously see. I did not want to make the same mistake twice.

Our lunch turned into a four-hour counseling session. The SWAT Commander asked questions to gauge where he believed I needed the most work and he provided me with tremendous guidance and feedback. He told me of several books, some dealing with negotiations, others to help with active listening skills, and a few which just required deep thought, that would help me along in my journey. He set-up introductions with a few current and past team members so I could learn even more.

Over the course of the next three years, I continued to work hard at my primary job but I took advantage of the guidance which had been provided to me. I read the books suggested. Some of them twice. I met with HNT members and picked their brains. I even volunteered at some of their training exercises, often times role-playing as the suspect on the phone and listening intently to what they said to persuade me to surrender. Being on the other end of the phone, role-playing for them was extremely valuable as I saw for myself how these professionals truly worked. And how they talked, or more importantly how they allowed me to 'vent' as the suspect during these training exercises, taught me some invaluable lessons.

In mid-1997, LVMPD hosted another HNT school and I again applied. Because of the importance of this class and the one-on-one time needed during scenarios, the class size is limited and letters of interest must be submitted. The HNT would review all applicants and select those who they felt would be the most promising. I learned later that I had been 'gifted' a spot in the previous class by the SWAT Commander as again, with my limited experience, I would have never made the selection process.

I hoped my eagerness to learn what the HNT members saw when I volunteered for their training exercises helped and I was fortunate enough to be selected. I vowed to learn from past mistakes and use the two ears I was given. What a difference three years of study, experience, and being humbled can make. Although I was familiar with the course material, it was like a new experience. I seemed to grasp the concepts so much better this second time around. It probably did not hurt to have had three years of experience of watching senior team members use the techniques for hours on end during the training.

The preparation paid off. At the end of this second class, I was selected to the HNT. It was only temporary though as I had to prove myself to be given a permanent spot. The timing was perfect. During the early part of 1998, we seemed to experience an influx of calls requiring our services. These calls ran the gamut; suicidal people, trapped bad guys, and the occasional hostage situation. As the new guy, I had the chance to fill several of the team spots but still did not have enough experience to get on the phone with the suspect as the primary negotiator.

On most teams, new team members arrive on events and help develop intelligence, conduct interviews with parties involved, and even listens to conversation the negotiator talking on the phone is having with the suspect. After gaining additional experience, the new team member is transitioned into being allowed to talk on the phone, under the wing of a senior team member, on all types of calls, except actual hostage situations. True hostage situations are rare and especially since at least one innocent person's life is hanging in the balance, this is no place for an inexperienced negotiator to start. The newer negotiators tend to gain their experience with suicidal subjects and barricaded suspects.

In 1999, I was promoted by the agency to the rank of Sergeant, but this had no effect on the HNT as it is rank neutral. Truth is, even though I was a Sergeant I still had less than two years of experience on the HNT and most of the team members had more experience so their opinions tended to carry more weight. It was also around this time that the Team Leader examined what it was that our team truly did and that was dealing with people in crisis. Less than 5% of calls the team responded to were actual hostage situations. While the title of Hostage Negotiation Team certainly sounded sexier, our team name changed to reflect what we truly were; the Crisis Negotiation Team (CNT).

While I'm certain the changing of the team name to CNT was not the cause, it was also during this same time frame that the workload began to increase. We were averaging 50-70 callouts per year and added two more people to each team to help. With the volume of calls we were handling increasing, it only took a few years before each person on the team, including myself, became fairly proficient in the various team roles. Each of the roles will be discussed in the next chapter. Because of the experience we were gaining, we had the opportunity to share our success stories, and even more importantly the lessons we learned from the mistakes we made, with surrounding agencies. Since LVMPD is a large agency, we had many examples to draw from. We had a sniper who shot an officer and shut down a city block after he took a hostage. We had a jumper on top of Hoover Dam and another on top of the Stratosphere Tower, the largest observation tower in the United States and the tallest structure west of the Mississippi River. We even had a suspect who shot two police officers, took a hostage, and demanded that he talk to his famous rapper brother-in-law before he would consider surrendering.

As I was gaining experience I was able to attend several negotiation conferences and training seminars to see what other agencies were doing and how they were doing it. One of the most impressive additions to a CNT, one that several other agencies had that we lacked, was a psych doctor. These teams had either a psychologist or psychiatrist assigned to their team, some paid and others received the doctor's services for free. While these doctors did not negotiate they did offer their professional advice. I brought this idea back to our team where it was met with mixed results. Some of the more senior members, who had been on the team for many years, explained how they had operated without a doctor since the team was formed in 1979 and did not see a need for some 'shrink' to tell us how to do our job. Most on the team felt that as long as we had the right doctor, someone who would respond to the events and offer tips when what we were doing was ineffective, it would be a great addition. The SWAT Commander, who made the ultimate decision, listened to both sides and decided we would try one of the psych doctors the agency used for pre-employment and see how it went. It was a huge success. Not only could the doctor listen to the person in crisis and explain the different personality disorders we likely were dealing with, but he offered suggestions on how we might be successful by using various approaches.

In 2003, our CNT began to go through some changes. Several people were promoted and a few retired. That forced some of us to move up and take on additional responsibilities. Our Team Leader, a wonderful woman with incredible talent not only as a negotiator but as a leader, was promoted in the agency and she had to leave the team. A new Team Leader was selected and I was honored to be chosen as the Assistant Team Leader. While I was fortunate to have been deployed on several hundred callouts and had the tutelage of talented negotiators and the team leader, I also knew six years of experience was not a lot of time in the negotiations world and I knew the tremendous amount of responsibility this role would require.

For the next two years I worked hand-in-glove with the new leader and the SWAT Commander to understand exactly what they wanted done on negotiation callouts and in what order. I also used my seven years of experience as a sergeant with the agency to help me with the leadership portion this role required, as it was critically important to make sure everyone was working together. As the Assistant Team Leader I really had the best of both worlds; I had the chance to help lead the team, make assignments, and run incidents in the Team Leader's absence but I also got to fill in and still negotiate when we were short-handed or when the Team Leader wanted to use my experience in a particular role at an event.

In 2005, the Team Leader was offered the opportunity to work for the police union which represented the agency's supervisors. It was an honor for him to get one of the only two positions for this assignment but it also meant he would have to leave the CNT. He took the new job and the SWAT Commander elevated me to the Team Leader position. To say I was humbled is a severe understatement. But again I was fortunate enough to have two years of experience as an

Assistant Team Leader with over 150 callouts to draw from during that time.

From 2005 through 2015, I had the honor to serve as the Team Leader. It was an incredible time but we were also incredibly busy. We had been averaging approximately 75 callouts per year and at times we were pushing 90+ CNT callouts per year.

Due to the increased number of callouts we were experiencing, the SWAT Commander allowed me to increase the number of negotiators on each team from 5 to 6, not including the team leader position. This may not sound like a lot but in essence, it was two more bodies to assist and on these events it is real easy to run short on bodies to accomplish all the tasks that need to be covered. And on many of these events we needed every body we had, and then some.

The CNT also grew in another way. Through the forward thinking of the SWAT Commander, a Search Warrant Officer was added to each team. This person would be an expert at search and seizure as well as be proficient at obtaining telephonic search warrants. We would no longer work under a 'consent to search' signed by a family member who sometimes would later sue the agency if their house was tear-gassed, citing they did not understand what they signed. Having a search warrant officer also prevented us from having to wait for the specific detective unit to be requested, respond, and conduct their investigation while we all waited for the search warrant. Although not always necessary having a search warrant in hand before SWAT breaks windows or employs other intrusive measures, helps indemnify the agency if we are later sued. Helping legally protect our officers and agency on the front end is also a smart decision.

During my ten years as Team Leader we responded to nearly every type of incident imaginable; from the downright comical to the completely heartbreaking. The people who made up the CNT were an incredible group who always gave each incident everything they had.

It was also a turbulent ten years. During those ten years, the position of SWAT Commander changed four times. We went from a SWAT Commander who used the CNT to its greatest potential to a SWAT Commander who seemed to use the team as a checkbox, claiming their brief use was ineffective so proceeded with a tactical resolution. It is not a knock on the latter SWAT Commander rather than a difference of opinion on the capabilities of the team and how they could both be best utilized, even on the same mission. Putting too much credence in either discipline can eventually become detrimental. The future SWAT Commanders were a balance of the two.

In the following chapters are summaries of incidents we have responded to. They are laid out how they occurred and what was done to resolve them. Some of the incidents had wonderful endings while others did not but through all of them, there are lessons to be learned, both good and bad.

Hopefully as you read through each of these incidents, you will be able to use some of what we did and add them to your 'bag of tricks'. In other incidents, I pray you will learn from some of the mistakes we made so you will not have to go through some of the same painful lessons.

In the end, I hope that learning from some of our experiences makes you a better negotiator or supervisor.

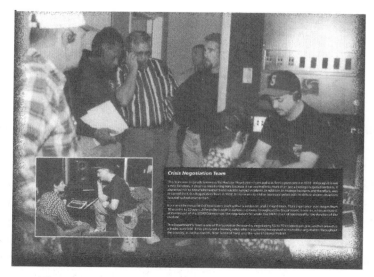

This was a picture of me, taken by an unknown LVMPD photographer and placed on a LVMPD calendar and distributed throughout the police department. It shows me as I speak on the phone during an actual hostage negotiation. Also shown is Rod Jett, the then SWAT Commander and other members of the CNT Team.

CHAPTER 1

SWAT OFFICER SHOT

Denise Gianninoto was a young 32-year-old woman who was living a happy life. She had a good job, owned her own home, had strong family values, and was dating a man, Emit Rice aged 35, who made her feel special. She was aware Emit had made some mistakes earlier in life, one of which was a burglary conviction which made him a convicted felon, but the man she knew seemed to have learned from these mistakes and had changed. She knew he had been previously married and had a six-year-old daughter but Emit's ex-wife and daughter lived in Arizona so he saw very little of his daughter. He had a strong work ethic and was employed as a union carpenter, which paid well. After nearly a year of dating, Denise decided in September, 2000 to take their relationship to the next level and asked Emit to move in with her.

Denise's home was located in the 3700 block of South Torrey Pines, near the area of West Flamingo and Rainbow, in southwest Las Vegas. It was a nice two-story residence with several bedrooms, offering them room to grow. But soon after Emit moved in, she began to see another side of him that made her concerned.

Denise discovered Emit owned a Smith & Wesson 9mm semi-automatic pistol. He had shared with her that he was a convicted felon so Denise knew he was not allowed to possess a firearm. When she confronted him about it, he admitted he knew he wasn't allowed to own one but said he needed a gun for protection. Denise explained she already owned a Colt .380 semi-auto pistol and believed one gun in the house would be sufficient. Emit would get angry and not want to discuss the firearm issue anymore.

In addition to Emit's gun, Denise made another discovery which caused her even more concern. Although Emit had never exhibited it prior to moving in, soon after they began to live together Emit became very possessive over her. At first his possessiveness seemed almost romantic but it increased to alarming levels. He would question her whereabouts and constantly call her at work to see what she was doing and especially check to see if she was meeting with anyone. Denise confronted Emit several times about this and it would escalate into loud arguments. It became so bad that Denise even discussed ending their relationship, which only created further arguments that ended in Emit apologizing and Denise conceding and agreeing to continue trying.

Unfortunately, bad grew to worse. Emit started coming home and drinking every day after work. He would drink beer from the time he came home until he went to bed. His drinking became another source of arguments between the two. Then, in January 2001, Emit was laid off from his union worker job. This caused him to enter a state of depression which only made the drinking worse. Denise explained the arguments between them increased, as did her desire to end the relationship. Emit promised to seek help, eventually seeing a doctor who prescribed him Paxil to aid with his depression.

Denise said she did her best to remain supportive of Emit, but his possessiveness, moodiness, and drinking continued to the point that she needed help. In February, 2001, she called her cousin, 29 year old Marissa Velenta, and asked her to move in with them. Denise used Marissa as someone she could vent to and ask advice. Marissa's presence seemed to only further aggravate Emit as he believed Marissa had moved in to try and split Denise and him apart. He began to argue with Marissa, blaming her for his relationship problems with Denise. Denise would have to intervene, making Emit feel his girlfriend would always take her cousin's side, which would only add to the stress.

In mid-March, 2001, the tension between Emit versus Denise and Marissa became so intense that during an argument with Denise over Emit's mistreatment of Marissa, Denise fled from her own home, fearing Emit would hurt her. Emit chased after Denise, catching her in a neighbor's front yard and knocked her to the ground. Other than the initial knock down, Emit did not punch or strike her. He just pinned Denise to the ground to allow him to finish yelling and making his point, something he did not see any harm in. After eight months of living together, Denise realized their relationship had crumbled past the point of repair and sought Marissa's advice on how she could end it. Little did Denise know that the relationship would deteriorate even further and much sooner than she anticipated.

On April 6, 2001, at approximately 9:30 p.m., Denise and Marissa were at the house, each enjoying a glass of wine on the back patio while waiting for the kitchen floor, which they had just mopped, to finish drying. Emit had gone out earlier in the evening for a night of drinking. When he returned home and walked inside, he was carrying a six pack of beer and found Denise and Marissa out back enjoying their evening. Emit went out back and an argument immediately ensued between him and the two women.

Emit turned his attention towards Marissa, again blaming her for his problems with Denise. His tone grew more intense, adding profane language directed at the younger cousin. Denise had heard enough and intervened, insisting Emit leave the house. Upon being ordered out of the home, Emit became violent and Denise was frightened. She yelled for Marissa to call 911 for help then tried to run away.

Marissa took the cordless telephone and ran into the backyard to call 911. Emit pursued Denise, catching her before she was able to flee the home. He dragged her back into the living room area and retrieved his Smith and Wesson 9mm pistol from the sofa but Denise was able to break free. She ran from the house to the next-door neighbor's home seeking refuge. Emit, chasing her with a pistol in one hand and the six pack of beer he had originally walked into the home with, caught Denise in the neighbor's front yard. He grabbed her by the hair, dragged her across the yard, then back into their own garage, still somehow holding onto both the gun and the beer.

As Marissa was on the phone with the 911 dispatcher, still hiding in the backyard, she was unaware that Emit had retrieved his pistol. She also did not know the two had run from the residence, that Emit had caught Denise, and that he was in the process of dragging her back to the garage. The dispatcher took the information Marissa supplied and the event was dispatched as a violent family disturbance. A patrol sergeant, with nearly 30 years of experience, was nearby when the call was dispatched and arrived only minutes after the call was dispatched.

As the patrol sergeant arrived he saw both Emit and Denise in the garage area. He could see Emit was holding on to Denise but did not see the gun. The sergeant, although not using the soundest tactical approach, pulled his marked patrol car into the driveway of the home and using his public address (PA) system, ordered the couple to exit the garage and walk over to his car. When Emit heard the order, he showed the sergeant his middle finger and closed the garage door as additional patrol cars began to arrive.

The patrol sergeant, upset over Emit's blatant disrespect of authority, ordered the dispatcher to recall the residence and instruct the couple to exit the home. The dispatcher complied with his request and recalled the phone number which had been used to call 911. When the phone rang, Marissa, who was still hiding in the backyard, chose not to answer which allowed Emit to answer. The dispatcher, as instructed, told Emit to exit the home. Emit was incensed and yelled to the police dispatcher that he had a gun, which the dispatcher promptly updated over the radio. The seasoned police sergeant, upon hearing the update, asked the police dispatcher to relay to Emit that the police had guns as well and to again order the occupants out. Emit could hear this radio broadcast over the telephone and informed the dispatcher with the game-changing update; he also had a hostage.

Officers went into the backyard and rescued Marissa where she had been hiding. Upon hearing the officers in the backyard, Emit yelled out, "Get the fuck away from here! I've got a gun and a hostage! I got the gun pointed at her fucking chest!"

At 9:53 p.m., after realizing how the incident had rapidly escalated, the patrol sergeant requested SWAT and Crisis Negotiators respond to the scene. While waiting for these assets to arrive, the police dispatcher was again asked to call into the residence. Emit again answered the phone call, warning the dispatcher to have police stay away. He reiterated that he was armed and only referred to Denise as "his hostage". Rather than rely on updates from the dispatcher, another patrol sergeant arrived and telephoned Emit. After a brief conversation between Emit and the second patrol sergeant, the telephone went dead. Future calls into the residence showed the phone number being out of service and no one knew why.

At approximately 10:14 p.m., just 21 minutes after their request, SWAT and Crisis Negotiators began to arrive. The first few arriving SWAT officers were ordered to "crisis dress" by their SWAT sergeant, who had arrived with them.

When SWAT officers arrive on an incident, they methodically don all of their protective equipment and receive deployment instructions. During a "crisis dress," the first few arriving officers grab just the bare essentials; a ballistic helmet and vest, along with their rifle, then deploy. After other team members arrive, these initial SWAT officers can go back and put on their remaining equipment. The "crisis dress" is typically used only on a confirmed hostage incident and is done should an emergency entry be necessary.

Having the first few SWAT officers equipped with the sheer basics allows for an immediate entry should the hostage suddenly be in a life-threatening situation; on the verge of being killed.

As negotiators began to arrive and obtained the briefing on the incident, the SWAT sergeant and four SWAT officers had "crisis dressed" and found the rear sliding glass door would be their immediate entry point until additional team members arrived and other primary entry points were considered.

During the negotiator briefing we learned the Crisis Negotiation Team Leader had been monitoring the event over the police radio and knew it had developed into a confirmed hostage incident. He contacted the local phone company and requested Emit's home telephone line be taken down, to prevent Emit from calling anyone or allowing for friends/family/media from calling in to him. While cell phones existed in 2001, they were not nearly as prevalent as they are today and while unknown to us at that time, neither Emit nor Denise had one.

Our team protocol dictated action by team members should only occur after arrival on scene, briefed on the situation, and authorized by the SWAT Commander. The reasons for this mandate are obvious. While the Team Leader had the best of intentions, it disrupted the conversation the on-scene sergeant was having with Emit.

While acknowledging this mistake, the relationship with the local phone company cannot be overstated. Without the phone companies' assistance, the suspect has the ability to make whatever outgoing calls he chooses from a traditional landline telephone. Should he be talking to someone else, negotiators have no way of talking to him, other than the "beep" indicating an incoming call should the suspect's phone be equipped with a "call-waiting" option.

By having a local phone company representative, ideally one who responds to the scene, negotiators can have the suspect's phone line taken down and a new phone number issued which only the negotiators have access to. Additionally, the suspect's phone can be set up so when he picks up his phone, the negotiator phone rings; he can't make any other outbound calls, forcing him to talk to negotiators. This is only if he does not have a cell phone. Should the suspect have a home phone and cell phone, negotiators have options available which include contacting the cell phone carrier and having the suspect's cell phone service suspended, forcing him to use the home phone. These are options and relationships which negotiation teams should explore prior to an event occurring.

Back at the negotiator briefing, intelligence on the incident was being developed, negotiator assignments were being made, and the phone company was being contacted to expedite restoring Emit's phone service. Just then, the unexpected occurred. Several gunshots were heard emanating from inside Denise's residence.

The SWAT sergeant on-scene, fearing the gunfire was Emit murdering Denise, ordered a "crisis entry". One SWAT officer smashed the rear sliding glass door and the four SWAT officers, along with the SWAT sergeant, made entry into the downstairs living room area. The SWAT officers quickly cleared the downstairs, trying to locate where the gunfire had come from. The lead SWAT officer, Officer Mark Fowler, not finding the suspect downstairs, quickly moved to the staircase area and prepared to ascend upstairs.

SWAT Officer Fowler posted on the staircase, waiting as his partner, SWAT Officer Robert "Jess" Kegley, was coming up from behind to join him. Emit suddenly emerged at the top of the staircase and began firing down towards the officers. One of Emit's initial 9mm rounds found its mark, striking Officer Fowler's left femur. The bullet's impact was so violent, it shattered the femur and caused Officer Fowler's left foot to rotate 180 degrees, pointing towards the rear. As Officer Fowler began to fall, he fired four rounds from his Hecker and Koch, MP-5 Sub Machine Gun while simultaneously yelling out that he had been hit by the suspect's gunfire.

Officer Fowler's partner, Officer Kegley, arrived during the firefight and saw Emit on the landing at the top of the stairs. He brought his MP-5 up and began to fire at Emit but his first round missed and his weapon then jammed. He quickly transitioned to his handgun but as he brought the pistol up, Emit had disappeared from the landing.

While two SWAT officers held their position, covering the staircase from the ground floor, two others conducted a "downed officer rescue" and extracted Officer Fowler from the residence where he was transported to the hospital for emergency care.

Emit had retreated from the staircase landing area into a bedroom where he held Denise. Obviously pumped up and full of adrenaline from the gunfight, Emit yelled down to the SWAT officers, "Fuck you! Come up here and shoot me motherfucker! I got the gun pointed at her chest. I'll kill the bitch!" Even though Denise remained a hostage, after being involved in a gunfight and having a fellow officer shot, it was reported the SWAT officers yelled back some choice statements of their own.

While the phone representative was attempting to reconnect Emit's home phone telephone, communication efforts were turned over to the crisis negotiation team.

From a negotiator's perspective:

By definition, this incident was not a true hostage situation, however that did not matter to Denise. A hostage situation consists of a person being held against their will, being used by the suspect to fulfill a demand. This situation with Emit and Denise is often referred to as a "pseudo-hostage" as it lacks a demand from the suspect. The suspect didn't "take" this person in order to have a commitment fulfilled. "Pseudo-hostage" situations are usually domestic related and highly volatile. The suspect needs nothing from police, except often times wanting the police to leave. These events are of high risk of homicide followed by a suicide. It's embodies the old saying, "If I can't have you, no one will."

As imagined, the scene was chaotic. A woman was being held hostage, a gunfight had occurred, a SWAT officer had been shot, and the only source of communication had been severed.

While waiting for the telephone service to be restored, we had a negotiator go forward with SWAT officers in an armored vehicle to attempt communication over the armored vehicle's PA system.

Sergeant Mike Bunker, the most senior negotiator on the team at the time, was chosen as the primary negotiator, due to his experience. I was assigned to coordinate all of the intelligence on the incident and later filled in as the secondary negotiator.

As SWAT officers were filling in and beefing up their foothold on the bottom floor of the residence and in outer containment positions, the forward negotiator was asked to begin to try and contact Emit using the PA system. Emit could hear some of what the forward negotiator was broadcasting over the PA and SWAT officers inside the residence relayed some of the responses Emit yelled back. Interestingly, Emit specifically asked for a "throw-phone", not a commonly known item in 2001.

After what seemed like an eternity of Emit not having phone service, the phone company was finally able to reestablish the residential connection, yet block it from making any outbound calls. Mike made his first phone call into the home at 11:05 p.m. and spoke to Emit. Unfortunately, the introduction did not go well.

When Emit answered the phone, he was understandably hostile, taking out his frustrations on Mike for the home phone not working. Mike tried to explain to Emit how he had just arrived at the scene but Emit seemed intent on directing his anger at someone and Mike proved a convenient target. As he did his best to calm Emit down, Emit revealed part of his dark plans; he was upset over the house phone not previously working as he said he wanted to call his six year old daughter in Arizona and say goodbye. This showed Emit's intent on committing suicide but he made no mention of Denise, leaving us all to wonder if he had determined her fate as well. As Mike struggled to maintain a dialog over Emit's rants, Emit began to swear at Mike then slammed down the phone.

After a quick group think of possible different approaches and objections we may encounter, Mike called back a few minutes later. The phone rang incessantly until it was finally answered, this time by Denise. She was surprisingly calm. She spoke for less than fifteen seconds before Emit took the phone from her hands and took over the phone conversations. He continued to lash out at Mike, using profanities directed specifically at him, claiming he was talking down to him. When Mike attempted to apologize and continue the conversation, Emit again hung up the phone.

Emit would repeat this type of behavior, answering the phone and swearing at Mike before hanging up, for the next several phone calls. Before ending each call, Emit would scream at him, still accusing him of talking down to him. In hindsight, it would have been a better option to replace the primary negotiator at that point, even if Mike wasn't talking down to Emit, as in the end, all that matters is Emit's perception and we had an innocent third party life on the line. Instead of replacing Mike, the team leader believed since it was early in the negotiation, Emit was just releasing some of his frustration and was using Mike as the outlet, so decided we would press on.

At 11:19 p.m., Emit answered Mike's phone call and provided a chilling warning. Although still irate towards Mike, Emit made it clear that if the police tried to come up the stairs, he would "kill the hostage", choosing the word "hostage" instead of Denise. He further reiterated he wanted to call his daughter to say goodbye. Depersonalizing his girlfriend by referring to her only as "the hostage" and wanting to say goodbye to his daughter were obvious bad signs.

After again being hung up on, Mike again called back into the home and for the first time, Emit expressed his anger towards someone other than Mike. Emit began to explain his hatred toward Denise's cousin, Marissa, and believed the problems he was having with his girlfriend were due to Marissa meddling in their relationship. Just as it appeared Emit would keep his ire directed towards Marissa, Emit again took issue with how Mike was talking to him, causing him yet again to hang up the phone.

After hanging up at 11:30 p.m., Emit refused to answer subsequent phone calls from Mike, forcing them to be picked up by the answering machine. The SWAT officers inside the house could hear the upstairs telephone ringing so knew Emit could hear the phone, he was just choosing not to answer it. On a domestic situation like this, not keeping Emit on the phone, keeping him occupied but also trying to find a peaceful resolution, is dangerous.

We were only twenty-five minutes into Mike trying to talk with Emit and Emit was now refusing to answer the phone. The forward negotiator in the armored vehicle was asked to again try to contact Emit over the PA. For fifteen minutes, Mike called into the residence, only to be greeted by the answering machine while the forward negotiator continued speaking over the PA.

Speaking over the PA gets frustrating as there is often times no response and it's easy to run out of things to say. One of the phrases often used when trying to contact a barricaded subject over the PA is to ask the subject to flip a light on and off so we at least know they can hear us. This sometimes works on a barricaded person who we had yet to make contact with. This phrase is not advisable to use in this situation when Emit is angry, has already spoken with us, and appears to simply not want to talk. Unfortunately, that was the phrase used. Over and over again. "Emit, if you can hear me, please turn the light on or off so we know you're ok". Having that continually repeated, at high decibels, would be irritating.

Emit finally answered the phone at 11:45 p.m., and he was understandably upset about being asked to turn the light on and off whilst the phone continually rang. To make matters worse, as Mike talked to Emit, no one told the forward negotiator we had established phone contact so the broadcast over the PA about turning the lights on and off continued. The left hand didn't know what the right was doing. We looked like buffoons and Emit made sure to tell Mike this, of course using stronger terminology, before hanging up again.

The subsequent telephone call into the residence was answered by Denise. All she was able to say was that she was ok and Emit again took the phone from her. As he was berating Mike for how he felt he was being talked to, he explained that he simply wanted twenty minutes to try and think things over. Considering his early statements about wanting to say goodbye to his daughter and his current irate condition, agreeing to a long period of "no-contact" is risky and Mike knew it. Mike had Emit agree to a fifteen minute break before hanging up at midnight.

Everyone in the command post held their breath for fifteen minutes, hoping things would remain quiet during that time frame and not have the silence shattered by gunfire, given Emit's earlier statements and the known risk for homicide/suicide. It became even more concerning when Emit broke his promise and refused to answer Mike's phone call at 12:15 a.m..

At 12:20 a.m., Emit finally answered Mike's phone call. It didn't go unnoticed that he answered at the twenty minute mark, like he had originally asked for. When Emit did answer, his demeanor was much calmer and he actually thanked Mike for allowing him to have the break. But of course he wanted more. He explained to Mike he was in the process of trying to work out some issues with his girlfriend and wanted five more minutes. Probably because this was the first time he was spoken kindly to, and possibly because he viewed Emit's reference to speaking to his "girlfriend" and not "hostage" as a sign of progress, Mike agreed to the additional five minutes.

At 12:25 a.m., Emit answered Mike's scheduled phone call. He remained thankful for the time Mike allotted to him and said he was still working things out with Denise, actually using her first name. This all was viewed as positive. Emit then relayed what was believed to be one of the core issues causing his irrational behavior; he shared he was fearful of the adjudication coming from his pending court case.

All eyes were suddenly on me. I had been responsible for providing all of Emit's background information. I had checked his local arrests, national arrests, (through N.C.I.C.), driver's license queries, pawn records, marriage information, and anything else I could think of. I learned about and shared the details to his earlier Burglary conviction but I wasn't aware of anything new as there were no arrests listed. Emit had also not mentioned anything earlier during any of our conversations with him. But because of this statement, I knew I missed something.

I quickly accessed the police computer system and logged into the court records to view upcoming cases. It was there I made a startling discovery. Emit had been served an indictment on two felony charges; Sexual Assault on a Minor Under 14 Years of Age and Lewdness with a Minor Under 14 Years of Age. The victim was his step-daughter from his previous marriage. My heart sank.

The court records program listed the prosecutor assigned to the case and even though it was after midnight, I was able to get the prosecutor's home phone number and called her. She explained to me the horrid details of the case and said she had recently been in contact with Emit and his attorney where they had negotiated a plea agreement. While the plea agreement had yet to be accepted by the judge, because of the details to the crimes he committed with his step-daughter and considering his ex-felon status, the prosecutor explained how Emit had agreed to accept a prison sentence of nearly twenty years. He was expected to surrender to 'walk-through' arrest the following week and would proceed to the sentencing after his plea.

Although Emit had not been arrested for these charges, hence not showing in his arrest record as the charges were initiated through an indictment, there was no excuse for me not initially checking court records for pending cases as these would have shown up. I quickly, and sheepishly, went back and shared with the SWAT Commander, Negotiation Team Leader, and other negotiators the information I had confirmed. This information was also passed along to Mike.

After two hours of negotiations, the relationship between Emit and Mike was still challenging; Mike tried to establish rapport and dialog but Emit would remain irate, believing Mike was condescending. Even though Mike was not the one who had continually harped over the PA system about turning the lights on and off and was not the person who failed to get the needed intelligence which would help develop themes to deal with Emit's issues, a change in the primary negotiator was long overdue.

Detective Michael Eylar, who had been serving as the secondary negotiator for Mike, was the natural choice to assume the role of primary negotiator, as he had already listened to the entire previous conversation. I was placed as Michael's secondary.

At 12:54 a.m., Michael placed his first call into Emit. Emit was confused at first, wanting to know what happened to Mike and asked to speak with him. But as Michael continued to talk, Emit seemed more accepting and didn't hang up the phone, which was a marked improvement.

Michael's approach and tone of voice appeared to work. Emit became more rational and just five minutes into their conversation he offered our first glimmer of hope; Emit said he planned on letting Denise come out. Although he didn't specify when he planned on releasing her, the fact that Emit brought this up was the most positive sign to occur since we began the event.

Emit remained comfortable with Michael, expounding on his concerns of the pending court case and the prison time he knew he would have to serve. Although we were happy Emit continued to talk, didn't appear as angry, and hadn't hung up on Michael, we did ask Michael to gently nudge Emit on when he planned on releasing Denise. Emit was very straightforward when asked, explaining Denise would come out in one hour. He continued his straightforwardness, explaining he would kill himself after Denise exited.

Michael took the opportunity to conduct suicide intervention; explaining how suicide is a permanent solution to a temporary problem. He agreed that serving the prison time would suck but explained that even though he may be locked up, he would still have many people who would care for him and he could still correspond with. Emit would not agree with Michael, just reiterating he would let Denise free but did intend to follow through with killing himself after her release.

At 1:09 a.m., just fifteen minutes after Michael had begun talking with him, Emit said he was going to send Denise downstairs to the waiting SWAT officers. This seemed odd as he had just explained it would be an hour. Emit said he would have to hang up the telephone so he could say his goodbyes to her as he acknowledged it would be the last time he would ever see her. Although this was risky, Michael agreed, knowing Emit was going to hang up if he wanted to anyway and agreeing to it allowed the rapport to build.

We did advise the SWAT Commander of the possibilities of homicide/suicide when Emit hung up which the commander broadcast to the SWAT officers.

After a tense four minutes, Michael called back and Emit answered, announcing Denise would be walking downstairs. Michael thanked him for this and the SWAT Commander briefed the SWAT officers positioned on the ground floor to expect her presence. Several minutes passed but Denise never appeared. Fearful, Michael placed several phone calls to the residence but each time the phone was picked up then promptly disconnected. We were all on pins and needles, wondering what was going on and how much we should push with repeated phone calls.

At 1:18 a.m., Emit answered the phone and again claimed Denise was exiting. Michael spoke to Emit for two long minutes when suddenly an upstairs door opened and Denise walked downstairs and into the arms of a waiting SWAT officer. Three and a half hours of having a gun trained on her, threatened with death by the man she had loved, Denise was finally safe.

After she was removed from the inner perimeter, we had the opportunity to debrief her, hoping she could provide us with something we could use to change Emit's mind on his intent to take his own life. Denise was obviously overwhelmed but said she believed Emit remained intent on fulfilling his desire. She cautioned us that in addition to the Smith and Wesson 9mm pistol he owned, Emit also had what she believed were one hundred rounds of ammunition for the pistol and two spare magazines. She also explained he was in possession of her Colt .380 semi-automatic pistol. This information was shared with the SWAT Commander who promptly briefed his SWAT officers.

We asked Denise about the delay when Emit first said she was coming out until she finally came out twelve minutes later. She explained when Emit first told her she could leave, she was free to do so but she was scared. We assumed she meant she was afraid for Emit, scared he would hurt himself when she left. Denise was quick to correct us. She said she was extremely afraid that when she started to walk out, she felt Emit would shoot her in the back. She said it took her the twelve minutes to work up the courage to walk out and finally just took her chances that Emit wouldn't shoot.

Michael had stayed on the telephone with Emit as Denise came down the stairs to the awaiting SWAT officers. While she was taken to a safe location, Michael praised Emit for doing the right thing. He then switched gears, trying to convince Emit that better days still lay ahead and asked him to come out and meet with him personally. Emit refused the meet offer, explaining he would not come out. He then shared the same information Denise had just relayed; that he had one hundred bullets and two magazines, implying he was ready for a shootout should police try to assault him. When Michael tried to reassure him that no one would come up the stairs, Emit said he didn't trust Michael and hung up the phone. This was the first time Emit treated Michael poorly.

At 1:28 a.m., two and a half hours after negotiators first spoke with Emit, Michael called back into the house and again talked to him. Emit became very stoic, explaining he was tired of playing games with us and he was going to follow through with his plan and kill himself. Michael tried to intervene, but Emit made one final eerie remark claiming, "It's been fun", then hung up the phone.

Michael could hear the finality in Emit's voice and redialed his number. Michael made several calls to the home but each one went unanswered. Finally, at 1:38 a.m., only eight minutes after ending his last phone call, SWAT officers downstairs reported hearing one shot coming from the upstairs area of the home. We all knew what that meant.

The SWAT Commander still had to go through the motions. Although Emit wouldn't answer the phone after saying he was going to kill himself and a single gunshot was heard, this was the same person who had open fired on several SWAT officers, striking one of them. He was still upstairs, in an elevated position of advantage, so they had to make sure Emit was not simply playing possum.

SWAT officers inserted a listening device but nothing could be heard. They deployed several gas rounds but still no movement or sounds were detected. At 2:16 a.m., SWAT officers were authorized to ascend the stairs which began the slow methodical search task. At 2:31 a.m., nearly five hours after the incident first began, SWAT officers on the second floor of the residence broadcasted they had located Emit deceased in the upstairs bathroom area from a self-inflicted gunshot wound to the head.

Although we as negotiators made several mistakes on this event, we were able to walk away from it with a partial win; Denise's safe release. I'm not certain that even had we played our cards perfectly on this event and developed a strong initial rapport with Emit, we would have been successful in having him exit and taken into custody without incident. I think Emit knew that in addition to committing the heinous sexual acts on his minor step-daughter, following it up with shooting a SWAT officer sealed his fate of knowing he would never be a free man. However, even with everything Emit had done wrong, we still did everything we could to get him out safe.

Lessons Learned:

We were very fortunate there were no additional police officers injured in this event as we put ourselves in a poor position from the start of the event. Police officers are taught during the first portion of the academy the importance of using good tactics when arriving on calls. We are also taught that family disturbances can be some of the most dangerous calls police officers respond to. When arriving on a call, police officers are taught to park several houses away from the incident and to approach the location, with their partner, in a way that provides them some cover yet still allows them to see and hear what is going on. They are certainly never taught to drive directly into the driveway of the residence!

No one ever asked the 30-year sergeant why he pulled directly into the driveway. No one asked why he chose to use the PA radio versus exiting his patrol car and give verbal commands to have Emit and Denise exit the garage. In this incident, we are probably very lucky the sergeant did not open his patrol car door to confront them as the sergeant did not see Emit armed with the pistol and Emit certainly would have had the drop on the sergeant.

When the dispatcher was told to call into the residence and was told by Emit that he was armed with a gun, it was not a wise choice for the sergeant to relay back that the police were outside and had guns too. Even though when officers first arrived they were unaware it was a hostage incident, trying to exert authority, and using a third party to do, (the dispatcher), will likely never produce positive results.

A second sergeant showed up on scene and was able to make telephone contact with Emit. As discussed, when the Crisis Negotiation Team Leader was enroute to the location, he contacted the phone company to have Emit's telephone line taken down. During these type of critical events, best case practice is to isolate the suspect's phone line, forcing him to only speak with the negotiator. But there are certainly a lot of "what if's" and every scenario is different. Just as this incident showed, a police supervisor had telephone contact with Emit. What if they had tremendous rapport? Is there any reason to shut down the phone line? Unless the suspect is doing something that shows a true need for the phone to be disrupted, these types of decisions should only be made at the scene.

Whenever the police first make contact with a suspect on these types of events, it is exceptionally normal for the suspect to lash out at the officer and make spiteful comments. As the event goes on, this anger normally subsides and a regular conversation can be had. Emit lashed out at Mike when their phone conversation began but Emit never returned to normal. It was clear there was a personality conflict between Emit and Mike as Emit believed he was being talked down to. Although none of us listening felt that way, the only person's opinion who matters was Emit's, as he was holding a hostage. We certainly did not want to further aggravate him. Looking back, we should have switched negotiators much sooner than we did. When we finally did switch and put Michael on as the primary negotiator, we saw a huge positive change in Emit's demeanor.

Some of Emit's anger towards Mike was due to voice commands he was receiving over the PA system, especially while he was on the phone with Mike. This was simply poor communications between the negotiators, not being clear with the negotiator announcing over the PA radio, on when to start and stop talking. It was also not helpful to simply repeat the commands of turning the house light on and off, over and over again. That would make anyone inside a house irritated. The negotiator who was operating the PA was new and was not sure what he should say. The team leader should have made sure the new negotiator was properly prepared before sending him to broadcast verbal instructions over the PA radio.

The failure to check pending court cases was huge. Had I done this check at the beginning of the incident, we would have likely known some of the reasons Emit was so adamant about ending the event violently. Emit knew he was going to prison and would be there for a very long time. Had we known that at the beginning, we could have tried to develop strategies to help soften this when it was brought up on the phone. To help prevent making these type of mistakes, we created a template of sources to be checked on all future events. While it might seem basic, it has helped us from making this same mistake twice.

*Suspect Emit Rice's booking photo. It
was obtained from LVMPD*

*A picture of the front of the residence
where the incident took place.*

A still photo I took from a video I helped shoot at the scene, several weeks after the event. It shows the view in from the rear sliding glass door the SWAT officers smashed to gain entry after hearing the gunfire.

A still photo I took from a video I helped shoot at the scene, several weeks after the event. It shows the view Emit Rice had when he saw SWAT Officer Fowler at the bottom of the stairs when he shot him.

CHAPTER 2

FREMONT STREET SNIPER

For those not familiar with Las Vegas, the location of the city's most famous attractions and gambling areas have changed over time. The current Las Vegas strip, located on Las Vegas Boulevard, is home to some of the world's largest and most glamorous hotels and gaming establishments. However, prior to the 1950s, this "strip" was nonexistent. Las Vegas was still famous for gaming during those times but those establishments were in the heart of Downtown Las Vegas, located on Fremont Street. These older casinos, such as the Four Queens, Golden Nugget and The California, still exist today and the area is currently being revitalized. Less than ten blocks east of downtown, yet still on Fremont Street, lies a series of daily/weekly rentals. These rentals are sometimes frequented by less than law abiding people. Such was the case on January 7, 2003.

On January 7, 2003, at approximately 3:25 a.m., LVMPD dispatch began to receive several 911 calls reporting 7 to 12 gunshots heard coming from an apartment complex located at Fremont Street and 15th Street. As those calls were coming in, the night clerk for the apartment complex was in the front lobby area and witnessed a black male adult run through the lobby area, armed with a rifle, firing shots indiscriminately. The night clerk also called 911 to report the suspect was last seen running out the backdoor of the lobby area, towards the rear alley.

Within two minutes of these calls, several single-man patrol vehicles began arriving in the area of the apartment complex, which consists of multiple three-level apartment buildings. One of the arriving officers pulled into the north alleyway and found a male on the ground with a gunshot wound to the head. As the officer was broadcasting this updated information, two additional single-manned patrol cars began to arrive at the front of the apartment complex, near the lobby area. These two units heard additional gunfire occurring, broadcast the information, and started deploying AR-15 rifles to prepare for an active shooter event. Several of these rounds were suspected of being fired toward the officer arriving in the alley who was checking on the man on the ground.

As the gunfire stalled, the officer in the north alley could see the victim was shot in the head and obviously deceased. As additional gunfire erupted, officers could hear it but did not know where it was coming from. It was emanating from the center of the complex area as the suspect, unbeknownst to the officers, was firing randomly. He made his way on foot through the buildings to apartment building "E", located on the southern end of the complex. It was at this southern building that the suspect went to the third floor, into apartment # 307. This studio apartment had one window which faced west towards downtown Las Vegas. The window also provided a view of the apartment complex across the street as well as a vantage of the front of the current apartment complex where additional police vehicles were beginning to arrive.

Undetected in this third-floor apartment, the suspect continued to shoot, firing multiple rifle rounds from the west facing window. He fired multiple rounds at the apartment complex directly south across the street, striking an unsuspecting citizen in the chest who was standing on his balcony. The arriving patrol cars out front also provided for ample targets of opportunity. The suspect continued his rifle fire, hitting one patrol car at least ten times. One of those rounds fired fragmented causing the jagged round to continue on until it found its mark, striking an officer in the leg.

To call this situation hectic would be an understatement. As officers were trying to locate the suspect and tend to the wounded - which included one of their own - a phone call came in to the same night clerk who called 911 to report seeing the suspect. Unbelievably, the man on the other end of the line claimed he was the shooter and told the night clerk he had demands and wanted national media attention. The night clerk immediately called out to nearby patrol officers and handed the office phone to the first officer who walked up, Officer Ed Reese.

As soon as Officer Reese was handed the telephone, the suspect asked Officer Reese the condition of the victim in the north alleyway, unaware one of the rounds he fired had also struck the man across the on the balcony across the street. When Officer Reese said he was unaware of the alleyway victim's condition, the suspect told him to go check. He told the suspect he wasn't able to check on the victim and when the suspect inquired why, Officer Reese replied back, "Because you keep shooting at us!"

It did not take long for Officer Reese to learn where the suspect was calling from. The suspect called the front desk area from the truncated phone line in the apartment he had run into, an older PBX type phone system which immediately displayed which room he was calling from; apartment building "E", apartment # 307, located on the third floor. Officers immediately began setting up containment and coverage of that room, remaining mindful of the suspect's firing capabilities through his west-facing window. If what had occurred was not bad enough, the suspect also spontaneously informed Officer Reese that he was holding a hostage in the room with him.

As all of this was occurring, patrol supervisors on scene immediately recognized the extreme dangers the suspect had placed the officers and citizens alike in and requested SWAT and crisis negotiators be called out. The callout was initiated at 3:43 a.m., just eighteen minutes after the first 911 call was received.

As SWAT and crisis negotiators were enroute to the scene, they monitored the radio channel for this event. It was easy to imagine the sheer pandemonium taking place at the scene as supervisors were quickly trying to ensure containment was in place, evacuations from the critical area were taking place, wounded were transported, crime scenes established, witnesses identified, and a command post established. Not to mention, Officer Reese was still on the telephone with the suspect.

At approximately 4:15 a.m., prior to SWAT taking over containment positions, several additional rounds were fired, believed to possibly have come from the window area of apartment #-307. Officer Reese asked the suspect about the gunfire and was told "those are warning shot for those dumb asses to stay inside." Luckily, no one was hit from his last barrage of gunfire. The suspect did convey, however, that he didn't want to go to jail for the rest of his life, a statement that, while minute, was a small piece of intelligence which could be used. He also referred to his hostage as a "she," threatening he would shoot her if he didn't receive news coverage. This demand was logged and passed along to the SWAT Commander who had just arrived.

Just after 4:30 a.m., most of the SWAT team and the crisis negotiators had arrived on scene. The SWAT officers were deployed and assumed inner perimeter locations. SWAT snipers were also placed around apartment #307. Negotiators had also been briefed and assignments made, which included who would talk to the suspect, identify those which would develop the much needed critical information on the suspect, hostage, and the relationship, if any, to the victims' shot.

At 4:43 a.m., SWAT had the situation contained and negotiators made their initial contact with the suspect.

From a negotiator's perspective:

Just as most of the other team members did, I monitored the radio traffic of the event while driving to the call.

Understandably, the radio was being used non-stop as it seemed each officer discovered additional critical information. Just prior to our arrival, one of the patrol supervisors selected a 7-11 store parking lot to stage the command post as well as a spot for negotiators to use. This 7-11 was located several blocks down so its location was ideal. On a side note, there is another 7-11 located directly west across the street from the apartment complex where the incident was taking place. While we simply didn't have the resources to evacuate it, apparently the idea of closing it since it was still in an area which could be struck by gunfire never occurred to the employees. The cavalier attitude of some people, who knew police were there for this shooting but went about their day which included needing to shop at 7-11, never ceased to amaze me.

Upon our arrival, we were informed by the SWAT Commander that his SWAT officers had full containment on apartment E-307, and had sniper coverage as well. Negotiators were briefed on the details of the incident from a patrol supervisor. The only change other than the details listed above, was that a Detective Sergeant had relieved Officer Reese and the Detective Sergeant was speaking to the suspect on the phone. We were also told of the subject's demands and that he would kill the female hostage if he did not receive news coverage of this incident.

After the briefing, we made assignments for the negotiators including Sergeant John Hayes as primary negotiator and I would serve as his secondary. Obviously, resolving the incident peacefully was the main goal. Next to completing that task, the SWAT Commander, Lieutenant Larry Burns, needed the suspect and hostage identified, information on the room's layout, and a list of the evacuations already completed.

John and I began monitoring the conversations between the Detective Sergeant and the suspect. Since there did not appear to be any real rapport established, we made the decision to transition. At 4:43 a.m., John was introduced to the suspect and began negotiations. Prior to taking over negotiations, John and I discussed our strategy. We agreed the best course of action would be to try and downplay what had already taken place while additionally "fish" for information on both the suspect and hostage.

John had a smooth transition and seemed to establish a rapport right away. Because this was a murder and kidnapping case, we also decided to tape record the conversations.

Nevada is a unique state in regards to its wiretap laws. We are one of the few states left that has a two-party consent. This means that barring a court order, each person on the end of the telephone must consent to the conversation being recorded. To apply for a court order, there are only seven predicate crimes which the statute allows for a wiretap provision to be applied for. Murder and Kidnap are two of those seven predicate crimes. Fortunately, Nevada statute recognizes emergency situations do exist and allows the Chief District Attorney to authorize an emergency wiretap interception under certain circumstances, with the written documentation provided to the court within 72 hours of the event.

While any conversations that the suspect has with us during negotiations could provide evidence of the crimes, the main reason we as negotiators ask for an emergency wiretap interception on a kidnap is to ensure we do not miss anything vital in the conversation.

Within a few minutes of the transition, the suspect voluntarily told us his name was Ricky Horne and that he was from the Pittsburgh area. Upon hearing this, additional assisting negotiators got right to work to help identify who he was and learn about his background. We did not have to dig very long as Ricky must have caught on to our "fishing" and gave us his full name and date of birth, making our job much easier.

As most negotiators know, inquiring about a hostage

is a bit dicey. We want to personalize the hostage, always using their first name and never using the phrase "hostage". We want to inquire about them, make sure they are okay and learn what we can, yet be mindful to not be so over-the-top that even the suspect realizes he holds something very valuable and can barter with. Trying to accomplish this intelligence gathering on a "stranger-type" abduction can be challenging to say the least.

As the intelligence began coming in on Ricky, John made his first inquiry on the female hostage, hoping since Ricky was so free with the information on himself, that he would offer the same on her. Unfortunately, Ricky only initially said that the girl was simply at the "wrong place at the wrong time", but assured us that he would not hurt her.

Realizing Ricky appeared guarded about giving information on the female, John moved the conversation back to Ricky himself. Ricky was very open and explained he just recently arrived in Las Vegas from Pittsburgh, PA and that he had a good job there, working for a large hotel chain. He said while in Pittsburgh, he had gotten into some legal trouble with cocaine and was placed in a court ordered drug rehabilitation home. Ricky said he became disgusted when the drug rehab home refused to give him any time off after seven months of staying there with good behavior so he fled to Las Vegas, knowing an arrest warrant would be issued. After arriving in Las Vegas, he found himself in a bind as he couldn't get a job because he knew his criminal background would be checked and the arrest warrant detected.

While John continued to talk with Ricky, negotiators developed additional information on him. We learned Ricky was a 31-year-old man who had an arrest record including narcotic violations and attempted murder, all in the Pittsburgh area. Although Ricky never conveyed this, assisting negotiators were able to learn that Ricky's mother lived in Las Vegas and a uniform patrol officer was sent to contact her and bring her to the scene. When she arrived, she shared with us that Ricky had two children, Kayla, an eleven-year-old female, and Ricky Junior, a five-year-old boy. Ricky's mom explained that the mother of both of his children was a drug addict and that she and the children are all back in Pittsburgh. She also shared that he had attempted to commit suicide on numerous previous occasions.

After getting the information from Ricky's mother, and without provocation, Ricky continued to open up about himself and the many problems in his life. He explained how he had attempted to commit suicide on seven different occasions, including trying to slit his wrists, attempting to jump from a bridge and even drinking roach spray.

Delving into the incident at hand, John broached the topic, trying to downplay the incident. Ricky went in the opposite direction, exclaiming how he had killed an innocent person for no reason at all. He even admitted he did not even know what the victim's face looked like. It was obvious that Ricky was referring to the victim in the north alleyway, and was still unaware of the victim across the street. It was also obvious that Ricky was receiving some of information from the news media, as every news outlet in the area was on the scene and providing live updates.

Ricky said because of all the problems he had encountered over his life, especially since he fled from the court ordered halfway house which caused an arrest warrant to be issued and because that prevented him from getting a job in Las Vegas, he was despondent. He was so depressed that he planned on going into the bathroom and killing himself. Ricky confessed he could not bring himself to commit the act and considered himself a coward. Unable to complete the suicide, Ricky said he knew that if he went outside of his apartment and fired gunshots at someone, he could provoke the police to come and shoot him. Ricky said he planned on just going outside and shooting someone in the leg to cause the police response but feared after he followed through and committed the act, that he may have hit the victim in the head. When asked why he felt this way, Ricky said he had been watching the local news and the news reported the victim was struck in the head.

John tried to downplay this, explaining how the news broadcast inaccurate information on a regular basis. John told Ricky the last information we had received was the victim was still in surgery. Since Ricky explained he was getting information from the news, we realized the negative implications the news media was causing for us and we made plans to disrupt Ricky's cable television service.

By 5:15 a.m., John and Ricky had been talking for nearly 30 minutes and the rapport appeared strong. Ricky was relaxed, easily conveying his thoughts. John used the opportunity to gather more information on the victim as we still had no idea who she was. Ricky volunteered the information with little coaxing, explaining her name was Tracy and that she was a local crackhead. John asked Ricky to let her go but he again refused, but as promised earlier, said she would not be hurt. Ricky did tell us, however, that that he had barricaded the apartment door with a dresser and the west window with the mattress from the room. When pressed further about Tracy, wanting to just hear her voice, Ricky explained that she was taped up and he was not willing to un-tape her. While Ricky's explanation made sense, given his propensity for violence by shooting at complete strangers, the concerns for Tracy's well-being was much stronger.

The SWAT snipers verified much of what Ricky had said. They could not see into the only window of the room, which faced west, as it was covered by a mattress. The SWAT entry team was contacted and they reported they could not hear a female's voice.

As John continued to speak with Ricky, assisting negotiators made additional inquiries on Ricky. Negotiators learned he had used his identification card to check into apartment #E-307 several days earlier and no one else was listed on the lease with him. Negotiators were still trying to learn more about his arrest warrant as well as more details from his earlier Attempted Murder charge in Pittsburgh.

Up until this point of time, we as a negotiations team had yet to have a chance to conduct an intelligence debrief and discuss progress of the negotiations. As luck would have it, at approximately 5:25 a.m. there became a lull in the conversation, and Ricky asked John to take a short break, which John agreed to.

While we were off-line with Ricky, we discussed during our brief team meeting additional intelligence that we needed as well as negotiation strategies. We also agreed we would continue to try and downplay Ricky's earlier gunfire and stay away from discussing the status of the two gunfire victims. Negotiators who were researching Ricky's background explained during the briefing that they were unable to find outstanding arrest warrants on him. Due to the information which Ricky relayed, it appeared that possibly the arrest warrant had just not been entered into the system so we assigned a negotiator to contact Pittsburgh and inquire further. Several minutes into the team meeting, the SWAT officers reported hearing shots fired coming from inside apartment #E-307.

SWAT Commander Burns, realizing that if the shots had already been fired, Ricky could have killed Tracy then himself but also realized he could simply be playing possum, so ordered us to immediately get back on the telephone. SWAT Commander Burns also had the SWAT entry team prepared to make a crisis entry.

John called back and was transferred to Ricky's room. Ricky answered the telephone like it was no big deal, explaining he just had fired several gunshots into the air but not at anyone. John tried to explain to him the dangers he posed when he suddenly began firing off gunshots but Ricky retorted that it would not be his bullets that would kill Tracy. Ricky said Tracy would only get hurt if the police came in shooting and hit her.

Listening to Ricky, we were thankful the crisis entry had not been ordered. Although the SWAT officers are exceptionally skilled and have tremendous experience at making dynamic crisis entries, making entry on an armed man who has already killed and feels he has nothing to live for, and holding an innocent person inside, always has its potential for injury.

As they continued their conversation, John praised Ricky about how calm he had remained. Ricky said he could not take all the credit as he admitted he was in the process of smoking a marijuana joint, had already taken some ecstasy, and had nearly finished drinking a gallon of Wild Rose wine. While we could hear the sound of Ricky inhaling, making his claim of smoking marijuana believable, his assertion of consuming nearly a gallon of wine seemed hard to believe, especially considering how lucid he sounded.

John began to talk to Ricky about his marijuana use, trying to convince him to slow down and stay focused. There was a marked change in Ricky's voice and he suddenly claimed he felt John was patronizing him, although he did not explain how. As John tried to explore what caused this sudden change of behavior, Ricky changed topics again and began to voice some of the anger he had towards the doctors in Pittsburgh. He blamed the doctors for not doing more to help him with his suicidal intentions, claiming it showed how neither they, nor anyone else really cared about him. Ricky said it was because of these doctors that he wanted his picture to be on the news for this incident, hoping these doctors would feel responsible for not doing enough to help him.

At approximately 5:40 a.m., Ricky began to explain how much he had done to help John. Ricky told John how he had volunteered all of his personal information which he did not have to do as well as ensuring that Tracy was okay, stating he had even offered her water. He assured John that he would not hurt Tracy and even blurted out that he would not rape her, a concern we always have when a female is being held against her will. Ricky told us all the positive things he did to set us up for his quid pro quo, explaining he wanted his photo to be placed on the news in exchange for all these positive he had done. John said he would make sure Ricky's picture got on the news but said it would require him releasing Tracy, which Ricky promptly refused.

The conversation with Ricky continued for twenty more minutes. He remained calm but just after 6:00 a.m., that suddenly changed. Ricky said he was watching the news and they reported the earlier victim Ricky had shot was dead. We started to scramble.

John explained he was in the command post and had not been told that information, something supervisors certainly would share if it was true. John also tried using his earlier explanation, how many times the media rushed to report information which later turned out to be false. Attempting to divert Ricky's attention from the news, John again asked about releasing Tracy. Although it was wise to try and change topics, asking Ricky to give up the one thing he knew prevented the police from assaulting his location was something we should have waited on. It was clear Ricky was worried about what was going to happen to him, especially since the news was reporting Ricky was now a murderer, and we were asking him to give up his trump card.

Ricky saw the shallowness of our request. It was the first time Ricky began to sound irritated and agitated since we began our phone conversation with him. Ricky explained he would not release Tracy because it did not benefit him. Not only was Ricky irritated, he also sounded hurt and said he would not release her because he felt that we cared more for Tracy than we did about him and he began questioning his own self-worth.

Instead of us picking up on how Ricky felt hurt, we continued to inquire about Tracy. Ricky assured us that he was periodically checking on her and reiterated he would not hurt her because she had nothing to do with this incident. He said she was simply "in the wrong place at the wrong time." John tried to capitalize on this and tried to rationalize with Ricky how it did not make sense to keep her, since she had nothing to do with what he was going through. Ricky listened to what John said but replied he would not let her go, again saying the only way she would be hurt would be if police stormed his room and in the ensuing firefight, shot her.

As John was talking with Ricky, we were receiving periodic updates from other negotiators on intelligence they had developed. One of the pieces of intelligence we gained was about the existence of Ricky's daughter, Kayla. I had written this information down on my notebook but we had yet to discuss as a team the relationship Ricky had with his children or how we felt the best way was to introduce the information.

It was my fault for writing the information down on my notebook and leaving it where John could see. As John was searching for additional 'hooks', or ideas we thought we could bring up to Ricky to resolve the situation, John looked over and saw what I had written. Without warning, John brought up Ricky's daughter Kayla. It was a gamble.

I was upset with myself for not covering up the information from John, to wait until we either learned more and knew it was okay to introduce or to discuss it in a team meeting during a break. I was anxious as I waited to hear Ricky's reaction to John's new discovery. To my surprise, Ricky did not overreact. He instead praised John, giving him kudos for doing 'his homework' and learning more about him. I was certainly relieved. John continued, trying to capitalize on using Kayla's name and explaining the strength of family. I think this is where we realized we may have pushed too far. Ricky suddenly side-stepped the family inferences and explained he knew that he only had two options; going to jail or going to the grave.

Our conversation with Ricky carried on. At approximately 6:20 a.m., Ricky mentioned a female named Denise Miles. We were already familiar with Denise, learning during our intelligence gathering that this was Ricky's quasi-girlfriend. One of the negotiators had even located her and had her at the scene conducting an interview with her. Although Ricky was unaware we were meeting with Denise, he expressed his desire to speak with her. John, unaware that negotiators already had Denise at the command post, attempted to talk around the subject but Ricky interrupted and argued he would not discuss anything else until he spoke with Denise and slammed down the telephone.

Since Ricky hung up, we used this time to have quick team meeting and discuss any new information as well as negotiation strategies. We explained to John that we had Denise at the command post and could possibly get a tape-recorded message from her. The negotiator who interviewed Denise also said it was their impression that Denise and Ricky were not in a serious relationship, that it was casual at best. Not wanting to leave a man who had already killed one man and critically injured another alone in a room with a female, we quickly ended the meeting and John called back to the hotel's PBX operator and was patched through to the room.

Ricky immediately inquired about Denise, again expressing his desire to speak with her. Ricky even alluded to the fact that he might be willing to come out of his room if he had a chance to just talk with her. John inquired about what Ricky wanted to say and he explained he just wanted to apologize for all the things he had done to her. This of course did not make sense, especially considering that in our team meeting we learned their relationship was very casual. As negotiators, it is also a red flag when the person in crisis suddenly requests to just say a few things to the person they care for as often times they want to use this opportunity to say their final words or lay blame to the person before taking their own life. Ricky's request to talk with Denise was something we wanted to stall on as his claim of possibly exiting the room afterwards was weak at best.

As time went on, it seemed like Ricky realized more and more the power he forgot he had about controlling the conversation. He had hung up on us earlier when he said he only wanted to talk to Denise. He started to use this power, akin to a little kid who did not get his way, and began to hang up the phone on us more often. Although Ricky's hang-ups allowed us brief moments where we could share new intelligence or strategies, we never liked being off the phone for fear of what Ricky could do. And every time we called back to him, we had to go through the same PBX issue and be transferred to his room. Calling his room directly was not possible.

During one of the times Ricky hung up the phone, we learned by having an officer stationed with the hotel PBX person, that Ricky was trying to make outgoing long-distance calls. Unfortunately the antiquated system would not show which numbers he was calling. The phone system did allow him to make several local phone calls but again, due to the age of the system, the system was unable to show us which numbers he called. Because of this disadvantage, we contacted the local telephone company and other electronic experts, asking them to respond to our location. We wanted to see if the experts could tell us who Ricky was attempting to call, as that would assist us with our intelligence efforts, as well as if they could establish a way for us to call his room directly.

As we continued our phone conversations with Ricky, he explained how he was still watching the news. He said the local news confirmed the victim Ricky shot was dead. John tried to minimize the shooting and revert back to his earlier explanation on frequent errors the news made but I believe Ricky knew the truth. And I believe we lost credibility with Ricky.

Ricky again hung up the phone. As a team we discussed being honest with the victim's condition, especially since Ricky indicated he already knew. As we were contemplating how we would have John soften the news, another negotiator brought up Ricky's claim of possibly surrendering if he spoke with Denise. We all agreed this was extremely risky, especially since they explained when Denise was interviewed, she was upset and hard to control. We discussed that in previous events, we had obtained a tape-recorded message from the person and played it, and decided that was the approach we should use. We were so focused on implementing the tape-recorded message plan that we forgot to discuss how John would address the murder victim when he got back on the phone.

John dialed up the hotel and was transferred to Ricky. As they spoke, negotiators obtained a tape-recorded message from Denise. As discussed, the message was to be one of positive reinforcements and her willingness to meet with Ricky as soon as he came out. But being in a rush to get the message back so John could play it, no one reviewed it. The negotiator who obtained the message did the best job they could while dealing with an emotional woman who was stubborn about saying exactly into the tape what was asked of her. It was also such a poor quality that the sixty second tape was hard to hear.

As John talked with Ricky, who continued his request to speak with Denise, her tape recording arrived. At the same time, we learned the phone experts had arrived and fixed the PBX issue, allowing us to dial directly into Ricky's room.

At approximately 7:00 a.m., John played the tape. Unfortunately, the tape recording quality was poor and came across as distorted when transmitted but Ricky could tell it was Denise's voice. I, along with everyone in the command post, was disappointed though no one was more disappointed than John. This was a huge chance for us and it seemed blown. Ricky expressed his anger, for not being able to hear the message clearly and for not being able to talk with Denise directly. We looked like clowns. But, if there was a positive side, at least Ricky was not asking about the victim's condition anymore. But we suddenly had a bigger issue to contend with.

Ricky remained upset about not talking directly to Denise. He then reemphasized how he was upset at the entire position he was in and was tired of it. Ricky said he knew he was going to jail and he would rather be dead, explaining he had mentally prepared himself to die. This is when Ricky made a statement which changed how John would talk with him.

Ricky told John he was ready to end the situation and was going to come out of the room, but would bring his gun with him and force the police to kill him. Although him coming out alive was important, it was more important to me that Tracy be unharmed, so I was good with Ricky's decision. But Ricky's statement obviously bothered John. When John heard Ricky make the threat of coming out of the room with his gun, John told him not to and to stay in the room. What?

John had been on the telephone with Ricky for over two hours. While Ricky had unjustifiably shot two people, there was also no denying he had a very troubled past. As he explained his mental health problems, his numerous attempts to commit suicide, his multiple claims that doctors refused to help him, his drug abuse issues, and his children's mother being a drug addict and unsure of the children's well-being, it was easy to understand his troubles. While this does not make up for the crimes he just committed, after speaking for over two hours with him and trying to facilitate a peaceful resolution, a bond had certainly developed between Ricky and John.

Ricky and John went back and forth several times, Ricky kept saying he was coming out into the hall with the gun and John telling him to stay inside. Those familiar with negotiation techniques might recognize this as being similar to the Stockholm Syndrome. Whether or not this was the case and knowing the man that John is, I believe he felt in his heart he would have been able to have Ricky taken into custody peacefully and with no harm to Tracy. With that being said, I believed then and still believe now that the hostage is our first priority and the suspect is a distant second. While it would be a shame for Ricky to force the SWAT officers to kill him, if we were able to secure Tracy unharmed, it would be a win.

I was writing notes to John, telling him to allow Ricky to come out by himself in the hallway. John read the notes and would tell Ricky to come out in the hall but leave the gun behind. Ricky refused. The two men seem to then argue over this point, when suddenly the negotiation took another wild turn.

As Ricky remained argumentative about coming out with the gun, John tried to reason with him. John finally told Ricky he would in fact go to jail for the events that occurred. Ricky said he knew this but John chimed in and told him not for anything that occurred in Pittsburgh. You could have heard a pin drop as Ricky became eerily quiet, waiting to hear what John would say next.

John went on to explain that we had checked with Pittsburgh and that there was no active arrest warrant. Ricky first let out a nervous laughter but then became inconsolable, explaining how he had just ruined his life, committing these crimes because he believed he had an arrest warrant in Pittsburgh. At one point, Ricky even dropped the telephone and could be heard screaming in the background. This continued on for over five minutes, concluding with Ricky hanging up the telephone.

We needed to get him back on the phone. Immediately. At 7:15 a.m., Ricky finally answered John's incoming call. He was still irate, explaining how he would've just gone back home to Pittsburgh and got his old job back had he known he did not have an arrest warrant. He again explained that he was going to come into the hallway with his rifle to which John pleaded with him not to. At one point, SWAT officers saw the front door of the apartment open only to be slammed shut when John pleaded with Ricky not to "go out like that" and to consider his girlfriend and children.

Just four minutes later, after the back-and-forth conversations between Ricky and John, John continued with him explaining he was still coming out into the hallway with the gun, SWAT officers again saw Ricky open the front door, this time leaving it standing partially ajar.

Ricky was still on the phone with John and said that he was very scared but knew that he had to go outside in the hallway and face his destiny, to finally ease his pain. The finality of the event began to set in with John as Ricky matter-of-factly told him he was very sorry for what he was about to do and for John to also tell Ricky's mother he was sorry. John knew in his heart exactly what was about to occur.

One very long minute later, SWAT officers witnessed Ricky exit the front door with a rifle in his hand. As they issued verbal commands to him, he unexpectedly dropped the gun and gave up. Just like that, the murder suspect was taken into custody without incident.

SWAT officers immediately entered the room to conduct the hostage rescue. To their surprise, the room was empty. Tracy had been nothing but a ruse. Ricky knew that by claiming to have a hostage, police would be cautious about forcing an entry. He was right.

During our subsequent debriefing of this incident, several questioned why John would tell a murder suspect to stay inside with a hostage versus allowing him to come out of a room alone, armed with a gun, knowing what would occur. While I also realize this is something many will disagree with since textbooks explain what to do in these situations, sometimes a man with a good heart believes even though the man has obviously wronged, saving his life was worth the try.

Lessons Learned:

The scene was exceptionally dynamic when we arrived and the briefing was a bit hurried but under the circumstances it was understandable. We had enough of the basic information to start and the transition of Ricky talking to negotiators went smooth.

It was an obvious hassle to call the hotel and have PBX transfer the call. While this was how the hotel was set-up, it was something we should have identified as a potential problem early on and had people respond that could bypass it. Not only would it have made our job easier, it would have given us the intelligence as to who Ricky was trying to call during the incident.

Early during the negotiations between Ricky and John, there became a short lull and the two wanted a short break. It was okay to take the break but was a huge mistake to not ask Ricky to simply leave the phone off the hook while taking the break. We know better than this through previous experiences and it should not have happened. Not only do we have the luxury of not having to call back through PBX, but we also keep an open phone-line into the room and can hear what is being said. Often times with keeping an open phone line, we gather valuable information as people forget the phone is off the hook.

We made several huge mistakes in dealing with the media and Ricky's inquiries about the victim's condition. From the first moment we learned Ricky was monitoring the media coverage on TV, we should have made arrangements to handle the flow of information. Although it was a hostage situation, we still could have either severed his cable feed or cut the power, especially since the telephone in his room did not require power, so Ricky could not keep following the event. We also could have had one of the police supervisors on scene to inform the media folks present on the challenges they were presenting by giving updates on the victims.

While the media certainly does not have to abide by our wishes, most of the time when we take the time to explain the reasoning to them, they are willing to help.

Writing about what to say versus having to deal with it at that time are two totally different experiences. It is much easier to state here that when Ricky confronted us with knowing the victim was dead from the news report that we should have dealt with the statement head on. Instead, in our efforts to minimize the situation, we tried to side-step the statement and make excuses but I believe it hurt our credibility with Ricky. He knew the truth. Again, it is much easier to type it after the fact than when dealing with it spontaneously.

Not only was hearing about the victims' condition hurting our negotiation, but just having the event constantly being broadcast on the news was feeding Ricky's ego, which is something he clearly explained to us he wanted. Disrupting the television service would have been advantageous to us.

When Ricky made his demand to speak with Denise, we thought that since we had been successful in previous negotiations using a tape-recording, we concluded this method would be the best route to take. We made this such a priority, and made it time sensitive, that we never bothered to view the tape contents to make sure it was what we wanted. We allowed Ricky to make us feel rushed. Had we slowed down, explained to the negotiator obtaining the tape exactly what we were looking for, it might have come back better. When the tape arrived, we should have played it and when we found it did not meet our needs, we should have sent it back out for another revision. Since this event, we have done this multiple times, and it is rare that the first rendition of a recording captures what we want. We routinely send tapes back and have them redone and re-reviewed until we get exactly what we are looking for. Although one might think that the person providing the tape would get upset, it seems like the time between requests helps even the most emotional person calm down.

Although it was my job as the secondary negotiator to help control the pace of the negotiation and help suggest things for John to say, I think it was a tremendous mistake for John to confront Ricky with the fact that he did not have an arrest warrant it Pittsburgh. When John made the statement, it was done during a time that Ricky was trying to control the conversation and was talking just 'matter-of-factly'. I believe John made the statement out of sheer frustration, trying to show Ricky that he did not always know all the facts. Although saying this to Ricky likely forced him out of the room, I feel it was an error to do so.

Lastly, with regard to John's comment for Ricky to not come out of the room if he was coming out with the rifle. Well, hindsight being what it is, I think John would even admit he should have encouraged Ricky to come out rather than telling him to stay inside. But John is also a skilled negotiator and wanted to try to end the event with no further bloodshed and there was no doubt a rapport between the two had formed. Although I had passed him notes suggesting the error of his way and reminding John that Tracy's safety was our first concern, during the heat of the moment, John was doing what he was trained to do; to save lives. I also believe that if Ricky had not come out as fast as he did, John would have realized the mistake he was making and self-corrected his stance.

This image shows the fortification the murder suspect, Ricky Horne, used with the room's mattress and dresser to block the door and window. It was part of the evidence used in the trial and became part of the public record.

This image shows the bullet holes murder suspect Ricky Horne fired into a patrol car when the patrol car arrived in front of the South Cove Apartments. It was part of the evidence used in the trial and became part of the public record.

Witnesses describe dodging bullets from sniper

Ricky Horne listens to testimony Thursday during his preliminary hearing. He faces multiple felony counts in connection with a January shooting spree that left one man dead, and another man and a police officer wounded.

JEFF SCHEID/REVIEW-JOURNAL

By GLENN PUIT

REVIEW-JOURNAL

One witness said a bullet parted his hair.

Testifying during a preliminary hearing Thursday for sniper suspect Ricky Horne, another witness said when he walked out of his downtown apartment Jan. 7, he saw Horne standing in an apartment foyer, bearing down on him with a rifle.

"He's pointing a rifle right at me," said Las Vegan Darryl Kibler. "I just jumped back in and closed the door and two shots hit the window."

One bullet smashed through the window, cutting Kibler's hand. Another whizzed through the crowded apartment without hitting anyone.

"Two more shots hit under the air conditioner," Kibler testified.

Horne, 31, is accused of going on a rampage with a rifle at the South Cove Apartments. The tense standoff at Fremont and 15th streets left a man dead and two men wounded. Horne was arrested by a police SWAT team, charged with multiple counts of attempted murder and one count of murder with a deadly weapon.

Killed in the shooting was 42-year-old Bryan Ricks, who was shot in the head. Carl Capers, 31, was gravely wounded by a gunshot to the torso, but he has been released from University Medical Center.

A Las Vegas police officer, Samual Carrillo, was struck in the hand by a bullet.

In court Thursday, Horne

► SEE HEARING PAGE 68

A photo clip from an article written in the Las Vegas Review Journal newspaper. It shows murder suspect Ricky Horne and provides some details to the crime.

A picture of the front of the South Cove apartments where the incident took place.

A picture of the window of room murder suspect Ricky Horne was in at the South Cove apartments where the incident took place.

CHAPTER 3

STRANGER ABDUCTION

During the first week of each December, Las Vegas hosts the National Finals Rodeo. The event is held at the Thomas and Mack Center, home to the University of Nevada, Las Vegas's, UNLV, Running Rebels basketball team. The arena is located on the southwest corner of the university. There is affordable student housing in the area but many of the apartments tend to be a bit dated. Such is the case with the apartments adjacent to the west side of the Thomas and Mack Center, on East Naples Drive.

The apartment complex located in the 600 block of East Naples Drive was constructed in 1975. The complex itself is a two-story brick building with eleven apartments on both the east and west sides of the building. The apartments in the complex are all studio apartments, relatively small in size, averaging approximately 438 square feet. There are apartments on both floors and every apartment in the complex has a sliding glass door as its front door and sole source of admittance to the apartment. Each apartment is surrounded by filled cement bricks, making it a very sturdy building.

Apartment #16 is located upstairs on the east side of the building, on the north corner. The sliding glass door of apartment #16 faces east and looks into the parking lot of the Thomas and Mack Center. It was the home of Gregory Grant, a 47-year-old male who lived alone in the apartment. He had lived there for over a year and kept mostly to himself. The only thing most neighbors noticed about him was that he was "weird" and knew to avoid him.

Edwin Martinez, 23 years of age, also lived in the same complex, upstairs, just four apartments south of Gregory. Edwin, who spoke broken English, had lived in the complex for several months and although he saw Gregory coming and going from his apartment, never talked to him as he had been warned by other tenants about Gregory being strange and advised to avoid him.

Gregory's earlier background seemed normal enough. In 1983 he enlisted in the U.S Air Force. Although some of his military assignments were never verified, Gregory claimed to have been assigned to the Air Force Security Police, now known as Security Forces. He further said he had received explosive training and had working experience as a military dog handler. He stayed in the Air Force for eight years but was discharged in 1991 for paranoid schizophrenia, a condition he was hospitalized for. He believed a cult was after him, trying to kill him, and also thought some officers from the various Las Vegas valley police departments belonged to this cult. One year later, he was arrested for his first and only criminal offense, Elderly Neglect, for failing to take care of his ailing mother.

From 1992 through 2003, Gregory had no documented contact with law enforcement and little was known about him during that time frame. He surfaced again in 2004, already living at the apartment complex on Naples Drive. In September, 2004, Gregory checked himself into a local Las Vegas hospital for depression but was later transferred to a Las Vegas mental health hospital after explaining to doctors how cult members were still trying to kill him and that area policeman were active members of this cult. By the beginning of October, 2004, Gregory had been discharged from the mental health hospital and was back living at the apartment on Naples Drive. Unfortunately, he was still dealing with his paranoia issues.

During the daytime hours of December 1, 2004, cowboys from around the world were bringing in the various cattle which would be used during the National Finals Rodeo event. In fact, the pen where the cattle were stored was directly east of Gregory's apartment, less than 75 yards away. But as the cowboys prepared their cattle, Gregory had concocted a plan to deal with the cult members he felt were around him, intent on killing him. He had prepared a written script, rehearsing it over and over in his head, which he would follow to the letter. That evening seemed the perfect time to hatch his plan.

Just after 8 p.m., Gregory exited his second-floor corner apartment and saw a neighbor four doors down, standing on the walkway of the second floor. Gregory was convinced this neighbor was a member of this cult.

The neighbor Gregory spotted was Edwin. Edwin was a young, slender-built man, standing 5'6" and weighed less than 130 pounds. He had only been in the United States from Mexico for a short amount of time and was doing his best to learn the English language. He lived in his apartment with a roommate, and they did their best to avoid Gregory. That evening, it would change.

Gregory exited his apartment, turning right and walking southbound towards Edwin. Gregory was carrying a dog leash in his hand. He approached Edwin and asked if he had seen his dog. It seemed peculiar to Edwin that Gregory approached him as the two had never spoken even though they lived four doors apart. Edwin didn't even know Gregory owned a dog as Edwin had never seen one previously. Gregory's question seemed innocent enough and Edwin, in his broken English, told Gregory that he had not seen the dog. Gregory thanked Edwin and Edwin turned to walk away. No one else was outside so Gregory put his plan into motion.

As soon as Edwin turned his back on him, with lightning speed, Gregory flung the dog leash at Edwin, somehow lassoing it around Edwin's neck. Gregory quickly cinched the noose tightly around Edwin's neck, cutting off his blood supply. As Gregory pulled the makeshift lasso backward, Edwin passed out. Gregory pulled Edwin's limp body north along the walkway into his corner apartment.

With Edwin still passed out, Gregory restrained Edwin's hands with a pair of handcuffs he had acquired for this preplanned event. After handcuffing him, Gregory pulled the dog leash through a hole he had cut out above the bathroom doorway, between two wooden studs. With the dog leash secured by the studs, Gregory fastened the end of the dog leash to Edwin's handcuffs.

Edwin began to awaken as Gregory was securing the dog leash to the handcuffs. Because of the length of the dog leash, it required Edwin to stand in the bathroom doorway, nearly on his tip toes, suspended from the opening cut above the bathroom doorway by this dog leash. Edwin likely could not have conceived of a worst possible day, waking up in a *Pulp Fiction* movie-type scenario.

Capturing Edwin, a person he believed was a member of the cult trying to kill him, was only part of Gregory's plan. Implementing the next steps would prove just as bizarre.

At 9:18 p.m., Gregory used a deactivated cell phone he had purchased at a local thrift store for his plan, and called 911. Although a cell phone may not have paid service, they still allow outgoing 911 calls to be made for emergency purposes.

Gregory spoke to a police dispatcher. His voice was shaky and he was obviously nervous. The police dispatcher answered the line, asking the routine question, "What is your emergency?" Gregory answered the question by explaining he had a bomb and a hostage, indicating he would not detonate the bomb as long as the police did not try to enter his apartment. He further explained to the dispatcher that he was in fear of his life and that he had knowledge of explosives.

As the police dispatcher tried to interrupt and ask questions, Gregory spoke over her, providing more details as though he was reading it from a script, which he secretly was. Without being prompted, he provided the dispatcher his full name, date of birth, and Social Security number so his identity could be verified. Gregory concluded the call by telling the dispatcher he was giving his permission for arriving officers to evacuate the area. He further said when the officers who arrived at the scene were ready to speak to him, they should contact him over a bullhorn and he would use his deactivated cell phone, call 911, and the police dispatcher could transfer his phone call to the officer wishing to talk to him.

Based on Gregory's 911 call, the police dispatcher created an event and several units were sent to his apartment complex which Gregory had provided the address to. Although dealing with a possible hoax or a mentally disturbed subject, the officers were still required to check out this highly unlikely event.

Four minutes after Gregory's initial 911 call, as officers were still being dispatched to the event, Gregory again called 911 to provide updated information. He told the dispatcher of a black pickup truck in his apartment complex parking lot that he believed was part of the cult which was after him and wanted officers to detain the occupants of that truck. In addition to taking down Gregory's update, the police dispatcher used this call as an opportunity to obtain more information, specifically about the hostage Gregory claimed in his earlier call to have.

While waiting for patrol units to arrive, the dispatcher inquired about the hostage. Gregory explained he had to take this person hostage because he was among some of the people that were trying to kill him. Unprovoked, Gregory assured the dispatcher that the hostage, although restrained, was safe. When the dispatcher asked for the hostage's name, Gregory honestly answered he did not know but turned to Edwin and asked for him to yell out his name. Edwin cried out his name and, realizing Gregory was on the phone with police, shouted "Help me police!" several times. The police dispatcher heard Edwin's pleas and realized this was either an elaborate hoax or the beginning of a very scary event. As the dispatcher tried to gather more information, Gregory insisted the police dispatcher transfer him to the Federal Bureau of Investigation (F.B.I) which she did.

Several patrol officers arrived to what they felt was a comical event. Surely, no one takes a hostage then calls the police to tell on themselves, much less back up their claim by adding they also have a bomb. As the officers arrived to the apartment complex, they made their way upstairs to Gregory's corner apartment. While the sliding glass door was covered with aluminum foil to obscure the view, the officers did find two different holes cut into the foil. One small hole was cut into the center area of the window to provide a small view in and out of the apartment. The apartment was dark inside so the officers were unable to see inside. The second hole, and likely the reason the officers didn't stay around long enough to examine the first hole further, exposed the top of a metal filing cabinet pressed against the side of the sliding glass door and the officers could see a very apparent explosive device on top of the cabinet. The device appeared cylindrical in shape, possibly several cylinder–type devices wrapped in tape with a wire protruding from the bottom of it. Suddenly the amusing police call for service became very real.

As patrol officers began evacuating nearby residents, at Gregory's request, his phone call was transferred to the Las Vegas FBI office. Since it was nearly 10 p.m., Gregory spoke to the sole duty agent working. The FBI agent only knew of Gregory's initial information and was not privy to what officers had discovered at his apartment as the call had been transferred before the officers discovered the device.

Gregory introduced himself to the FBI agent and began to explain how a cult was after him and how he was forced to take a hostage. He tried to convince the FBI agent how real everything was and that he was truly in fear for his life. He told the agent that for the event to end safely he would need a ranking member of the FBI to respond to his apartment because many of the Las Vegas valley police officers were also cult members and could not be trusted. The FBI agent, most likely used to strange calls coming in, didn't take Gregory seriously. Without hearing what the patrol officers found, who would? Gregory sensed he was not being taken serious and told the agent to transfer him back to LVMPD dispatch as he wanted to speak to an actual hostage negotiator. The agent promptly transferred the call back to the 911 police dispatcher, probably thankful to not have to speak to Gregory anymore.

After being transferred back, Gregory told the police dispatcher he wanted to speak to an actual hostage negotiator. The dispatcher accurately informed him that the negotiators were not on-duty and they would need to be called out. The dispatcher said she was in the process of having the negotiators respond but asked Gregory, while he was waiting, if he wanted to speak to one of the officers at the scene. Gregory agreed to talk to an officer.

Police officers were still working on conducting evacuations when the police dispatcher broadcast over the radio that she again had Gregory on the phone and he was requesting to speak to a hostage negotiator. The patrol sergeant for the area, who was on-scene assisting with the scene coordination, asked for Gregory's call to be transferred to his cell phone. In Las Vegas, we train the supervisors to appoint an officer with good communication skills to establish conversation with the subject, leaving the sergeant available to coordinate and supervise. While this is trained, sometimes in the heat of the moment, it is not always followed.

The patrol sergeant began speaking with Gregory. Gregory tried to relay his story. After explaining why he believed his life was in danger from the cult, he cited several demands which had to be met before he would release the hostage and not detonate the device. Some of Gregory's demands included not only having a ranking FBI agent present but also a specific local media reporter and a pastor he knew from a local church.

The sergeant, still trying to monitor the police radio, oversee the evacuation, and coordinate other police activities, quickly realized the difficulty of completing these tasks while paying close attention to Gregory's demands. Gregory was also getting frustrated. One of the officers had focused a spotlight on his window, specifically at the small hole Gregory used for viewing out, and the strong light prevented him from seeing. As the sergeant was multi-tasking, Gregory complained about the spotlight, which was just one more issue the sergeant had to contend with.

As difficult as it was to manage all of these tasks, the sergeant knew they were dealing with a suspected explosive device because his officers had seen the bomb through the window. Up until that point in time, the only intelligence they had about a hostage also being present was from what the police dispatcher reported hearing over the phone. To try and gain confirmation on the hostage, the patrol sergeant asked Gregory if they would bring his hostage to the window, using the phrase "hostage". Using this term is something that should always be avoided.

Gregory was very receptive to the sergeant's request but said he was unable to move the hostage to the window, explaining that the hostage was restrained. Gregory did, however, offer the sergeant an alternative. Gregory told the sergeant he could deploy a police sniper to the top of the Thomas and Mack Center, and by looking in through the hole of his front window with a sniper rifle, would be able to see the hostage.

The sergeant realized the magnitude of this event and while the hostage's presence could not be confirmed, Gregory being inside his apartment with a suspected explosive device and refusing to come out was a barricaded incident. SWAT and crisis negotiators were requested.

As complex as the scene had become, the patrol sergeant was thankful it occurred when it did, as had it happened the following evening, over 14,000 people would have had to be evacuated from opening night of the National Finals Rodeo. The Thomas and Mack Center was clearly within the bomb evacuation perimeter and to try and accomplish a task that large would have been an incredible undertaking.

Also realizing the tasks which needed to be completed prior to the arrival of SWAT and crisis negotiators, the sergeant finally delegated communication duties to an officer on scene, who spoke with Gregory until negotiators arrived. SWAT and Crisis Negotiators arrived at approximately 12:30 a.m.. SWAT officers deployed and assumed inner perimeter areas and negotiators were briefed on what had occurred to that point.

From a negotiator's perspective:

I received the basic details of the event when we were requested to respond to the incident. I thought some of the initial information may be inaccurate as a random hostage taking is a rare event and the details of this event seemed a bit farfetched.

Although several of the studies vary on the actual percentages, it is safe to say that less than 20% of all barricaded incidents throughout the United States are true hostage events. The key to the incident being a bona fide hostage incident is the person being held against their will is being used by the suspect to fulfill a demand; give me money and a get-away car and I'll release the hostage. A quid pro quo.

Upon arriving at the command post, which was set up further down the street at Naples Avenue and Swenson and outside of the blast perimeter, we received our briefing on what officers knew up until then. We were told about Gregory's military claims and the mental health information he relayed so we knew we would have quite a bit of work to do to try and verify this. We made assignments for negotiators to contact Nellis Air Force Base, located in the northeast portion of Las Vegas, to make hospital contacts as well as with mental health, knowing it would be difficult for them to release information as many times it is considered "doctor/patient" privileged.

Considering the incident, we felt a negotiator who had a military background would be best suited to talk with Gregory, as that seemed to be the only semi-concrete information we had and wanted to use someone who could develop a rapport with him. I didn't have any military experience and the only person on the team at that time with any military background was Sergeant Clint Nichols. Clint was selected to fulfill the role of primary negotiator.

At 12:50 a.m., as we were concluding our briefing, we learned a patrol officer was on-line with Gregory. Gregory had again called 911 from his deactivated cell phone and the dispatcher transferred him to the patrol officer's phone number she had. Clint was able to have the patrol officer introduce him to Gregory, explaining Clint was the negotiator he had previously requested, so the transition went smooth. Unfortunately, this initial call was to the patrol sergeant's cell phone so the entire team did not have the ability to monitor the conversation on our usual command post negotiator phone system. Clint did activate the speaker phone so those in close proximity could hear, including the negotiator fulfilling the Scribe position, to ensure any critical information was logged.

Gregory was very cordial while speaking with Clint, seeming relieved to speak to an actual negotiator, as that was part of his initial plan. After the initial greetings, Gregory was quick to explain what happened and repeat his series of demands. Gregory explained he knew Edwin was surveilling him and that Edwin was a member of the cult which had planned to kill him. Rather than argue, Clint continued to listen. Gregory continued to speak with Clint, citing how he needed this cult exposed and how he didn't trust the local police departments as cult members had infiltrated their ranks.

Gregory reiterated his earlier information, explaining

to Clint that he had a bomb but would not detonate it if his demands were met. Gregory told Clint of his military experience as well as his knowledge of explosives to ensure his information was taken seriously. Gregory repeated his earlier demand, that he wanted three people brought to the scene; a ranking member of the FBI, a member of the local media - preferably a newscaster Gregory named who specialized in U.F.O. sightings - and the pastor from his church. Gregory said if these three people responded to the scene and he was able to have a conference with them, he would release Edwin and not detonate the bomb.

Clint reassured Gregory, saying he understood Gregory's demands and repeated them back to him. Clint took the opportunity to explain to Gregory the communication problems with Clint not being able to call him and Gregory only being able to call Clint back by dialing 911 and being patched through. Clint offered to have a phone delivered to Gregory but Gregory refused, saying he would not open the door and was also worried a listening device would be planted into the phone.

Gregory's behavior was certainly bizarre but it was also clear he had done some research. Not many people are aware that deactivated phones always have the ability to call 911. To make sure there were no complications with his communication plan, Gregory shared how he had purchased two deactivated cell phones from the local thrift store to have as a backup should one of the phones fail. He was also right about the ability of police to have a listening device inserted inside a phone delivered to him.

Clint was able to keep Gregory on the phone for nearly 15 minutes, attempting to establish a strong rapport. Gregory's tone remained fairly monotone, never getting excited. He did explain to Clint he needed to take a short break and even though Clint tried to keep Gregory on the phone, Gregory hung up.

As negotiators, we always attempt to keep a hostage

taker on the telephone for many reasons, one being if they are talking, odds are they are not hurting the hostage. Unfortunately, after Gregory hung up, we had no way of calling him back. We were at the mercy of when he chose to talk. But we took advantage of this first break to make sure the negotiation phone in the command post was ready and that dispatch had the new phone number to transfer Gregory's call. We also discussed negotiation strategies as well as talked about any new intelligence developed.

After several minutes, which felt like an eternity, Gregory called back into 911 and was patched through to the negotiation phone in the command post. Using this special phone system allowed us to keep Clint and the secondary negotiator isolated and undisturbed in a dedicated room yet allowed us the ability to have the conversation sent to two outside monitoring areas. One of the monitoring areas was the room the SWAT commander, Lieutenant Larry Burns, and I were in, the other being outside of the command post to a secure area where other negotiators and investigators, who if not assigned tasks, could monitor the conversation and work to develop on intelligence based on information they heard.

Clint's conversation with Gregory continued to go well. Gregory was very open, answering seemingly any question posed to him. At 1:10 a.m., twenty minutes into their conversation, Gregory shared with Clint that the cult he had been speaking about had been trying to execute him since 1991. He said there was video evidence and a hologram but police refused to investigate it. He further explained his self-admittance to a local hospital in 2004, again reiterating how the cult was after him during that time as well. It was clear to all of us how delusional Gregory was and that this had been going on for many years.

Clint attempted to inquire about Edwin, but Gregory would only say that he was fine, then return to what he had been talking about. Gregory brought up his military service in the Air Force and Clint was able to further strengthen their bond, explaining how he too had served in the military. Clint was able to ask questions about Gregory's Military Occupation Specialty (MOS), or known in the Air Force as Air Force Specialty Codes (AFSC). Talking their military jargon and about the various countries each had been stationed in was easy for both men and showed the wisdom in placing a fellow veteran as the primary negotiator.

As Clint and Gregory spoke, Gregory's tone remained monotone, never getting worked up about the situation he was in or what was going on around him. He did inquire about the status of the three people he asked for; the ranking FBI agent, his pastor, and the local news reporter. Clint was honest and able to convince Gregory that he took his request seriously but he had only asked Clint for their presence twenty minutes prior and since it was nearly 1:30 in the morning, it would take a bit more time.

Assisting negotiators were busy trying to run down any information on Gregory, especially his military claims. It was critical to learn if Gregory had the military experience, and especially the explosive knowledge he claimed. Unfortunately, calling Nellis Air Force Base at 1:30 a.m., the only person they could reach was a nineteen-year-old airman who did not have the faintest clue where to begin to look for any of the information on Gregory's background. Asking this young airman to wake up a supervisor to access this information was also a difficult task as this young soldier did not want to get into trouble.

While negotiators attempted to confirm Gregory's Air Force records through base personnel, we asked Clint if he could explore Gregory's military background since Gregory seemed open to talking about it earlier. With little coaxing, Gregory stated while in the Air Force he had worked as a Law Enforcement Specialist, including being a canine handler. He also said he had the chance to work with explosives but did not elaborate. His knowledge of explosives was what we were hoping Gregory would talk about but we also wanted to be careful to not come across as not believing him or to challenge his bomb making abilities.

During their conversation, Clint bluntly asked Gregory why he left the Air Force as it seemed like he enjoyed the assignment. Gregory explained he did enjoy serving but said he was discharged due to a paranoid personality disorder. Gregory seemed upset, explaining because of this diagnosis, he was not entitled to any compensation from the military but did say he received disability pay from the Social Security Administration. Hearing this information provided negotiators with another outlet to search for intelligence but again, due to the early morning hours, would prove difficult.

It was nice for Gregory to open up about his military background but what we really needed was more information on Edwin. We sent a request to Clint to inquire about Edwin but every time he did, Gregory would only respond that he was fine. This was a bit concerning as Edwin's voice had not been heard for over four hours, when Gregory first called into 911. It was also during one of these inquiries that Gregory exposed a troubling statement about himself, confessing to Clint he was "homicidal, suicidal, and paranoid"; not a comforting statement especially considering he was holding a person hostage whom he believed was planning to kill him.

Clint's demeanor with Gregory was kind and understanding. He would offer praise to Gregory during the times Gregory was cooperative, trying to help build him up. Clint also attempted to downplay the situation and tried to convince Gregory since no one had been hurt, the crimes he would be accused of would likely be relatively minor. As bizarre as Gregory may have been, his response to this attempted downplay proved just how intelligent Gregory actually was. Gregory retorted that although he did not have the NRS book in front of him, (he actually used the phrase "NRS" which is the acronym for Nevada Revised Statues), he knew he would be guilty of Kidnapping, Assault, and

Possession of an Explosive Device. Gregory proved he was very knowledgeable of the law. And one of the deciding factors of mental competency in the State of Nevada is of the person knew the difference between right and wrong. Gregory certainly demonstrated his knowledge of this.

Taken aback by Gregory's accurate explanation of some of the charges he would exposed to, Clint did his best to continue to downplay the situation. Gregory cut Clint's conversation off, telling Clint he knew the incident would end with one of only three options; Gregory going to prison, going to mental health, or going to the coroner. Gregory did offer a glimmer of hope saying he didn't want to be executed by the police, claiming it would "ruin his day", a statement both he and Clint were able to share a brief laugh over, also indicating Gregory's unlikely plan of committing "suicide by cop".

Since Gregory was so open and never seemed to get emotional with any of the questions, Clint took advantage of the situation and asked Gregory why Edwin was in his apartment. Gregory again repeated the story of how Edwin was a member of the cult trying to kill him and Gregory spotted Edwin on the walkway area in front of the apartments. Gregory said he carried a dog leash and approached Edwin, whom he did not know by name, and asked Edwin if he had seen his dog. Gregory explained when Edwin replied no and turned around, Gregory whipped the dog leash around Edwin's neck and began pulling him back towards Gregory's apartment. Edwin said he pulled Edwin four apartment lengths and while in front of his own apartment, noticed the dog leash had tightened so much that Edwin had passed out. Gregory said he quickly handcuffed Edwin then secured his handcuffed hands to the dog leash, after he had first affixed the dog leash to a hole he had previously cut next to a stud above his bathroom door.

Clint told Gregory his skills were very impressive and remarked that with the rodeo in town, Gregory could likely get a job with them. The two men again shared a moment of levity. Immediately afterwards, Gregory again assured Clint that Edwin would be released after the three people he asked for arrived. Gregory continued and said Edwin would not be hurt as long as the police did not try to enter his apartment. Gregory also made another troubling statement, saying he believed the incident could end in a homicide or suicide but that he was not overly concerned as he believed he was already dead. Gregory's statement about believing he was already dead was extremely disconcerting to us.

After SWAT and Crisis Negotiators had first arrived and received our initial briefing, which included the presence of the suspected explosive device, SWAT Commander Burns requested the Las Vegas Bomb Squad respond to provide technical assistance. While waiting for the Nellis Air Force Base airman to locate any records on Gregory, because of his military training and suspected military explosive knowledge, the Nellis Air Force Base Explosive Ordinance Disposal (EOD), had also been requested.

Edwin was obviously in a life-threatening position. There were also times when Gregory would hang up the cell phone and we could not hear what was occurring inside the apartment. Because of this, SWAT Commander Burns had requested our Technical and Analytical Section (TASS) to respond and install listening devices to allow us to hear conversations inside Gregory's apartment. Planting the microphones without the team being detected proved to be a challenge but just prior to 2:00 a.m., they were able to successfully install the devices.

While Clint continued to talk with Gregory, we delivered a note requesting Clint to continue to personalize Edwin, using Edwin's first name frequently. Continuing to refer to Edwin by first name would make him more of a person and less as an object. In addition to frequently using Edwin's first name, Clint continued to inquire about him, asking Gregory if he could speak with him. Gregory explained it would not be possible to speak with Edwin as Gregory would revealed he would have to move from his place of concealment and said he would be exposed to a police sniper if he got close to Edwin.

At approximately 2:30 a.m., two hours into their negotiation, Clint informed Gregory that both the media and the FBI were present at the scene and that they were just waiting for the pastor to arrive. All of the local media outlets were present to cover this hostage situation. The newscaster Gregory had asked for was not at the scene but since he did not ask, we did not tell him this specifically. Clint then told Gregory it would be a show of good faith on his behalf to release Edwin, reminding Gregory he still had the upper hand since he possessed the explosive device. Gregory refused to budge. Gregory said after the pastor arrived, he would speak to all three of them in a closed-circuit television conference and would then release Edwin. This television conference was something new Gregory added and we were dumbfounded.

Clint went on the defense, explaining we had lived up to our side of the bargain but this new close-circuit conference request was something new and had not been previously discussed. In his same monotone voice, Gregory said he thought the entire time it was implied he would need to speak with the three people he requested as it would do no good for the three people to just be present at the scene. We should have noticed that this was simply how Gregory would operate, always bending and manipulating rules and agreements.

Clint attempted to use logic, explaining that to conduct Gregory's proposed television conference would violate his earlier stated rule of not wanting anyone near his apartment or he would detonate the explosive. Gregory retorted, answering that officers would be able to connect into his cable-television box, located on the side of the building, which would allow for a closed-circuit television conference to occur. It was obvious Gregory had thought this out. It was also obvious that Gregory did not know what he was asking for was physically impossible to do. This also further exposed some of Gregory's delusions.

At 3:00 a.m., nearly six hours after the incident first began, Clint found himself trying to reason with someone who was not reasonable. In his attempt to check on Edwin's welfare, Clint conveyed to Gregory that his bosses would never agree to a television conference without an assurance Edwin was unharmed. Edwin's voice had still not been heard from since the initial 911 call and given some of the statements Gregory had already made, including feeling homicidal, there was a true concern for Edwin.

Gregory said he understood Edwin was an instrument for him to gain access to the media, FBI, and his pastor, ("instrument for him to gain access" were Gregory's words). Gregory agreed to let police see Edwin, instructing Clint to have a police sniper look in through the small opening cut into the aluminum foil covering his front door. When Clint tried to explain how time consuming it would be to accomplish Gregory's idea of verification through use of the police sniper, Gregory retorted that he was not in a hurry.

As Clint and Gregory continued to talk, Gregory made additional statements which caused all of us in the command post tremendous concern. One comment Gregory made came in the form of a warning. Gregory warned that if police tried to hurt him, he felt justified in hurting Edwin. As Clint tried to assure Gregory we had no intent of hurting anyone, Gregory interrupted and said he knew the police were planning a rescue and was worried about officers storming his apartment and throwing flash bangs, (Gregory used the terminology "flash bangs"). While some of us questioned Gregory's mental state, several pointed out how well thought out, and accurate some of his statements were.

The SWAT snipers reported they were unable to see into the apartment. The hole in the aluminum foil on the front door was simply too small. The glare from the patrol car spotlights off the glass made the task even more difficult. Unfortunately the phone connection between Clint and Gregory began to fade and we suspected the issues were due to Gregory's deactivated cellphone, possibly with the phone's battery. At approximately 4:00 a.m., the phone call eventually dropped.

We had the forward negotiator bullhorn Gregory, asking him to call back into 911, explaining Clint wanted to talk to him. Gregory called into 911 but due to telephone issues, possibly with overloaded circuits into Dispatch or the command post, they were unable to transfer his call. Amazingly, the phone issues continued until 5:30 a.m., when Gregory's call was successfully transferred to Clint. During those ninety minutes, Gregory was able to call into 911 and speak to a dispatcher but for unknown reasons, the call could not be transferred.

We sent a negotiator, not Clint, to the dispatch center, with the intention of at least having a negotiator able to talk with Gregory. We kept Clint in the command post as we felt the phone issue would be resolved quickly. In the meantime, the dispatcher talking to Gregory relayed to Clint what Gregory wanted said. This was certainly not the optimal way to communicate, and especially not with a hostage's life in the balance. But it was Murphy's Law that in the most critical of times, we would have a catastrophic failure!

We had representatives from the phone company at the scene trying to fix the issue but they had no idea what was causing it, especially since they had no idea what type, or even how old, the thrift store cell phone Gregory was using.

We asked for reports on what could be heard through the listening devices which had been deployed. Those monitoring the devices said they could hear faint conversations but not enough to truly make out what was being said. On a positive note, they reported the conversations appeared to be between two different people and the tone seemed calm. It was a small consolation to know that there were at least two voices inside, indicating Edwin was alive.

While waiting for the negotiator to arrive at the dispatch center and begin negotiations with Gregory, SWAT Commander Burns explained he needed more information on Gregory's location inside the apartment as well as on the device. One way it could be accomplished was through the use of a robot but at that point in time, our agency did not own any robotic equipment. SWAT Commander Burns contacted Nellis Air Force Base EOD and learned they had a remote robot and he requested they respond to assist.

While we had not been completely out of contact with Gregory, it was frustrating to play the "telephone game" with Clint telling the dispatcher what to say and her relaying the information back and forth. One of the key items Clint had passed along to Gregory was that the pastor he had requested had arrived, but the dispatcher reported Gregory seemed unfazed upon hearing the news. Clint also reiterated the offer of having a phone delivered to Gregory but Gregory promptly refused.

While it was reported by the dispatcher that Gregory seemed nonchalant about the pastor's arrival, we felt that this was the last of the trio he had requested and hoped it would prompt Gregory to move negotiations along.

We interviewed the pastor and he was perplexed as to why he had been requested. The pastor said he thought he knew of the Gregory we were referring to but he certainly had no relationship with him and could not even recall a time they had engaged in a conversation. Instead of trying to figure out the mystery of Gregory's request, we obtained a very positive tape recording from the pastor. The pastor recorded the message, explaining he was at the scene and wanted to meet with Gregory. He also reassured Gregory he would ensure his safety. We delivered the pastor's tape recording to Clint so he could review it and know the most appropriate time to play it.

As luck would have it, just as the negotiator at the dispatch center was preparing to take over the conversation with Gregory, the phone system was restored and Gregory's phone call was successfully transferred back to Clint in the command post. To this day, we still have no idea what caused the outage nor why service was suddenly restored.

When the phone call was finally transferred, one of Clint's initial goals was to convince Gregory of the seriousness of the phone issue and try to have him accept a "throw phone" from us. As soon as Clint brought this up, Gregory was adamant he would not accept it, explaining how he knew if he opened the door, the police would assault him. There were no other ways to deliver a phone as the front sliding glass door was the only opening to the apartment. All of us in the command post remained frustrated as we had no idea if we would experience another cell phone outage.

Clint began to get frustrated with Gregory unwilling to accept the phone. Clint explained they would likely have future issues with dropped calls but Gregory said he was patient and was not in a rush, further aggravating Clint. Clint had been talking with Gregory for over six hours and was feeling the effects. Clint then moved on to the topic of the pastor.

Clint explained how the pastor had arrived but Clint was unable to have Gregory talk to him due to the phone issues. Clint likely phrased it that way to help show Gregory the importance of accepting a phone from us. Clint said he wanted to prove the pastor had been present and at 6:15 a.m., with permission from the SWAT Commander, played the pastor's tape recording. At the conclusion of the approximate 60 second tape, Gregory simply thanked Clint for the message. This was not the response we were hoping for.

We were thankful to at least have telephone contact with Gregory. We were also busy trying to help coach Clint as his frustration levels were evident. We were so pre-occupied with what we were doing, we were unaware the EOD robot had been delivered and that Nellis AFB EOD Bomb Squad was moving it into place.

Unbeknownst to negotiators, the EOD robot had been remotely moved in front of Gregory's apartment, with a camera peering inside. Gregory brought up the camera and its unnerving presence but Clint, unaware it was there, told Gregory he had no idea what he was talking about. While this was a miscommunication issue, Clint was able to work through it. Clint turned the situation around on Gregory, telling him these types of things should be expected since he had gotten everything he had asked for and Gregory still seemed unwilling to follow through. Although this is not the type of tone typically used during a hostage negotiation, Gregory did not offer resistance to Clint's statements.

At 6:22 a.m., less than ten minutes after their arrival, images from the EOD robot began to beam into the command post. The Las Vegas Bomb Squad and Nellis AFB EOD examined the suspected explosive device then moved the camera to view inside the hole cut into the aluminum foil covering the front glass door. What we witnessed over the camera was startling.

Edwin was seen on the camera, just as Gregory had described. His hands were bound behind his back and he was suspended by some sort of chain, which was later found to be the dog leash, attached above the doorway of the bathroom of the studio apartment. It was the first time anyone actually saw Edwin and although shocked at the position he was in, we all felt relieved to have conformation that he was alive.

The robot's camera was also able to provide SWAT Commander Burns with the layout of the apartment. The camera revealed the front sliding glass door opened into the living room with a kitchen on the left and a bed on the right. Straight through the living room was the bathroom door, the one Edwin was suspended over.

Every so often, Gregory's head could be seen by the camera, bobbing up over the kitchen counter. This showed he was sitting on the floor, beneath the kitchen counter but right next to where Edwin was located. Although the SWAT snipers couldn't see in, SWAT Commander Burns was able to broadcast to all SWAT officers the location of both the hostage taker and the hostage, describing what he witnessed over the camera.

Clint continued to talk with Gregory but it was clear his frustration was getting worse. Clint reminded Gregory everything he had done for him, fulfilling every demand Gregory posed. He assured Gregory the three people he asked for, the reporter, FBI agent, and pastor, were all waiting for him and gave his word he would be allowed to meet with them.

Gregory spun the conversation, saying it was Clint's primary goal to have Edwin released yet it was Gregory's goal to deliver an important message to the trio. Clint explained he wanted to help Gregory deliver his message and even offered to tape record a message from Gregory and deliver it to the media until Gregory was able to come out and deliver another message himself. Gregory refused the offer. We seemed to be in a stalemate.

Through use of the robot, we verified we had a confirmed hostage situation. It appeared everything Gregory had been telling us, how he had kidnapped Edwin, how he restrained him, and the presence of the bomb, were true.

We began to consider the situation. Edwin had been suspended from the doorway for over nine hours. Although we had the three people Gregory asked for present, we seemed no closer to negotiating a peaceful resolution with Gregory. Whatever we did at Gregory's request, he seemed to add something or claim it was not done to his exact specifications.

Another troubling piece of information was gleaned from EOD personnel; when the sun rose, the sunlight's reflection off of Gregory's sliding glass door would prevent the robot's camera from seeing inside. But with the negative information, a positive bit came in as well. The Las Vegas Bomb Squad and EOD personnel examined the images of the suspected explosive device and they reported to SWAT Commander Burns that they were 85% certain it was not an actual explosive device. Considering Gregory's military background, was anyone willing to take that 15% chance?

As Clint continued to try and convince Gregory that he had met all of his requests and continue working forward, Gregory began to complain more about the presence of the robot. Gregory said the robot looking in on him made him feel like he was about to be executed. When Clint tried to reassure him, Gregory claimed that Clint unnecessarily escalated the situation by allowing the robot to be brought up and Gregory said he did not want to do anything Clint suggested. This was a huge step backwards in rapport building.

Clint promised to have the robot moved away, an obvious stressor for Gregory, if he would just allow Edwin to leave. Clint reminded Gregory that since he was still in possession of the bomb, the police would not come in and Clint would still make sure Gregory would be able to meet with the three delegates he chose. Gregory flatly refused.

Just before 7:00 a.m., nearly ten hours after the event first began, SWAT Commander Burns asked us for an update on our progress. The commander had been previously monitoring the negotiations but had to step away to meet with the bomb technicians. We provided an honest assessment; that while we tried to deliver everything Gregory had asked for, it seemed he would continue to be noncommittal, never satisfied with anything we delivered and always upping the ante. Commander Burns told us to continue our negotiation efforts.

SWAT Commander Burns made a broadcast to the SWAT snipers and provided them with a description of where both Edwin and Gregory were located inside the apartment. It sounded to me as if he was vectoring in coordinates to the snipers, using markings on the front sliding glass door as reference points.

At 7:14 a.m., Commander Burns again asked for an update on the negotiations. While we were maintaining a dialog with Gregory, we had not made any progress. It seemed as though Commander Burns was formulating a plan and asked us to keep him updated should there be any change in the negotiation.

At 7:32 a.m., SWAT Commander Burns approached us for the third time. He explained that with the hostage being kidnapped and restrained for over 10 hours and especially since Gregory showed no intention of releasing Edwin regardless of the concessions given to him, he planned on conducting a hostage rescue using an explosive breech and it was imperative we keep Gregory on the telephone. We conveyed the plan to Clint and he understood his mission.

Commander Burns kept his eye on the monitor, providing the SWAT officers updates on any movements Gregory made. At 7:39 a.m., once he verified Gregory was crouched down behind the kitchen counter, on the left side of the room, SWAT Commander Burns gave the order and we heard a giant explosion.

There seemed like a slight pause in the action, then on the monitor we could see SWAT officers flooding in through the area where the front sliding glass door to the Gregory's apartment used to be. It was only a matter of a few seconds later that the SWAT entry team officers broadcasted the suspect was in custody and they had safely rescued Edwin.

As we were conducting our negotiations, Commander Burns finalized a plan with the SWAT officers. The plan they implemented consisted of a water charge being placed on the front sliding glass door. When detonated, the glass fell and snipers had an immediate view inside. They had already trained their rifles to the area they knew Gregory to be from the coordinates given to them by SWAT Commander Burns. The slight pause was deliberate; the SWAT Commander's plan included a sniper shot should Gregory move towards Edwin, which would be blocked if SWAT entered immediately upon detonation.

After SWAT officers secured the scene, the area was released to the Las Vegas Bomb Squad. When the bomb squad entered the apartment, it only took them a few minutes to determine the suspected explosive device was simply four road flares wrapped in duct tape with a wire taped to the end.

Although it was a protracted event, there was a tremendous amount of teamwork which allowed it to be successfully concluded. The crisis negotiators did their part to try and end the incident peacefully and keep Gregory calm. Keeping Gregory occupied gave SWAT the time necessary for them to develop a plan. The TASS section provided assistance with their listening devices which could help alert us if dynamics inside the room changed. The work done by both Nellis EOD and the Bomb Squad could not be overstated as they not only helped identify the bomb as a suspected hoax but also provided a robot which provided the camera feed necessary to implement the tactical plan.

No one was more thankful than Edwin. He knew the life-threatening position he was in and later confided he did not think he would make it out alive. The one admission Edwin later made, which provided a brief moment of levity that was so desperately needed; Edwin said, referring to Gregory, "They were right. He is strange."

Interestingly, my primary assignment during this time was as a sergeant in the Robbery Section. The Robbery Section handled kidnappings, so this would have been our case. So even though the need for crisis negotiators was over, I had to put on my other hat and assist with the kidnap investigation.

After we finished our investigations, we charged Gregory Grant with Kidnap with Weapon, Attempt Murder with Weapon, Coercion, Bomb Hoax, and Bomb Threats. The case was delayed for years.

Gregory's attorneys claimed he was incompetent which caused court ordered competency hearings and countless other delays. In 2015, eleven years after the incident occurred, Gregory was finally deemed competent to stand trial and was promptly found guilty on all counts after a short trial.

I'm sure Edwin was also finally able to celebrate.

Lessons Learned:

When patrol officers first arrived, Gregory had called 911 and was on the phone with the dispatcher. The patrol sergeant asked for Gregory's call to be transferred to his phone. The reason we teach supervisors to delegate this task to an officer with good communication skills is because the sergeant is present to supervise. As the sergeant soon found out, it is nearly impossible to carry on a dynamic conversation, employ good active listening skills, document critical comments made by the suspect, and be responsible for the police actions occurring.

Another area for improvement, even for those who have no specific training in crisis negotiations, is for the person to be cognizant of the phrases used when communicating with a suspect who has a hostage. The term 'hostage' should be eliminated and instead replaced with the person's name. It helps identify them as a person, not an object. There are many other words or phrase which should be avoided. One such example is avoid asking about the suspect's demands. Although Gregory had planned this entire incident, most hostage situations occur in the spur of the moment. Using words such as 'hostage' or 'demands' may remind the suspect of power he may not have realized he had.

In this incident, we desperately needed access to military information on Gregory. As we learned, if a critical incident occurs after normal hours, it is often difficult to access important information as the people who have access to it have gone home.

The power of pre-incident relationships cannot be overstated enough. By meeting key people who have, or can grant access to critical information, problems similar to those we experienced in this incident can be avoided. After this event, we met with and now have a working relationship with the Air Force Base Commander as well as those we can contact during off hours. This even holds true when dealing with medical information. A volunteer psychiatrist assigned to the Crisis Negotiation Team has access to medical records that very few police officers would be able to obtain. The important part is to establish these relationships now, before a major event occurs.

Looking back at this event, we should have replaced Clint with a different primary negotiator. We initially chose Clint because of his military background and the rapport it allowed him and Gregory to establish. As time went on, it was clear Clint became frustrated with Gregory and putting a different negotiator on, even one with no military experience, would have been better.

Lastly, we exhibited poor communications towards the end of the incident when the EOD robot was deployed. It was likely because we were not paying attention that we failed to notice SWAT moving the robot move towards Gregory's door. Clint had a great deal of experience and was able to handle Gregory's reaction to the robot well, but our failure to pay attention and know about the robot could have been catastrophic. It is essential that a tactical liaison person be designated to ensure SWAT always knows what negotiators are doing and vice versa.

A picture of the device the kidnap suspect, Gregory Grant, claimed was a bomb. It was part of the evidence used in the trial and became part of the public record.

A picture of the location kidnap suspect, Gregory Grant, hid while holding the victim hostage and negotiating from. It was part of the evidence used in the trial and became part of the public record.

The barrier kidnap suspect Gregory Grant put on his front sling glass door to prevent anyone from looking in, except for the small hole he cut into it. The hole allowed the robot to see inside. It was part of the evidence used in the trial and became part of the public record.

The doorway into the bathroom where kidnap suspect Gregory Grant held the victim, Edwin Martinez. It shows the dog leach the victim was attached to. It was part of the evidence used in the trial and became part of the public record.

This was a still photo I took from a video which was I given, shot by Lane Swainston. The still photo shows the moment of detonation when SWAT officers used an explosive to blow open the front sliding glass door to Gregory Grant's residence to allow them to go inside and rescue the victim.

Gregory Grants booking photo. It was part of the evidence used in the trial and became part of the public record.

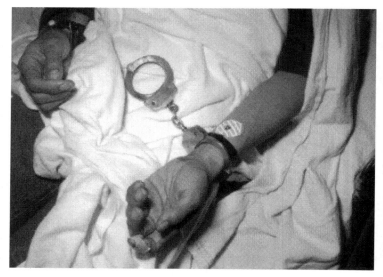

Handcuffs while they are still on the kidnap victim, Edwin Martinez. They were put on him by kidnapper Gregory Grant. This photo was part of the evidence used in the trial and became part of the public record.

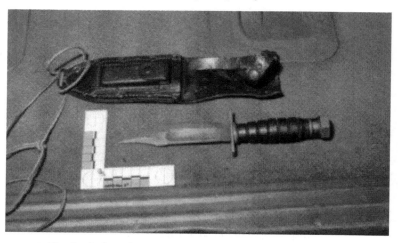

The knife found in Gregory Grant's room, which he used to hold the victim hostage. Photo was part of the evidence used in the trial and became part of the public record.

The view in from Gregory Grant's front door. It shows the counter from which Gregory hid behind as well as the doorway with the dog leach attached to it where Edwin was restrained. This photo was part of the evidence used in the trial and became part of the public record.

The abrasions kidnap victim Edwin Martinez suffered while being handcuffed and suspended from the doorway. This photo was part of the evidence used in the trial and became part of the public record.

Two knives which Gregory Grant used to hold kidnap victim Edwin Martinez. The picture also shows papers on top of the stove which is the script Gregory Grant read from when he called 911. It is the hiding place he sat in. This photo was part of the evidence used in the trial and became part of the public record.

This was a still photo I took from a video which was I given, shot by Lane Swainston. The still photo shows SWAT officers entering Gregory Grant's apartment after the explosive breech detonated to rescue the victim. This photo was part of the evidence used in the trial and became part of the public record.

CHAPTER 4

STRATOSPHERE JUMPER

The Stratosphere Hotel is a hotel and casino located on the north end of the Las Vegas Strip. The hotel was built in 1996 and stands 1,149 feet tall. The building has 109 floors and is topped with a large glass enclosure which houses an observation area and a restaurant. It holds the title for the largest observation tower in the United States and the tallest building west of the Mississippi. Sadly, because of its height, several people have used the structure to jump to their death. To help prevent this, around the top of the structure, the hotel erected wrought iron fencing to stop people from accessing the outer areas, requiring them to instead gain their views from inside the glassed observation area. Unfortunately, this does not always keep everyone out.

On August 02, 2006, at approximately 1:00 a.m., hotel security saw a white male adult on the outer edge of the hotel and notified the police. LVMPD uniformed patrol officers arrived and met security on the top floor of the hotel. Hotel security had no information on the subject so the patrol officers went out and made contact with him. They were separated by the wrought iron fencing. When they made contact with the subject, he would only identify himself as "Dale". Although Dale was on the outside of the wrought iron fence, he was also lying on the angled glass on the top of the hotel, forcing him to hold on to a heavy wire to prevent falling. After nearly an hour of patrol officers talking to Dale, trying unsuccessfully to convince him to come inside, patrol supervisors notified the SWAT Commander, Lieutenant Larry Burns, and asked for assistance.

Because there was little a tactical team could do, only the CNT along with the mobile tactical operations center,

TOC, were requested. The call for negotiators was initiated at 2:17 a.m..

At approximately 2:45 a.m., negotiators arrived and received their briefing for the incident at the TOC. SWAT Commander Burns determined a small contingent of the negotiation team would meet patrol officers near the rooftop area and conduct a debriefing with them. After receiving the additional details, the primary and secondary negotiators would move up and relieve the patrol officers talking to Dale. The remaining negotiators would stay at the TOC and be in contact with those on the roof of the hotel on the dedicated negotiator police radio channel reserved for negotiators as well as through use of cell phones. The negotiators in the TOC would obtain additional intelligence and follow up on information as it was obtained.

At approximately 3:00 a.m., the contingent of negotiators made it to the Stratosphere rooftop area. Upon meeting with the patrol officers, Dale had been positively identified by them as Alfred "Dale" Petersen, who preferred to use his middle name. The only other information the officers learned was that Dale said he was going through a divorce.

The primary and secondary negotiators were then moved up towards the area where Dale was, relieving the two uniformed patrol officers who were talking to him.

From a negotiator's perspective:

Learning about Dale's pending divorce explained why we believed he was despondent. I had been through not one, but two divorces, so the team felt I would be best suited to be the primary negotiator. The team most likely believed Dale and I could commiserate together, which made me feel a bit awkward as I had never hung from the side of a 1,100-foot building before either of my divorces

While dealing with suicidal people was very common for our team, in 2006 it was still relatively rare for us to respond to potential "jumpers". Up until this time jumpers consisted of less than 5% of the potential suicidal people we had responded to. We had also never responded to a jumper at any structure as tall as the Stratosphere.

Because we rarely dealt with potential jumpers, we were naïve to some of the safety practices, as you will see. For some strange reason, after this incident the number of jumpers we responded to increased.

Prior to approaching Dale, I went over several ideas for ways I would introduce myself and begin the conversation in my head. This transition, or "handoff", is important as rapport needs to be established quickly and as the saying goes, you never get a second chance to make a good first impression.

As for the theme I thought of using, I have always been open about the struggles I had experienced with both of my divorces and have used that honesty when dealing with people in crisis facing a similar issue. As the other saying goes, misery loves company, and I have found that where appropriate, when I share some of my personal struggles, the person in crisis tends to relate and a bond begins to form between us.

At approximately 3:00 a.m., I approached Dale's location and was introduced by the patrol officer who had been talking to him. The secondary negotiator stayed quietly behind me. The only police type identification attire I wore was my negotiator shirt as I did not want to appear threatening or too authoritative and I intentionally did not carry a police radio or earpiece so that I could concentrate strictly on my conversation with Dale. I knew anything vital would be relayed to me by the secondary negotiator. Unbeknownst to me, the secondary negotiator did not bring a radio or earpiece so continually had to walk away to get updates, which was a bit distracting to Dale.

After the introduction, I began my conversation with Dale and the patrol officer walked away. The transition went as well as could have been expected. I told Dale that I was concerned about where he was sitting as he had to hold on to a wire to prevent from falling. I asked him if we could at least provide him with a more secure rope to use but he refused.

As I began my conversation with Dale, I told him I wanted to work with him and to try to find a resolution together. Dale agreed. That was a small sign of progress. With one agreement under my belt, I pushed and asked if he would come several feet up from where he was at to sit on a ledge. I reminded Dale there was still a fence between us. He refused. Ok, not as promising as I had hoped.

Talking with Dale, I tried to find some common ground, talking about something we both could relate to and build rapport. While talking, the police helicopter began flying near us with its spotlight on. Naturally, this concerned Dale as he felt that somehow the helicopter's presence meant the police were going to do something to him. I assured him that was not the case.

SWAT Commander Burns had already been advised by negotiators on the roof of the problem the police helicopter was causing. Commander Burns contacted dispatch and learned the chopper was in the area searching for someone on an unrelated call, but the commander was able to convince the helicopter pilot to orbit in a different area.

We do not allow subjects to control police tactics, but this was a small concession that we were able to make. Truthfully, it was a non-issue to the helicopter crew as they had finished their search and were going to leave the area anyway. As any good negotiator would do, I took some credit for having the helicopter moved. I told Dale I knew it bothered him and it was important for me to do whatever I could to help work things out with him. Dale was appreciative of the helicopter's departure and thanked me for doing it. He said it was the first time in a long time that anyone did anything for him. My 'white lie' helped me build some rapport and credibility with him.

Thirty minutes into our conversation, a bond began to form between Dale and I. We were both just two men, each wearing a T-shirt and jeans, conversing about life 1100 feet above the ground. The only thing which separated us was the wrought iron fencing and during our short talk, I had been successful in convincing Dale move up a few feet and sit on the small ledge next to the fence.

I believe Dale felt comfortable with me. He began to share that he had recently been divorced and because of it, had to sell his home. It appeared to me that the initial intel we had received regarding Dale's recent divorce could be the main stressor causing this current activity. I decided to test the waters and told him that I too had been divorced, not just once but twice, and had to sell my homes each time. While this event was not about me, I hoped that by explaining some of my past may help Dale feel I could relate to him and his situation better. The gamble paid off. Dale replied, "Then you know how bad it sucks".

I told Dale it appeared we had more in common than we first realized and perhaps it was fate which brought us together. I asked him if he would be willing to come inside where we would talk further. I explained that by talking inside, maybe over a cup of coffee, we could explore several ideas on how to improve the situation he was in. Still talking, I reassured him that he was not in any trouble and he would not have to worry about the risk of going to jail. Many people in these types of situations worry about incarceration should they decide to surrender but often times they are simply referred to a mental health professional and no charges are ever filed.

The area I was sitting and talking to Dale from was extremely dark. He could see me because I was very close to him, only separated by the iron fencing. The lights from the Las Vegas Strip provided enough ambient lighting that we could both see each other clearly but could not see much further than ten feet behind us. Through the cover of darkness, neither of us knew that the remaining negotiators were gathered in the dark, meeting with a group of firefighters that had been summoned and were discussing a potential rescue plan.

The firefighters were from the Clark County Fire Department's Heavy Rescue Squad. Although they also possessed the same firefighter training as other squads, this squad receives specialized training on a multitude of situations. Dealing with people stranded in high places is one of the areas they have trained for.

The SWAT Commander had requested the Heavy Rescue Squad and asked this team to meet with negotiators on the roof to assess the situation. The firefighters discussed several different scenarios and how they could provide the best assistance. In each of the rescue options, the group of firefighters would approach Dale, each wearing a rescue line. Wait. What was a rescue line?

The negotiators learned that the firefighters were experts in "high angle rescue". Part of this squad's standard operating procedure included that any time they worked in these types of situations, each firefighter is mandated to wear a rappel harness with a rope attached and anchored to a safety point. Since our negotiation team did not deal with jumpers very often, we were ignorant to some of the safety practices we could have initiated.

The group of negotiators and firefighters continued to meet and discuss how they could effectively approach Dale and attempt a rescue as I continued to talk with him and have him climb back over the fence to safety.

At approximately 3:45 a.m., Dale told me that he had to "take a piss," and asked me what he should do. I told him if he just came back over the fence, I would take him to the finest bathroom in the entire hotel. While this made him smile, he told me that he was not coming back over the fence. He said he had been on the roof for nearly three hours and really had to use the restroom. Trying to problem solve, I told Dale I could get him a cup to use when he suddenly said, "Forget it, I'll go right here." Dale stood up and while balancing on the small ledge, he turned away from me, unzipped his pants, and began urinating. I was thankful that he had the common courtesy to turn away from me, but I could not help wonder what tourists walking below must have thought was falling on them.

After relieving nature's call, Dale told me in a very matter-of-fact manner that he did not come out onto the rooftop to get attention or cry for help. He simply said that he had been in pain for a long time and this was something that he wanted to do to end the pain. He said what made the decision difficult was he did not know what was "waiting for him on the other side"; I believe he was talking about the afterlife of heaven and hell.

Dale began speaking about his divorce and his son. As I let him talk, I felt his mood suddenly change. It appeared he was working up the courage to jump. As I was talking to Dale earlier in the event, one of the negotiators informed me that Dale had at least one child. The negotiators were trying to obtain additional information on his child, especially the child's name, so I could personalize it.

Trying to break Dale's fixation with what it appeared he was about to do, I brought up my divorces. I told Dale that although my divorces were painful, I considered myself exceptionally lucky as I was the father of two beautiful children. I was hoping Dale would make the connection. I then did something I had rarely done before. I took out my wallet and pulled out a laminated photograph I kept of my two boys. I showed the picture to Dale and reminded him of the importance a father plays in his children's lives, even if they do not live with him.

As I continued to try and reason with Dale, I confided with him that I too had gone through dark times because of my divorces. I told him as I worked through it, I realized

I could never do anything that would take the father away from my two sons. They were the most important things in my life. This gamble appeared to work as Dale began to ask about my children and he spoke about him being a father. I shared only what I felt comfortable with but what I did share appeared to be enough as Dale was listening.

Dale continued to listen to what I said. As we were talking, he suddenly reached into his pants pocket and pulled out a cigarette. He lit the cigarette and seemed to smoke the entire thing in two large drags. He continued to engage in small talk, asking questions about police procedures and wondering how much the incident was going to cost the city. I downplayed his concerns but felt that engaging in the small talk would help strengthen our rapport.

It had been a while since my last surrender request so I wanted to test if the rapport I had established with Dale was enough to have him surrender. I again asked him if he would be willing to come over the fence so we could finish chatting inside. My rapport was not as strong as I had hoped. He again refused. Dale informed me he knew he had only two choices; that he could come over the fence or jump. He said if he obliged me and came over the fence, he limited his options.

It was just after 4:00 a.m. and Dale and I had been speaking for an hour. He shared with me how he had attempted to commit suicide six months prior but failed. He said during this suicide attempt he had used zip ties to bind down his arms and legs after putting saran wrap over his face and head. He believed that during the attempt his own body's "fight or flight" kicked in and he somehow broke free from the ties and his attempt failed. To me, this failed attempt reinforced how serious Dale was about dying.

At approximately 4:15 a.m., Dale confessed he had used up his last cigarette and asked me if I could get him another one. I realized that this was a potential bartering item and told him I would have someone check on that. It was at this point the negotiation changed in a direction that no one could have predicted.

Dale took this opportunity to share with me where he had been for the past two years. Believing he was about to share inside information about being a criminal mastermind, I asked Dale to explain further. He said he learned people were spying on him and were using sophisticated cameras to aid in the surveillance. Dale explained that when he discovered the location of one of the surveillance cameras, they would disintegrate into his hands when he touched them. My vast police experience quickly concluded Dale's problems were not just confined to his divorce.

Dale continued, explaining that police and government agencies were following him. He said he once tried to write down the license plates of the vehicles following him but the paper he was writing on began to change the plate numbers he just wrote. Dale believed he was being set up and he could not take it anymore. Sadly, he said he did not have the power to stop those setting him up. Nothing Dale was saying made any sense.

I used my best active listening skills, hoping Dale would come back around to talking about the divorce. At least that was something I could understand and converse about. Unfortunately, he continued to talk about the spies that were after him.

Dale finally changed topics and asked again about the cigarette he requested. I told him I did not know but would go check on it. I made Dale promise that if I went to check on the cigarette, he would have to give me his word that he would not try to hurt himself while I was doing so. Dale agreed to the promise. He explained how badly he needed the cigarette but I knew it was not bad enough to ask him again to climb over the fence. I also knew using the excuse of checking on the cigarette would give me an opportunity to receive any updates the negotiators learned of.

While I know it's not fair to judge person in crisis, I

could not help but feeling a bit betrayed. I know it was my own fault as I made the early assumption that this entire incident with Dale was due to his divorce and the pain that he was going through. In my attempt to develop rapport and ultimately try to help save his life, I opened up and shared my own personal struggles with Dale. Who would have known he would listen, only to start talking about the dissolving spy cameras?

The personal information I shared did seem to help as it strengthened the bond between Dale and myself. I admit I felt a bit disappointed to learn his relationship issues were only one aspect of Dale's problems. His mental health issues would prove to be so much larger and would much more difficult to help with. While I am not a doctor, I have learned through my dealings with our team's psychiatrist that people with mental health issues like the ones Dale was expressing, believe what they are experiencing is real. Whether it is paper which alters information or cameras that dissolve, to argue with a person over their delusions is poor tactic. It is a better approach to simply let the person explain and remain nonjudgmental.

I walked away from Dale and into the dark area where my secondary was already standing with several of the other negotiators. My secondary negotiator had left my side early in the negotiation to check on any new information or developments then lost track of time while assisting in the rescue plan conversation.

Upon reaching the group, I asked for the cigarette. They had been aware of Dale's earlier request. I explained I would use the cigarette and attempt to get any kind of concession from Dale that I could. Someone in the group handed me a single cigarette but then told me they had been working on a plan. They said they devised a plan as they did not believe this negotiation was going to be successfully resolved verbally.

The plan they crafted would commence the next time that Dale asked for a cigarette. They explained that as Dale reached through the wrought iron bars to take the cigarette from my hand, I was to grab onto his wrist and pull him against the fence. The other negotiators would be waiting nearby in the shadows and would be ready to help. When I grabbed him, the other negotiators would help pull Dale towards the fence then place a handcuff on Dale's wrist. They would secure the free end of the handcuffs to the wrought iron fence, preventing Dale from jumping.

After Dale was handcuffed to the fence, the Heavy Rescue Squad would move into place and take over. They would use mechanical jaws to pry open the wrought iron fence and pull Dale through. They explained they had rehearsed this plan and was certain it would work.

Upon hearing this plan, to say I was shocked would be an understatement. I asked them if they were serious. The group said they were very serious and the Heavy Rescue Squad had been practicing on a different area of the roof for the past thirty minutes. They had timed their practice maneuvers and could accomplish prying the fence and pulling Dale through in a matter of a few seconds.

I remember being so stunned that in addition to asking the negotiators if they were serious about this plan, the only other question I asked them was if the SWAT Commander Burns was aware and approved of their plan, which I was told yes. Being so surprised about learning of this imminent plan, I forgot to ask the negotiators if they had developed any additional information or intelligence. I should've taken more time to process their plan. As I turned and began to walk back towards Dale with the single cigarette, the team leader gave me one last reminder; that they would implement the plan on the delivery of the next cigarette.

As indicated in the opening section of this chapter, up until this point our team did not respond to a large number of potential jumpers. I personally believe handling a potential jumper is one of the hardest negotiation categories we deal with. When dealing with a person barricaded in a house or car, there are so many tactical options the SWAT Commander has at their disposal. What options do they have on a jumper? Go over and push them? The most common tactic used on jumpers is to get close enough and grab them. I have never been a fan of this technique as it would be Murphy's Law that as soon as we put hands on them, the subject jumps or falls, causing some to argue it was a police precipitated event. Even worse, without the proper safety equipment, nothing prevents the subject in crisis from grabbing one of the negotiators and pulling them over the edge with them.

It was 4:40 a.m. as I left their meeting and walked back to where Dale was located. As I reached my previous location, with the cigarette in my hand, I held it up for Dale to see. As predicted, he reached through the fence, retrieved the cigarette, and used a lighter he already possessed to light it. As I reengaged Dale in conversation, the other negotiators and the Heavy Rescue Squad continued to rehearse their plan.

For the next ten minutes, Dale smoked and finished his cigarette. This cigarette took much longer for him to smoke than his previous one. Maybe he was just trying to savor it. While Dale was smoking, I put on my best "full court press". I was doing everything I could to convince Dale to come over the fence and allow us to finish our conversation inside. He refused.

At 4:53 a.m., after I spent nearly two hours talking to Dale and attempting to resolve the situation peacefully, Dale did what the negotiation team had hoped for. He asked me for another cigarette. I knew his verbal request would initiate a chain of events that I quite frankly was scared to death of.

As I turned around, one of the negotiators was walking towards me holding a single cigarette out in front of him. Trailing him, but concealed in the dark shadows on the rooftop, were two other negotiators. As this group walked towards me I knew what was about to happen and understood what my role was. I also knew I did not have the chance to meet with the team again and renegotiate a different plan. It was "go" time.

I took the cigarette from the negotiator and he gave me a slight head nod. As weird as it may sound, I knew the head nod was a signal, something I can't explain, but I knew that it meant they were ready.

I turned and walked back towards Dale with the single cigarette. I tried to put on my best smiling face as he began to reach through the wrought iron bars of the fence. I know my hand had to be shaking as I was reaching it towards Dale's hand to give him the cigarette, hoping to God that when I grabbed him, he did not slip away and fall.

As Dale took the cigarette, I latched onto his wrist with both of my hands, with all of my might. Dale immediately let out a death curling scream and started pulling back, trying to rip his hand away from mine. What seemed like minutes was actually only two to three seconds as the three other negotiators ran up and helped hold on to Dale. One helped grab the arm I was restraining while another grabbed one of Dale's other limbs. The third negotiator, as planned, placed a set of handcuffs around Dale's restrained wrist and secured the other side to the wrought iron bar on the fence. As all of this was occurring, Dale continually screamed, "I'm going! Let me go!" pulling with all his energy to fall the 109 stories below. As Dale was screaming, I tried to reason with him but realized it was pointless. I did feel a little bit relieved, knowing that the first part of the plan was done. To make a successful conclusion, the Heavy Rescue Squad would have to complete the second part of the plan.

As soon as Dale was restrained, the firefighters immediately appeared. As planned, they used their mechanical device to spread open the wrought iron bars of the fence. I was still standing next to Dale, trying to calm him down as the Heavy Rescue Squad made a large hole in the fence. My relief immediately turned immediately to fear when one of the firefighters yelled to me, "Hey, you're not tied off!"

For just a brief moment in time, I did not know what the firefighter was yelling about. I quickly glanced over and saw safety lines protruding from each of the firefighter's belts. I suddenly understood the firefighter's concern. For some strange reason, instead of quickly moving away, I just stared at the hole in the fence saw how far down the ground was. Thankfully, one of my partners moved me back.

As the firemen successfully pulled Dale through the opening they had cut and away from the hole, we approached them, properly handcuffed Dale, and moved him inside. This was of course after I believe I took a minute to reward myself by hyperventilating, realizing how stupid my actions were.

I tried to regain my composure and went over to again talk with Dale. He had been placed on a stretcher and was awaiting transport to a local hospital for mental health evaluations. I thanked Dale for not jumping and informed him, that as I had promised, he would not be going to jail. I told him he would be transported to a hospital and receive help from a doctor, and I knew he would get better. Dale said his not jumping was not for his lack of trying but praised me for being a man of my word and not taking him to jail.

It would have been interesting to have made follow-up contact with Dale, to see how he was doing. Not long after the incident, we heard he moved out of state, and we had no future contact with him. I know I am not the only negotiator on our team that still sees the Stratosphere Tower and reflects on that evening. I also know how thankful, as a team, we are to have learned from the mistakes we made and implemented procedures to prevent them from occurring again.

Lessons Learned:

I believe our mistakes began early in this event and started with the location where we established our TOC. We are very fortunate to have a mobile tactical operations center with state of the art equipment contained within. Unfortunately, I think we became too tied to it and its capabilities when we decided to leave a command position and some negotiators inside it while others went to the top of the tower. The computers installed inside the TOC have programs which make obtaining intelligence an easier task. Sometimes we rely too much on technology and forget we can obtain some of that same information over the phone or radio.

There was also plenty of space at the top of the observation tower from which an ad-hoc command post could have been established. It would have been close enough to stay informed yet far enough away that Dale could not have seen it nor heard what was being discussed. I feel having one group working from the TOC and a second group making plans from the rooftop, trying to keep the commander informed via telephone could have been improved by simply moving the commander to the top of the tower.

Likely the biggest lesson we took from this incident are the safety practices we violated. As stated, until this incident, it was a rare occasion that we dealt with jumpers. We had no idea the value of ensuring each team member on the roof wear a rappel harness and stay attached to a safety line if they are operational. This event could have easily been disastrous. While it would have been heart-breaking if Dale had jumped, it would have been tragic if one or more negotiators were pulled down with him because they did not wear any safety gear.

Since this incident, it has been mandated that all negotiators attend "high angle" training before they are allowed to respond on a jumper. During the training, team members learn how to don a rappel harness. They work with experts using rope systems that give the team members confidence operating from tall structures.

The movement of the secondary negotiator during this incident was addressed. The secondary negotiator is a critical component of the team and a huge value to the primary negotiator. Not only does the secondary receive and pass along important updates to the primary, but helps coach the primary when conversations take a wrong turn. If an additional body was needed during the rescue planning, another could have been requested. The secondary negotiator's role is too important to lose to a planning discussion. It is equally important the secondary negotiator bring their necessary equipment. By not bringing their radio and earpiece, the secondary negotiator had no other way to obtain updated information than to walk over and retrieve it.

Another lesson learned was the importance of having a tactical team nearby. While the four negotiators were able to execute this plan, it is certainly something that was never trained or practiced. And while the crisis negotiation team practices their verbal skills during regularly scheduled training, they do not have the same skills as the tactical team. These "hands-on" type incidents are best handled by the expert tacticians who routinely train for them.

Lastly, we view grabbing a potential jumper should only be used as an extreme last resort. For some of the reasons indicated above, there are incredible risks with attempting this. Attempting any potential jumper rescue should be done in concert with the tactical team, and only after strong consultation with the tactical commander.

This was a still photo I took from a video which was I given, shot by Lane Swainston. The still photo shows me walking with suicidal jumper Dale Peterson, after he was pulled off the ledge and placed into handcuffs. I handed him to two LVMPD patrol officers and we walked from the roof.(officer's names are unknown)

This was a still photo I took from a video which was I given, shot by Lane Swainston. The still photo shows me holding onto the suicidal jumper, Dale, after I grabbed him when he reached for a cigarette. It also shows members from the Clark County Fire Department's Heavy Rescue Squad, as they ran up and started cutting the iron bars to rescue Dale.

The Stratosphere Hotel

CHAPTER 5

MGM HOTEL JUMPER

Las Vegas is known for doing things on a grand scale. The MGM Hotel, more formally known as the MGM Grand Las Vegas, is certainly one of these grand scale items. Situated on the southern end of the Las Vegas Strip, it sits on over 120 acres of land and has nearly 7,000 hotel rooms. Over 100,000 people pass through its doors on a daily basis. In front of the hotel, even their mascot, Leo the Lion, is of grand scale. At 45 feet tall and weighing over 100,000 pounds, Leo the Lion is the largest bronze statue in the United States. However not everyone who frequents the hotel is hoping to enjoy all the amenities the hotel has to offer.

On Friday, August 04, 2006, at approximately 3:45 a.m., a black male adult found a ladder in an 'employee only' area, and climbed to the top of the front tower. This front tower area houses some of the casino area and has no guest rooms. At approximately seven stories high, it towers over the Leo the Lion statue which faces the intersection of Las Vegas Boulevard and Tropicana, arguably one of the busiest intersections in Las Vegas. Even at that early hour of the morning, the volume of pedestrian and vehicular traffic through the area is high. Adorned to the top of this tower, and evenly spread out, are four statues of Greek Gods, each cemented into place. The male subject stood at the top of the tower area, between two of these statues. Even though it was dark outside the man was clearly illuminated by the hotel lighting.

During the onset of the incident uniformed patrol officers ascended the tower, without any type of protective gear to protect them from falling, and attempted to convince the man to come down. Unfortunately, the subject only identified himself as Jonathan and said he wanted to jump and die. When the officers tried to talk to him, he would say things to them that did not make sense including, "Sun up is judgment time" and "The city is going to burn!" Even more alarming was Jonathan told the officers he was going to grab some nearby power lines to help achieve his death wish. Officers were uncertain if his threat about grabbing the power lines was tied to his statement about "the city is going to burn". Patrol supervisors contacted hotel officials to work on having power to those lines turned off.

The problems of having a jumper on the corner of one of the busiest corners of Las Vegas were well known to the on-scene patrol supervisor. Jonathan not only attracted a large gathering of pedestrians but was also causing people driving by the area to stop in the middle of the street to watch, causing additional traffic issues. In addition to increased pedestrian and vehicular traffic, Jonathon's antics had also drawn the attention of local news media personnel who began responding to the area to report on the event. News coverage of a potential jumper on the Las Vegas Strip is not good for the police department nor for the positive image Las Vegas works hard to maintain. At 3:56 a.m., hours the patrol supervisor requested SWAT and Crisis Negotiators.

From a negotiator's perspective:

I received the call out request just after 4 a.m.. As with most people at that hour, I was still snug in my bed and half thought I was dreaming since this was only two days after the Stratosphere Hotel jumper saga; we simply do not get that many jumper callouts.

As I got near the MGM Hotel, traffic was heavy as many hotel workers were starting to arrive, even at that early hour. It was much worse since patrol officers were trying to divert traffic as many lookeeloos were stopping in the intersection of Las Vegas Boulevard and Tropicana, offering what they thought the subject should do. Their ever so helpful advice consisted of yelling for the man to jump.

At approximately 4:45 a.m., SWAT and negotiators arrived on scene. The briefing we received was limited but it was the all the information the officers on scene had been able to develop.

The patrol officers reported they only knew the subject as Jonathan, who claimed to be and had the physical appearance of being 18 years of age. Officers had located a man in the nearby area who claimed to be Jonathan's stepbrother, Victor. It seemed awfully suspect to us as we were told Victor claimed he did not even know his stepbrother's last name. Victor did say he and Jonathan had been smoking marijuana until 10:30 p.m. the previous evening. That part was believable.

Victor claimed Jonathan lived with him at a nearby weekly motel. He said after a recent fight between the two of them, he forced Jonathan to leave and Jonathan had been homeless ever since. Victor said Jonathan did not like the officers from our police department because they continually harassed him and had him arrested on petty vagrancy type charges. He said he heard from a friend that Jonathan had been drinking ever since he left their marijuana smoking event. Victor said he saw a large presence of police vehicles, walked to the area, and noticed it was his brother on top of the hotel threatening to jump. We were unable to verify any of the information that Victor provided to us and he was unable to provide any additional information.

During the briefing, we were also informed of Jonathan's previous comments which included, "sun up is judgment time", and "the city is going to burn", but no one knew why he made them or what they meant. The patrol supervisor said they had contact with hotel security and were in the process of having the power lines near Jonathan turned off.

I was selected to be the primary negotiator on this event. I would wear a bodybug and, along with a secondary negotiator, would go through the employee access areas, and climb the ladder to the roof of where Jonathan was located.

A bodybug is a covert audio transmitter, more commonly known as a "wire". These devices were used in the 1990s and early 2000s, traditionally by undercover officers, to allow officers assisting in investigations to hear what was being said by the officer undercover and the parties they are meeting with. The bodybugs later gave way to improved devices as technology progressed. With that said, many agencies still have bodybugs they no longer use, making them more easily obtained by crisis negotiators teams without impacting department budgets.

The bodybug is a small, battery-powered device with a tiny microphone attached. They are so small that they can easily be concealed underneath a shirt. When activated, the microphone picks-up audio signals and transmits the signals to a listening post away from the area. Many command posts have audio receivers included inside which enable the conversations the negotiator has with the person in crisis to be monitored. They are a very effective tool.

Learning from some of the mistakes we made two nights prior, I would follow a small contingent of SWAT officers who would lead me to Jonathan's location. The SWAT officers would provide any "hands on" tactics if they became necessary.

Applying additional lessons learned from the Stratosphere Hotel jumper, myself, the secondary, and all of the SWAT officers on the roof would wear rappelling harnesses. When we reached the employee access area, we all donned them, then climbed the ladder to the roof area. Once on the roof, a designated safety officer located a secure anchor then affixed safety ropes to all of our harnesses.

The specific area Jonathan was standing in was approximately 150 feet from our location. It could only be accessed by walking across a small platform. Prior to attempting to make contact with Jonathan, I asked the

SWAT team leader, who was present with us on the roof, where I was allowed to move to. The team leader explained he preferred I talk from the location we were standing and attempt to have Jonathan walk to us. He said if necessary, I could walk a third of the way towards Jonathan, pointing out a spot I was not to cross. This was exceptionally helpful as I knew just how far I could move up to try and influence Jonathan without compromising my safety.

The two patrol officers who had been previously trying to talk with Jonathan had come down and attended our briefing so there was no one to introduce me to Jonathan. As the safety officer was securing the ropes to our harnesses, I discussed my opening contact strategies with my secondary negotiator. We discussed the best way to begin our conversation to try to put him at ease since I had a small SWAT team behind me. Their presence would make anyone uneasy.

The SWAT Team Leader Hixson told me he would keep most of his men out of sight, having them stand just behind a pillar where we were located. From this hidden location one of the SWAT officers would provide updates to the SWAT Commander, who was positioned below still but close enough to observe the situation. He also explained he would keep three of the officers behind me so Jonathan would know I was not there alone.

I had gone over what I was going to say and was ready to make contact. Due to the distance Jonathan was from me, along with the noise from passing vehicles and advice yelled from helpful passersby, we were concerned he may not be able to hear what I was saying. We radioed down our hearing concerns but decided we would initiate contact to see if any type of amplification would be needed. Just prior to my starting, the SWAT Team Leader reminded me of the area I was not to cross. He also pointed out a closer area and explained if Jonathan walked towards me, past the area he pointed out, I was to move out of the way so the tactical team could move up to take him into custody to prevent him from running back.

I realized how much safer I felt than just two nights prior while on the rooftop of the Stratosphere. I had a safety rope attached to my rappel harness and a fully trained tactical team behind me providing protection. It gave me additional confidence.

At 5:15 a.m., I motioned to my secondary negotiator and we both walked a few feet in front of the three SWAT officers. He and I each simply wore a Crisis Negotiation Team t-shirt and blue jeans while the SWAT team members wore their traditional tactical garb. I was hoping the physical distance away from the SWAT officers, along with our difference in clothing, would help Jonathan recognize the difference between "them and us". We were the good guys sent to talk to him. The SWAT guys were there to force him. As I took those few steps forward, I could not help from wondering why I seemed to be the negotiator selected to deal with those subjects in crisis which had obvious mental health issues. I was curious if the SWAT Commander was trying to tell me something.

I introduced myself to Jonathan and I could see his behavior was certainly unique. He was extremely agitated and he began cursing at me. His physical behavior alternated between spreading his arms and flapping them like a bird flying to raising his middle fingers at me while cursing. I tried to continue to talk to him but he began to do what I could only describe as a cross between karate and bizarre dance moves. Keep in mind, the ledge he was performing from was only eight inches wide, making it very easy to fall from.

After a five-minute physical demonstration, one which left me speechless, Jonathan began to scream out his earlier statements of "sun up is judgment time", and "the city is going to burn." Neither myself, my secondary, nor anyone at the command post, who could see Jonathan's moves and hear what he was yelling, knew what these phrases meant or if they had any significant meaning.

My secondary, who was equipped with a police radio set and wearing an earpiece, received advice from the psych doctor in the command post to simply encourage Jonathan to talk. This was good advice but much easier said than done. Jonathan returned to his karate/dance moves with the occasional screamed phrases. It seemed like the best course of action was to just let him be and tire himself out a bit.

After nearly ten minutes, Jonathan started to calm down and began to stand still. I made a second attempt at an introduction, trying to explain I was there to listen and help him. Jonathan was not interested in what I had to say. For twenty more minutes, he resumed his previous behavior. He would alternate from his dance/karate moves to screaming profanities. At one point, Jonathan got into a fighting stance and began doing deliberate karate moves, not aimed at anyone in particular, just apparently to show others he knew how to do them.

The command post asked if we felt a change in primary negotiators was appropriate. I discussed this with the secondary negotiator, about simply swapping roles, but we felt Jonathan's anger and behavior was likely not directed at me. It appeared he was just expressing himself and believed he would continue this behavior with anyone who talked with him. We asked the command post's permission to continue trying to talk with Jonathan which was granted.

At approximately 5:50 a.m., Jonathan, without explanation or any movement from us, moved twenty feet further away from us. He stood underneath one of the cemented Greek God statues, which unbeknownst to us, had several power lines behind it. Jonathan suddenly grabbed the power lines. We all cringed, expecting Jonathan to be suddenly electrocuted, but luckily, hotel officials had shut the power off to those lines and had failed to inform us. Although relieved, Jonathan's actions further proved to us though that his threats of suicide were sincere. After not getting the desired result from the power lines, Jonathan took off his shirt and returned to his karate demonstration.

In my time as a police officer and as a negotiator, I have encountered numerous people with mental health issues. I do not ever recall ever dealing with someone quite like Jonathan. He had immense energy to match his bizarre behavior. He also did not seem like he was interested in anything any one was saying. Not from me or from the passersby's who were still yelling up to him. Police officers on the ground did their best to cordon off the area but there was little they could do to stop people who were driving by from yelling hurtful comments at Jonathan.

Realizing that Jonathan had been screaming for over an hour as well as the physical exertion he was demonstrating, I assumed he had to be thirsty. I know I was from just watching him. As with any concessions negotiators think of, permission must still be obtained from the SWAT Commander, or incident commander depending on the organization, prior to offering them anything. The SWAT Commander, Lieutenant Larry Burns, heard what we were talking about over the radio and authorized me to offer Jonathan a bottle of water. I hoped my gesture would develop some type of rapport, which up until then, was nonexistent.

Just after 6:00 a.m., during one of Jonathan's verbal tirades, one of the phrases he yelled out included the fact that he was a soldier. Nothing else I had attempted thus far had worked and both myself and the secondary were running low on ideas. I yelled back to Jonathan that I heard him and acknowledged I knew he was a soldier. While Jonathan didn't respond, he did appear to make sudden eye contact and I wondered if the phrase meant something to him. Believing I may have broached a topic that Jonathan found interest in, I continued with the "soldier" theme. Unfortunately, Jonathan reverted back to his earlier karate-type behaviors.

I used the permission I had been given earlier and offered Jonathan a bottle of water. Jonathan acted as though he had not heard me. He stopped his karate routine and began to push on the nearby cement statute, attempting to push it off the building. Realizing the statute was cemented in and likely weighed in excess of 500 pounds, I did not believe Jonathan would be successful in his endeavor. He stopped pushing on the statue and began slamming his body into it, and although unlikely he would dislodge the statue, I did not want to see him hurt himself.

As he was slamming his body into the statute, Jonathan yelled out that he knew that we just wanted to kill him. This was one of the first phrases he said that I could understand the meaning of. I yelled to Jonathan that what he said was simply not true. I tried to use the "soldier" theme again, acknowledging he was a soldier. I then pointed towards the SWAT officers behind me, telling Jonathan that they were my soldiers. Suddenly, Jonathan paid attention to me.

As I continued to try to engage Jonathan in additional conversations, he started making more statements that did not make sense. He said he was "waiting for his ship to take him home", and referred to "judgment day". I did not understand everything Jonathan was saying but I did realize the inferences he was making appeared to be related to death.

Jonathan yelled out to me and explained that there were no good people left in the City of Las Vegas. He said he felt bad for me because he knew I was going to go to Hell. While I was hoping Jonathan was not forecasting my damnation, I was at least thankful he was starting to engage me in conversation and now saying things I could finally understand.

I tried to draw Jonathan into an actual dialog while including the "solider" theme since that seemed to pique his prior interest. I attempted this by telling him there were actually many good people in the city including "my soldiers", as I pointed towards the SWAT officers behind me. I told Jonathan that whatever he did, to please not hurt "my soldiers", implying the SWAT officers worked for me.

Jonathan called some of my bluff, asking where my uniform was since I was dressed in only the Crisis Negotiations t-shirt and blue jeans while the SWAT officers were in their full tactical gear. Not knowing what else to say, I told Jonathan that I did not know that he was going to be there today so did not put on my uniform. For some strange reason, Jonathan seemed to listen to what I said and it appeared this was our first attempt at establishing a rapport.

For the next twenty minutes, Jonathan and I spoke back and forth, nothing with any real substance, but I did mention the "soldiers" several times. Jonathan then said he wanted to go back to Kenya, Africa. Thinking he was in a delusional state, and quite frankly being taken off guard, I offered to take him there. As soon as the phrase left my lips, I knew it was a mistake. I bit my tongue and prayed Jonathan would not call me on it.

I hurried and switched gears, returning to the "soldier" theme. I kept talking about "my soldiers" and asked Jonathan if he would come down with me off the roof. I obviously misjudged our level of rapport as Jonathan's response was to spit then told me to shut the fuck up. I was growing frustrated as nothing I was suggesting seemed to matter and I was running out of ideas. The secondary negotiator seemed just as stumped.

Instead of returning to the "soldier" routine, which appeared had run its course, I ventured into uncharted waters and brought up his step-brother Victor. Jonathan looked at me in a strange manner and questioned who Victor was. I tried to backpedal. I explained to Jonathan that I had been told that Victor was his stepbrother. Instead of just dropping the topic, I pressed forward, explaining how sure I was that Victor was worried about him. Jonathan still looked puzzled and now wanted to see Victor. I realized we had been had and Victor was likely no relation to Jonathan but I had now painted myself into a corner. The only thing I could think of saying was that Victor would meet with him, but only if

Jonathan came off the roof. Thankfully, Jonathan dropped the subject. To say this event was a poor showing of my negotiator abilities would be an understatement.

Unfortunately, I was stressed from bringing up the entire conversation about Victor and quickly wanted to get away from that topic. So, what incredible idea did I bring up? Sadly, I went right back to the damn "soldier" theme.

I told Jonathan I was concerned for my soldiers, that they needed some rest. I explained to him how they could not leave until he came down from the building. Damn. How did I go right back to the same topic Jonathan had scolded me about earlier? The best thing I knew I could do was to shut up. I knew when all else failed, staying silent often helped me. It allowed me to recollect my thoughts and get back on track. By being silent, it also offered Jonathan an opportunity to talk as I am often guilty of talking when I should be listening.

A funny thing happened when I stopped talking. Jonathan suddenly grew quiet. He stopped cursing. The karate also ceased. He just stood there. Motionless. He was not cursing at me. This was the first time we had witnessed Jonathan calm.

I had done enough damage so I knew not to talk. I whispered to the SWAT team leader to pass me a bottle of water and to ask each of his men to start drinking a bottle of water. I finally had an idea.

It was nearly 6:30 in the morning but since it was the first week of August, it was already over 90 degrees. Jonathan had climbed to the roof of the MGM and had been screaming for almost three hours. He had to be thirsty. Rather than ask him if he was thirsty, I just started drinking my bottle of water, as did the SWAT officers.

I wanted to offer Jonathan some water but I also did not want to digress since Jonathan was finally quiet. So we kept sipping our water. Jonathan was watching. I finished my bottle of water and threw the empty bottle back towards where the SWAT officers were standing. Almost on cue and without asking, they handed me a fresh bottle. Jonathan was really paying attention to what we were doing.

I used a much softer voice and thanked Jonathan for allowing the soldiers the much-needed break. I told him I knew he too was a solider and was also entitled to a break and for some water. Trying to show him respect, I asked him if it would be okay if my soldiers walked over to him and brought him some water. Jonathan seemed to accept what I was telling him and began walking towards us. Suddenly, for some unknown reason, he changed his mind and turned back around. He stomped back to where he had been standing and began screaming incoherently at the top of his lungs.

I had no idea why Jonathan stormed off. As bizarre as it may sound, I knew in my heart it did not have anything to do with the solider comments. Reading the chain of events makes it sound like Jonathan's outburst were tied to the solider terminology but watching his demeanor, that was not the case. I realize that is a bold statement and I wish I could pinpoint what caused his outbursts, but I wanted to go with my gut feeling. I really believed the solider analogy was working.

Las Vegas is a town famous for gambling and I understand by doing this, I could be actually gambling with Jonathan's life but I asked the SWAT team leader if he could ask his men to start drinking from their water bottles again. Jonathan had stopped screaming and was watching us again.

I rolled the dice and kept my fingers crossed. I simply said to Jonathan, "Let's go eat and drink like soldiers", and started walking briefly away from him towards the SWAT officers. As luck would have it, Jonathan simultaneously put his shirt on and began walking towards our direction. To be honest, I was shocked. I kept praying he would not change his mind and retreat back. I continued to praise him for doing the right thing, ensuring him there were no tricks. I promised him that I was a man of my word and that we would eat and drink together.

Just like that, it was over. At 6:55 a.m., almost three hours after he first climbed onto the roof, Jonathan voluntarily walked to me and the awaiting SWAT officers and was taken into custody without incident. Since there was no other way off the roof, he was placed into a harness and safely lowered down by the SWAT officers.

Once on the ground, Jonathan and I enjoyed an energy bar and bottled water together, just as promised. Afterwards, he was not arrested, but taken to the hospital for mental health evaluation. I never did ask about "sun up being judgment time". I figured it was better some things just be left alone. We never had any further problems from Jonathan after that day.

Lessons Learned:

We had learned from previous incidents the importance of leaving the first responder in place until we are ready to transition to the negotiation team. On this incident, the two officers who had climbed onto the rooftop knew SWAT and negotiators had arrived so they came down to brief us on what had occurred. While it was good they came down since they were not wearing any safety equipment, they could have introduced us, then climbed down and debriefed with other assisting negotiators.

We have found that just because the negotiation team arrives does not mean the officer talking to the subject needs to be replaced. There have been several times when we have arrived on an event and noticed the first responder had developed a strong rapport and had great dialog with the subject. One these incidents, we simply rolled in and became his secondary negotiator and provided support. Why should we replace someone who is already doing a good job and start from scratch? Besides, one of the reasons negotiators are more successful than the first responder that initiated conversation is because we roll in with a tactical component. We can sometimes say the exact same things the first responder did but because we have the SWAT team with us in all of their gear and armored vehicles, the subject seems to cooperate more. That is one of the reasons both disciplines respond together and work as a team.

For the patrol supervisor on scene, calling for the specialized resources early in the incident was a smart move. Should things go sideways quickly and someone, (suspect, officer or nearby citizen) gets seriously injured or killed, a lawsuit is likely. There are two key questions that will typically be asked of the on-scene supervisor. The first question is usually, "Did you know you had a fully trained tactical and negotiation team you could contact?" That answer is almost always yes. The second question, and the one which is the hardest for the supervisor to answer is "Why did you not call them?"

Another issue identified on this event was my inability to think on my feet and come up with better communication topics and my failure to be quiet and allow Jonathan to speak. It is often beneficial to allow the subject to speak as this is their time to vent. It is also nice for the secondary negotiator to help feed the primary negotiator ideas when running out of ideas and to remind the primary to allow the subject to talk but the responsibility for conduct falls on the primary negotiator. It is true that missions succeed and fail based on the totality of the entire team but in self-reflection, these were two areas I truly struggled on and needed to improve.

There were several mistakes made during this incident but thankfully we were at least smart enough to implement procedures to help rectify problems identified during the Stratosphere jumper. The use of a rappel harness, a safety line, and the tremendous assistance received from the tactical team were just a few of the lessons we learned from the previous incident which not only helped us successfully resolve this incident but kept us safe in the process.

This was a still photo I took from a video which was I given, shot by Lane Swainston, who was flying above the scene in a helicopter. The still photo shows the location where the jumper Jonathan, was located. He is on the left side of the photo, beneath the sphere, and myself, along with SWAT officers, are on the right side of the photo.

This was a still photo I took from a video which was I given, shot by Lane Swainston, who was flying above the scene in a helicopter. The still photo shows the location where the jumper Jonathan, was located. It is an overall of the scene.

This was a still photo I took from a video which was I given, shot by Lane Swainston, who was flying above the scene in a helicopter. The still photo shows a close up of the jumper, Jonathan, beneath the sphere, as he was screaming.

I took this photo at the scene. It shows the location where the jumper was.

CHAPTER 6

HEARTBREAK ON THE HIGHWAY

Brian Ramirez was a successful middle-aged man who at 45 years of age had gone through some of life's difficult times but always managed to bounce back. He had been married to Laura Ramirez and together they shared a beautiful daughter, Heather.

Brian and Laura had their differences, which unfortunately, resulted with a divorce in 2007. Heather had just graduated high school and went off to attend college at University of California, Irvine.

Brian was learning to deal with the divorce and had begun to see Vivian. Vivian had also gone through a recent divorce and had a teenaged daughter named Shaneka. Brian and Vivian had known each other for several years and began dating as Brian's marriage to Laura was coming to an end. After an eighteen-month dating relationship, Brian and Vivian married in 2007, not long after Brian's divorce to Laura was finalized.

Brian had served in the U.S. Army for nearly 25 years, retiring as a supply officer. After leaving the Army, he was hired by a high-end Las Vegas security firm who, among other jobs, provided security details for classified areas within Nellis Air Force Base.

Life was looking up for Brian. Although he had gone through a divorce, he had a daughter in college, worked out at the gym on a regular basis, and had a great job. Unfortunately, a series of events occurred which caused Brian's life to spiral downward.

Although divorced from Laura, the two maintained an amicable relationship. Laura was diagnosed with brain cancer and shared with Brian she did not know how long she had left to live. If Laura's news was not devastating enough, Brian was then fired from his well-paying security job.

The company Brian worked for had access to sensitive information and patrolled classified areas. Because of this the security officers were required to pass a periodic polygraph test. During the most recent testing, Brian was caught changing his answers regarding steroid use.

The news of Laura's brain cancer and the loss of his job caused tremendous stress on Brian so he sought out help. His help came in the form of a bottle. Brian began drinking. Heavily. His relationship with his wife Vivian had begun to sour but dealing with this third source of stress was something Brian did not want to take on and he refused to talk about it.

Brian was a good man. He was conservative and a bit private. Vivian worked to make him into a different man. She encouraged Brian to get tattoos, something he had never done. The tattoos she ultimately convinced him to get were not routine. On Brian's bicep area, printed large enough for anyone to see was "VIVIAN'S FANTASY". On his opposing bicep, an even more degrading tattoo, "VIVIAN'S BITCH".

Brian's tattoos were not the only new additions Vivian wished for. Their adult time changed drastically as well. Vivian enjoyed having Brian dress in bondage type outfits as she took digital photographs of him in compromising positions. Deep down it appeared Brian regretted ever taking part in the photographs, considering them to be humiliating.

With everything Brian was experiencing, he was making a conscious effort to turn his life around. He had been in to see a counselor to talk about his problems. He even landed an interview for a job with the Nevada Capitol Police, a position he was excited about.

On January 16, 2008, Brian and Vivian decided to blow off some steam and went to a local casino to enjoy an evening out. Before arriving at the casino, Brian stopped at a liquor store and bought a bottle of Jack Daniels whiskey from which the two shared several drinks. They continued on, arriving at the hotel to enjoy a show. While at the show, Brian continued to drink. He drank so much that Vivian confronted him, which caused an argument.

The drinking argument became so intense, Vivian and Brian agreed their night out was ruined and they would return home. By this point, Vivian estimated Brian had consumed at least seven shots of whiskey, making him difficult to deal with.

While walking to Brian's truck, Vivian claimed Brian pushed her and grabbed her arm. She said she became infuriated that he had put his hands on her. Vivian said she was so mad that upon reaching the vehicle, she kicked out the truck's windshield with her high-heeled shoe. If he was angry before, Brian was now seething. His Dodge truck was one of his prized possessions.

The couple continued to argue as they drove toward their home, located in northwest Las Vegas. When they arrived, they both went upstairs and into their bedroom. Vivian's daughter, Shaneka was also home, asleep in her room.

Vivian prepared to go to sleep but anger got the best of Brian. He went into his closet and retrieved his stainless-steel Smith and Wesson .357 revolver. He emerged from the closet and fired four bullets into their home computer, located next to their bed. Brian's gunfire was most likely aimed at attempting to destroy the computer's hard drive which contained the compromising photos of him. Earlier, during their argument, Vivian had threatened to send the degrading photos to Brian's parents.

After he shot the computer, Vivian ran toward Brian and the two struggled over the pistol. Shaneka, whose bedroom was across from her mother's, awoke to the gunfire and subsequent struggle. When she went into her mother's room she found him towering over her. Shaneka heard Brian yell at her mother, "You know what you've done," as he fired a fifth round into the computer. Brian's statement gave further credence that he shot the computer over the embarrassing digital photos it housed.

Shaneka could see Brian holding her mother down with his left hand while he had the revolver in his right hand, pointed at her back. Vivian turned and found her daughter had entered the room and yelled for her to call the police. Brian realized the situation was spinning out of control. He knew if the police responded, he would be a suspect in several felony charges including Assault with a Deadly Weapon and Discharge of a Weapon in an Occupied Structure. Brian pleaded with Shaneka to not call the police. It was too late. Shaneka had already witnessed enough and knew her mother was in danger. She ran downstairs, grabbed the cordless phone, and darted across the street to call from a safe location. Unfortunately, across the street was too far for the cordless phone to connect, so her call to police could not go through.

Back inside the house, Brian's world was still spinning. He was not about to stick around to see what would happen. In addition to his .357 revolver, which contained only one live round after his gunfire, he also grabbed his Glock .40 semi-automatic pistol. He ran out the door with both pistols, got into his black Dodge truck, and fled the scene.

Brian forgot his Dodge was very distinguishable and easy to spot. Not only was it customized, it was painted black with large yellow stripes on both sides of the truck bed and the Dodge "Rumblebee" logo. To help further identify it, the vehicle bore personalized license plates.

Shaneka watched as Brian fled in his truck then ran back inside to check on her mother. She found her mother still on the floor but not injured from the gunfire.

Vivian could not believe what her husband had done. She knew he was going through a great deal and had even earlier spoken to her about committing suicide but she thought with the counseling, he was improving. Regardless of what Brian was going through, Vivian was scared. At 12:04 a.m., she called 911 to report what happened.

Brian had left. He stopped at a nearby convenience store, grabbed some snacks, and filled his truck up with gas. He left the store, got onto the freeway, and drove southbound, back towards the center of town.

It appeared he was planning a long drive, possibly to drive out of town and meet with his daughter Heather, or his father Ben, both of whom were in California. Brian loved his daughter and father with all of his heart. He held his father in such high regards, he wished he could have been more like him. Unfortunately, the 911 call to police had already been made.

In addition to explaining what had occurred, Vivian provided the police dispatcher with the description of Brian and his truck, including the truck's unique paint scheme and the vehicle's personalized license plates. She also told the dispatcher Brian was armed.

Five minutes after Vivian's emergency call, uniformed patrol Officer Jeff Robertson arrived at her home to obtain additional information. After hearing the story from Vivian, Officer Robertson advised the dispatcher that Brian was a suspect in several felony crimes. Upon hearing this, additional patrol officers began combing the area in attempts to locate him.

At approximately 12:19 a.m., just fourteen minutes after the 911 call was made, uniformed patrol Officer Howard Crosby located Brian driving his easily identifiable Dodge truck south on US95 towards downtown Las Vegas. Officer Crosby was soon joined by several other patrol vehicles after they realized Brian was suspected of being armed and dangerous. They elected not to try and stop the vehicle until the police helicopter, which radioed they were only a few minutes away, joined them should Brian try and flee.

Brian was no fool. He could see the multiple patrol cars in his rear-view mirror and knew what was about to happen. While driving the speed limit and waiting to see what the police were going to do, Brian used his cell phone and called

Vivian.

Back at the residence, Vivian's cell phone began ringing and instead of answering it, she showed it to Officer Robertson, who was still there completing a police report. The cell phone's caller ID displayed it was Brian who was calling her. Officer Robertson answered the cell phone and began to speak with Brian.

Brian told Officer Robertson that he wanted to talk to his wife. Officer Robertson explained that Vivian didn't want to talk to him and instead asked Brian to please return to the house so they could work out what had occurred. Brian, very matter-of-factly, explained to Officer Robertson he could not return to the house because he had screwed up and he knew what was in store for him.

Brian told Officer Robertson he was being followed by police cars. Officer Robertson asked him if he would be willing to pull over and cooperate with the officers. Brian told Officer Robertson that he had no plans of cooperating with the police then hung up the phone.

Officer Crosby and fellow officers were still following Brian on the freeway, providing updates on his location. They also learned via a radio broadcast from Officer Robertson that Brian had just called the house and explained he had no intent of cooperating. Officer Robertson also told the officers that Brian's wife believed he was suicidal.

While southbound on US95 at Boulder Highway, after being joined by the police helicopter, Officer Crosby signaled for Brian to stop by activating his red lights and siren. Brian refused and continued driving.

Officers who were monitoring the radio traffic predicted Brian might not stop and had gone to the next southbound exit, Russell Road, and laid out spike strips. Their location was perfect. Brian continued driving southbound and while passing the Russell Road exit, assisting officers pulled the spike strips into the path of his truck. Brian ran over the strips which began to deflate several of tires. Brian still had no plans of surrendering.

Immediately after hitting the spike strips and realizing his tires were going flat, Brian opened the rear sliding window of his truck and pointed his .357 revolver towards the pursuing units. With a loud report, Brian let off the last remaining round in his revolver. Officer Crosby felt something strike his patrol car and broadcast this over the radio. With Brian now shooting at them, it changed the dynamics of the call.

With his tires running flat, Brian limped his truck along the interstate, taking the next exit - Sunset Road. He tried to continue driving westbound on Sunset but with his crippled tires, it forced him to stop in the middle of the first intersection. At 12:40 a.m., in the middle of Sunset and Marks Street, less than 1/8 of a mile from the interstate, the armed barricade began.

Police personnel on scene all began working on their priorities. Officer Crosby and his partners used their patrol cars for cover and began at gunpoint to order Brian out of the vehicle.

Although it was after midnight, many of the nearby businesses were still open. One of the patrol supervisors asked the police dispatcher to call the businesses and have them shelter in place. The shift lieutenant also recognized the dangers Brian posed and announced to the officers that if Brian fled on foot, they were ordered not to permit him to enter any business. Every officer on the scene understood what that order meant. If Brian ran towards a business with the gun, they were to employ deadly force and shoot him.

The scene had instantly become chaotic. The shift lieutenant requested SWAT and Crisis Negotiators be enroute.

The police officers were yelling for Brian to surrender but he just sat calmly in his truck and redialed Vivian's cell phone. His phone call was again answered by Officer Robertson, angering Brian. Officer Robertson had been monitoring the police radio so was aware of Brian's location and what had transpired.

As Officer Robertson began talking to Brian, he noticed Brian's tone was much more resolved. Brian knew he had gone too far, sharing with Officer Robertson that he "screwed up". Brian explained that he always wanted to be a police officer but this incident would now prevent him from ever attaining that goal. Brian's conversation grew much darker as he told Officer Robertson of his certainty that he would die that evening, explaining the police were going to have to kill him.

Officer Robertson said anything he could think of to defuse the situation. As the officer was talking, something he said seemed to make a difference to Brian. He was able to convince Brian to throw one of his pistols out of his vehicle. Although we will never know, it was likely Brian threw the .357 revolver out of his truck as he knew it was unloaded after he fired the final round during the police pursuit. He was still armed with the .40 Glock which contained a full magazine of live ammunition.

Officer Robertson continued to talk with Brian over the cell phone. Sadly, officers on the scene continued to yell out verbal commands for Brian to exit the truck, which only caused Brian to become confused and distracted.

As the two men continued to talk over the phone, Brian repeated his ominous prediction of being certain he would die that evening. He even alluded to how his death would come. Brian said he didn't want to hurt the officers but knew if he just pointed his pistol at them the officers would be forced to kill him. He also reminded Officer Robertson he had received extensive firearms training from his previous security firm employment and clarified that he was a 'good shot'.

Officer Robertson was doing a good job communicating with Brian. This was demonstrated by not only Brian continuing to talk with him but also his ability to convince Brian to throw one of his pistols from the truck. No one else had achieved a concession from Brian.

Brian did ask to speak to Vivian but Officer Robertson had been cautioned earlier to not let this occur. He was warned that if Brian spoke to Vivian, there was a strong likelihood he would use the opportunity to say his final words to her then kill himself.

Supervisors at the car stop knew Brian was on the phone with Officer Robertson but they were frustrated Brian would not communicate with them. Hoping to force Brian to talk with them, supervisors ordered Officer Robertson to disconnect his call with Brian, which he did. All this did was make Brian upset. He even redialed the number several times but supervisors ordered Officer Robertson to not accept his calls.

The supervisors on scene wanted Brian's attention. And they got it. Angered by having his phone call with Officer Robertson disconnected, Brian stepped out of the truck. When he exited, he pointed his Glock .40 pistol to his head and demanded to speak with Vivian.

The officers used their patrol cars for cover while each trained their weapons at Brian. One officer tried to speak with Brian using the patrol car's PA system instead of yelling at him. They were trying to do whatever they could to prevent Brian from engaging them in a firefight. The officers knew SWAT and negotiators were enroute and were just trying to stall for time. However, time was ticking and Brian was growing impatient.

Brian repeated the earlier threats he made to Officer Robertson. He warned officers at the scene by yelling, "Don't make me point this gun at you". As they tried to calm Brian he yelled out to the officers, "I know you have families, I just want to shoot myself". For the officers on the scene, SWAT and crisis negotiators couldn't arrive fast enough.

While waiting for SWAT's arrival, officers watched Brian reach into the cab of the truck and put on a black leather coat. It appeared to the officers Brian was prepared to stand out in the cold for as long as it took for him to accomplish his mission. And it was cold. The temperature was in the mid-20s.

At 1:30 a.m., SWAT and negotiators began to arrive. As SWAT was preparing their deployment plan and negotiators were being briefed as to what had occurred, Brian became even more agitated. He was upset because no one would answer the phone when he called Vivian from his cell phone. Frustrated, he threw down his cell phone, smashing it. He continued his tirade and began to threaten the patrol officers by telling them, "There's no turning back. Don't make me shoot you". Brian obviously wanted to die.

From a negotiator's perspective:

I received the callout request, quickly got dressed, and began my drive. I monitored the patrol channel and listened to the radio updates. I did not live far from the incident so was the first negotiator to arrive. As I got out of my vehicle to head to the command post, I could not help but notice the thermometer read 19 degrees. I realize it may sound trivial but it simply does not get that cold in Las Vegas very often. I was thankful we would be able to talk to Brian from the interior of the warm command post. Boy was I wrong.

We received a briefing of the event and negotiator assignments were made. Detective Eric Ravelo, although relatively new to the team at the time, was selected to serve as the primary negotiator. Since Eric was relatively new, I was designated as his secondary negotiator to help coach him during the incident.

Prior to our deployment, we received an update from the SWAT Commander, Lieutenant Larry Burns. He explained the SWAT officers were going to move towards Brian in two armored vehicles. They would use their vehicles to block Brian's truck since even with flat tires, he could get in and drive off, albeit slowly.

Our initial plan was to call Brian on his cell phone and begin our negotiation. Unfortunately, he smashed his phone as we were arriving which negated that plan. The new communication plan required Eric to use the PA system in the armored vehicle and talk to Brian. The armored vehicle was also equipped with a small microphone. Officers believed we would be able to hear Brian's remarks through the microphone's speaker. As we spoke to Brian from inside the armored vehicle, SWAT officers would be stand to the rear of the armored vehicles should they need to intervene.

After we briefed our plan, we began to move into position. It was 2:00 a.m. and nearly two hours after the event first occurred.

Brian paid very close attention as the two SWAT vehicles moved up, blocking the front and rear of his truck. He was obviously alarmed and stood at a readied state with the Glock pistol still pressed against his head. I told Detective Eric Ravelo to talk to Brian as we moved up, hoping Eric's voice would not only draw his attention but hoped it would calm him down a bit.

Eric did an excellent job as he began talking to Brian. Using the PA system in the armored vehicle made Eric's job more challenging as it is difficult to be personable and develop rapport over a loud speaker. To complicate matters even more, it was nearly impossible to hear Brian's responses over the small microphone mounted in the armored vehicle. I strained to listen and help Eric understand what Brian said but Brian's voice was often simply too faint. Eric had to keep asking Brian to repeat himself, which added to Brian's frustration.

I was outfitted with a bodybug transmitter so negotiators at the command post could hear the progress of the negotiations. I also had a police radio and wore an earpiece which enabled me to receive updates from the command post. With the difficulties we were experiencing trying to hear what Brian said, I asked the command post if they could devise a different communication plan. They began to explore other communication options.

Although forced to deal with our limited ability to hear Brian's complete conversations, Eric did a remarkable job with establishing a rapport with him. With the armored vehicles directly in front and behind him, we had a clear view of Brian through the front windshield of the armored vehicle. Since Brian could see both Eric and I in the vehicle, it allowed Eric to use his body language as he spoke to Brian, which was helpful.

Eric communicated with Brian well but Brian remained guarded. He asked who I was and Eric explained that I was his partner, which he accepted. The entire time we spoke, he remained observant of the SWAT officers who were gathered to the rear of both armored vehicles.

To help aid with hearing Brian, we asked the SWAT officers if they could turn the ignitions to the armored vehicles off. They turned them both off which allowed us to hear a little better but we also lost our heat. I guess since the SWAT guys had to be cold, we did too.

As Eric spoke to Brian, Brian made it very clear to us and everyone else listening that he intended to die and would force the police to kill him. He reiterated he knew he would achieve this goal by just pointing his pistol at the SWAT officers. We needed Eric to redirect the conversation.

We had been told of Brian's love for his daughter, Heather. Eric exploited this, reminding Brian of all he was yet to experience with Heather. Talking about his daughter and the future possibilities seemed to take Brian's mind away from his ideas of committing "suicide by cop".

Eric asked me if he should bring up Vivian. My gut said that was a bad idea as we believed she was the root of the problem. I told him we should wait until we get further information from the negotiators doing research in the command post. Once we brought her up, we would be forced to deal with it. If Brian brought her up, I knew Eric could tap dance around the issue and feel Brian out before going down the rabbit hole with him. I also knew the negotiators in the command post would be researching Vivian and Brian's relationship.

Eric continued talking with Brian. It appeared to me that Brian was actually paying attention to what Eric was saying and the conversation was good. As good as it was though, Brian never moved the pistol away from his head. It also appeared the cold weather was beginning to get to him as he began to dance around to try and warm up.

As we continued to talk to Brian, assisting negotiators had Officer Robertson transport Vivian and her daughter, Shaneka, to the command post so they could be interviewed. They were interviewed separately to not only verify the story, but to hopefully gain information which may be beneficial in our negotiation with Brian. The command post was also staged far enough away so that neither of them could see Brian.

Vivian and Shaneka provided the negotiators many of the details outlined above. There was one peculiar thing negotiators noticed during their interview with Shaneka. She continually complained about being at the scene and questioned how long everything was going to take as she wanted to return home. She had been told her step-father was standing in the intersection with a gun to his head, threatening to kill himself yet she was so blasé. Her callousness was something that made us all question the relationship Brian had at home. Not only with his step-daughter but his wife as well.

At 3:00 a.m., Eric had been talking with Brian for an hour. Although Eric brought up key points that seemed to capture Brian's attention, there were several times Brian would remind us that he was going to die that evening and he would make the police kill him. It seemed that each time Brian brought up his desire to be killed by police, he inched his way closer to the armored vehicle. Not only did Eric and

I notice him getting closer but the SWAT officers remained acutely aware as well.

The cold weather had its effects on everyone. Eric and I were cold and we could see the SWAT officers moving around outside of Brian's view, trying to stay warm. The temperature appeared to be having an adverse effect on Brian as well. There were several times we could see his body trembling and it appeared it was the cold weather causing this, not his nerves. He was only wearing a leather coat over a short-sleeved t-shirt and a pair of blue jeans.

At 3:19 a.m., the cold weather really got to Brian. We could see him passing the pistol from one hand to the other, but always keeping it pointed to his head. He continued to move around in an attempt to stay warm.

Brian moved the gun away from his head to change which hands would hold the pistol. While changing hands and the gun briefly pointed upwards, it suddenly discharged. The gun going off startled Brian. It scared the hell out of me. As soon as it went off, Brian began apologizing, explaining that he did not mean to do it. Although apologetic, he put the gun right back to his head.

I believe it was Brian's cold, trembling hands that cause the accidental discharge of the pistol. Others believed Brian intentionally fired a round, possibly as a test fire in the prelude of forcing a police intervention. Whatever the case, Brian fired a .40 caliber round into the air near an extremely busy intersection and freeway. He could not continue to fire rounds without the police taking action.

Eric really stepped up the pace. He continued to talk to Brian about the possibilities life still held for him. Brian replied that if we gave him a cell phone and allowed him to make a call, he would put the gun down. This was a request we would consider, but who was he going to call and what was he going to say? It was our experience that many of suicidal people choose to call a loved one to say goodbye before committing the act.

Eric pressed on, continuing to talk with Brian. Actually, Eric did almost all of the talking. This was not his fault as Brian seemed to just get quiet. This one-way dialog continued for nearly an hour. At 4:15 a.m., I asked Eric if he could inquire about Brian's silence. Brian explained that he wanted to stop talking to rest his voice for a bit. This did not mean we had to stop talking. In fact, it would be silly if everyone stood motionless and did not speak while Brian stood in the intersection with a gun to his head.

As Eric talked it was hard to judge if what he was telling Brian was sinking in. In addition to being unsure if Brian was listening, we noticed Brian repeated his earlier behavior and began to inch his way back towards the armored vehicle we were in. Eric talked to him, and told him to move back to his truck. He got to within 6 yards of our vehicle and I believe the SWAT officers had the same fear we did. He was closing the distance to force the SWAT officers to take action. When the SWAT officers remained behind cover, Brian suddenly got down onto his knees, gun still at his head. We knew what he was about to do. But Eric raised his voice and got Brian's attention. I'm not sure what he said, but Brian unexplainably got back up and walked back to his truck. The gun stayed at his head.

We started to consider our position. Eric had been talking to Brian for over two hours during which Brian explained that he was going to force the police to kill him. Twice during their conversation, Brian intentionally backed himself close our vehicle, knowing SWAT was staged behind it and appeared to want to provoke a confrontation. We also had to consider he fired a gunshot into the air, which could be viewed as a test fire to work up his courage. Most importantly, we did not appear any closer to peacefully resolving the incident.

Eric and I discussed these facts amongst ourselves and felt we should flip-flop roles. I had already heard everything said and Brian was familiar, if only by sight, with my presence. What did we have to lose? We discussed this option via cell phone with the SWAT Commander Burns who concurred. He agreed that Eric had done a stellar job, but just hearing some of the same thing but from a second voice might help be all that was needed to convince Brian to put the gun.

At 4:26 a.m., I officially swapped positions with Eric. I briefly introduced myself to Brian as Eric climbed into the rear of the armored vehicle and assumed the secondary negotiator position. Brian did not question the switch of negotiators. I believe he was too stressed, cold, and tired to care.

Brian was a little blunter with me. As I was working on establishing a dialog, Brian said he had no problems talking to me but said that if I could just deliver him a cell phone we could be done. It was not that he liked me, he just wanted a phone. I tried to explore the telephone request and asked him who he planned on calling? Brian answered he would "talk to whomever he wanted to and if that person told him what he wanted to hear", he would put the gun down. It was obvious through his cryptic remarks that he did not want us to know who he wanted to call.

Did Brian want to call Vivian to see if their marriage was still viable after what happened or did he plan on blaming her for what happened? Did he intend to call his daughter and/or father, the two people that he loved the most and say goodbye? It just seemed more harm than good could come from any phone calls Brian wanted to make so we planned on stalling.

I continued to talk with Brian, telling him how much his family, especially his daughter and father meant to him. I reminded Brian if he was to do something to himself, who would be there to walk his Heather down the aisle when she got married? I tried to get as personal as I could, pulling at every heart string for every positive event I could think of.

Brian appeared to listen to what I was saying but he also said he wanted to call Vivian and again asked for a phone. He showed his hand a bit by explaining who he wanted to call. Maybe we could use Vivian to our advantage.

I asked Eric to contact the command post and ask obtain permission from the SWAT Commander for negotiators to get third party intermediary (TPI) tape from Vivian. I knew the negotiators would still have her near the command post area. I was hoping that if we received a warm, reassuring message from her I could play the tape and use its message to help convince Brian how much his wife cared about him. He would also know that she was nearby and I would explain that he could meet with her when the incident concluded. If our theory was true and it was Brian's plan to either say his final goodbye or leave Vivian with a nasty statement before he killed himself, using the tape would help prevent that. In any event, I knew that if I had a loving message from Vivian, I knew how I could work it into my negotiation.

Eric called and obtained SWAT Commander Burns' approval. Negotiators went right to work and obtained the tape recording from Vivian.

While we waited for the TPI tape, I knew there was no guarantee that when I played it, I would receive the response from Brian I was hoping for. It was a bit of a gamble considering that Vivian seemed to be the source of the argument which led to the barricade. If she was the source, I felt that if I sold the tape properly before playing it, I could read Brian's reaction. I felt if I told him I had it, wanted him to hear it and he showed a positive reaction, I could play the tape and use it to help convince Brian there was hope as well as many things to live for. I also knew the clock was ticking.

The sun would rise soon, stealing the dark areas SWAT officers were concealing themselves in. It would also bring more vehicular and pedestrian traffic to the area for people headed to work on a Thursday morning.

SWAT Commander Burns was aware of the many issues at hand and wondered if this incident could be successfully negotiated. Taking everything into consideration, the SWAT Commander explained his plan over the radio. The commander said if Brian moved the gun away from his head, the SWAT officers were going to initiate an intervention.

I listened to the intervention plan as it was laid out. If Brian presented a window of opportunity, SWAT officers would simultaneously deploy several less lethal options devices while maintaining lethal coverage should their options not work. I had been talking to Brian for twenty minutes but knew I had ramp up what I was saying and how I was saying it.

At 4:55 a.m., Brian told me that he needed to urinate. I offered to take him into one of the nicest bathrooms in the area. I always use that line. Brian and I both shared a laugh as we knew he would obviously not agree to that. Brian told me he did not have any other choice other than to urinate in the middle of the street. I told him I understood. The SWAT officers heard this conversation and announced over the SWAT radio that if Brian removed the pistol from his head to manipulate his pants and urinate, they would use the opportunity to initiate their intervention. As hard as it may be to believe, Brian was able to complete the task one-handed, keeping the Glock pistol pointed at his head with the other.

I knew if Brian presented them the opportunity, the officers were ready with their plan. I wondered to myself what was taking so long to get Vivian's TPI tape. Finally, at 5:22 a.m., the tape arrived and I had the commander's approval to play it. I quickly reviewed it so I knew what she said and how I would sell it.

I opened the dialog by explaining to Brian how much I knew he wanted to talk to Vivian. I reassured him that she was nearby and how much she cared about him. Brian shook his head - no, he did not believe she cared for him. I did not let his head shake deter me. I continued talking, telling him how much family meant and that he and Vivian could get through anything. I told him how every marriage has its ups and downs and even shared some private thoughts about my own marriage. Brian appeared to accept what I was saying and I knew it was the opportune time to play the tape.

I pushed play on the tape recorder and broadcast the sound over the PA system. The negotiators who obtained it did a phenomenal job coaching Vivian on what to say. As soon as Brian heard Vivian begin to speak, he became emotional and started to cry. This was the first time we saw Brian so emotional and I knew the tape was having its desire affects. Brian shook his head several times as Vivian's message played, concentrating on the words she said. The tape recording was done perfectly.

I used the message Vivian conveyed to further demonstrate how much Brian meant to her and how much he was loved. I confessed to him how I had wronged my spouse but because of her love and forgiveness, how our marriage grew even stronger. I used my personal situation as an analogy, forecasting to Brian how much better their marriage would be. Brian obviously liked what I was saying as he began agreeing with me and nodding his head yes. This was another first during this negotiation.

Time continued to tick by. It was 5:35 a.m. and although Brian still had the gun to his head, he seemed to listen intently to what I was saying, agreeing with most of its content. He also appeared more relaxed as he removed his finger from the trigger of the Glock, and indexed it along the side of the slide. One minute later, Brian did something else he had not done. He occasionally pulled the gun away from his head, briefly pointing it towards the ground before returning it to his head. It seemed like we were really making progress.

My cell phone rang and I could see on the caller ID display it was SWAT Commander Burns calling me. Since I was right in the middle of this conversation with Brian, I handed my cell phone back to Eric. Eric answered my phone and spoke with the Commander Burns. I did not pay any attention to Eric's telephone conversation as I was focused on Brian. He and I were making tremendous progress and the finish line was in sight.

Five minutes after he removed his finger form the trigger, Brian was still listening closely to what I was telling him. I began to shorten my message, repeating a few short phrases which reassured Brian how much he was loved by his family and of the bright future that still lay ahead.

Brian had moved closer to the armored vehicle, standing only a few feet in front of the windshield I was behind. When he moved up this time, it was not done in a threatening manner. He made eye contact with me and he was moving closer as I softened my voice and my message. He removed the gun from his head and pointed it down to the ground. All hell broke loose.

In an instant, as they had been instructed, the SWAT officers began their plan. I watched as the team of officers rolled out from behind the armored vehicle, led by an officer carrying a ballistic shield. One SWAT officer fired three wood baton rounds from a 37 mm gas gun. The rounds fired found their mark, striking Brian in the chest area.

After witnessing Brian being hit in the chest by the wood baton rounds, I watched him lean forward, apparently from the impact. Everything from that point seemed to move in slow motion. The SWAT officers began their approach as the less lethal rounds were fired.

I watched in disbelief as Brian began to recover from the impact of the wooden baton rounds and started to rise. As he was rising, I saw him raise the loaded Glock .40 pistol towards the approaching SWAT officers. I wanted to scream for Brian to stop as I knew he was about to fulfill his ultimate goal.

Brian continued to swing his arm upward and pointed it at the approaching SWAT officers, putting their lives in imminent jeopardy. SWAT Officer Peter Montesanti, whose assignment in the plan was to provide lethal coverage, fired two rounds at Brian from the Colt .223 M4 rifle he was carrying. The first round stuck Brian in the head, killing him instantly.

This all occurred a few feet in front of me as I watched through the windshield. Just seconds prior to this, Brian and I were deep in conversation and appeared we were making progress. As much rapport, bond, and connection I felt we had established, I ultimately was powerless from stopping Brian who was determined to end the event the way he wanted to.

Just moments before the shooting, I was shivering from the cold, having a heart-felt conversation with someone who started as a stranger but evolved into someone I cared about. Witnessing Brian's lifeless body on the roadway, with the severe head trauma he experienced, I was numb. I wasn't cold any more. I was just numb.

I knew and understood the SWAT officers made the right decision and I was thankful SWAT Officer Montesanti was there to protect his fellow teammates and the rest of us who were present. A part of me felt guilty for not doing more. As I learned more about him and especially after speaking to Brian, I knew he was a good man who had been dealt a bad hand in life.

After the incident, we conducted a debriefing. I wanted to ask Commander Burns why he authorized the plan as it appeared we were close to resolving the incident. I did not ask as I could see on the commander's face the weight he carried from the decision. I also knew there would be ample time in the future for us to discuss the event in private. Some of what I discovered will be detailed in the lessons learned section.

For many days and months after the incident, I unfairly played the game in my head of "I wonder if I would have just said…" I believe in the end the event played out just the way Brian wanted it to. I think he was working up the courage to pull the trigger and the SWAT officers approaching him gave him the excuse he needed to finish his plan. With that said, there has never been a single time in the past nine years that I have driven through that same intersection and wondered "what if".

Lessons Learned:

In nearly every incident across America, patrol officers are the first ones to arrive at every event, including suicidal subjects. They do an incredible job at containing the situation and slowing the momentum. These same officers resolve far more of these incidents than those which require a response from specialty units, i.e.; SWAT and crisis negotiators. I make this point so the next few following comments are made simply as areas for improvement, not to find fault.

As Brian was being pursued by patrol officers, he had called Vivian's cell phone which was answered by Officer Robertson. Officer Robertson informed the dispatcher that he was in telephone contact with him so everyone on the event was aware as well.

Brian was on the phone with Officer Robertson when he finally stopped his truck in the intersection. Confusion mounted when patrol officers continued to scream verbal commands at Brian while he tried to stay calm and continue his conversation with Officer Robertson. Officers on the scene were yelling for Brian to throw the gun down and get out of the truck while Officer Robertson attempted to convince him to stay on the phone and peacefully work with him. This is confusing for anyone, let alone someone who is in the middle of a crisis. An on-scene supervisor should consider the entire event and make a decision so only one officer talks.

A supervisor had yet to make the decision on who would converse with Brian. This is not an easy decision to make as there are several variables in play. One strong consideration should include the rapport Officer Robertson had developed with Brian. They developed a close enough bond that Officer Robertson was able to convince Brian to throw one of the handguns out of the truck. While it could be argued that he only threw the gun out because it was empty, none of the other officers had been able to gain any type of concession.

Another factor to consider during the supervisor's decision making was how he would monitor the progress of the negotiation if Officer Robertson was having a telephone conversation with Brian from across town. Unless Officer Robertson had a partner with him who could provide updates, this would be difficult.

Using the power of hindsight, a good decision could have been to allow Officer Robertson to talk with Brian but ensure a second officer was present to provide updates. Officer Robertson should also have been instructed that if he was able to convince Brian to surrender and step out of the truck unarmed, that Officer Robertson would be quiet and allow an officer on the scene to provide verbal commands as to not confuse Brian.

If this plan was used, it would be important for officers at the scene to remain quiet while Officer Robertson spoke to Brian. When he exited the car, one officer would be appointed as the 'verbal' officer, to help prevent numerous officers yelling commands.

Supervisors at the car stop knew Brian was on the phone with Officer Robertson but they were frustrated because Brian would not communicate with them. Without having a plan in place or knowing the relationship already established, they ordered Officer Robertson to disconnect his call. The decision angered Brian which caused him to exit his truck with the gun to his head, complicating matters more. With the suggestions listed above, a better plan could have been implemented.

On a positive side, the patrol supervisors are commended for the containment they implemented as well as the thorough evacuations they conducted. Brian chose a large, busy intersection, with numerous open businesses nearby. The supervisors were able to determine which businesses could be in the line of fire and direct evacuations while still monitoring the conversations an armed, suicidal man was having with officers. Not an easy task to complete.

Negotiators made contact with Brian over the PA system and tried to listen to his remarks over a small speaker. Not only were the private matters the negotiators were talking to Brian about amplified for everyone to hear, it was nearly impossible to hear his responses with the armored vehicles running. The plan had been to call Brian on his cell phone but he smashed the phone just prior to negotiators moving into place. Several other communication options existed but were not implemented.

One communication option could have been to simply provide Brian with another cell phone. The dedicated cell phone used for this purpose is either carried in the command post or with the crisis negotiations team leader and is a regular cell phone with some simple functions activated. One of the functions placed on the cell phone, which can be implemented by nearly any cell carrier, is to restrict the phone from making any outgoing phone calls. Cell phones can be programed with this feature however one phone number is mandated to be allowed to call; 911. The phone also accepts any incoming phone calls.

By setting up a cell phone in this manner, negotiators are the only ones who possess the phone number to this cell phone that will be delivered to the subject. This prevents any outside people from calling in to them and disrupting the negotiation. By locking down any outgoing phone calls, it prevents the subject from calling anyone except 911 operators, who will then only patch the subject's phone call through to the designated negotiator. This helps negotiators immensely as it isolates the subject from talking to anyone but a negotiator.

We advise the dispatch supervisor prior to deploying the cell phone so they can brief other dispatchers. We also instruct the dispatchers that when they receive the call from the subject, to transfer the call to the designated negotiator but to stay on the line and "mute" the dispatcher's side of the call. This allows us to record the call without a court order since they made their called into 911.

After making sure the cell phone is properly set up with a fully charged battery, the easiest way to deploy the phone is to put it into a small padded case with holes drilled into it to allow ringing sounds to emanate through the case. The case is then brought forward to SWAT officers and announcements given over the PA system explaining the phone will be delivered either by throwing it through a window or door, hence the phrase "throw phone".

Another type of throw phone, although much more expensive and proprietary to each company's dedicated crisis negotiation equipment is a normal appearing telephone placed in a padded case. A phone line runs from the throw phone back to the command post. The dedicated system in the command post is connect to the throw phone and it is brought forward and deployed the same way as the cell phone; simply thrown through a door or window.

One advantage to using this type of system is whenever the subject picks up the throw phone, it automatically rings the negotiator side. The throw phone does not have the ability to make out-going calls nor can it receive calls, except those coming from the negotiator's dedicated line. It is a "closed system."

Another advantage to using this type of throw phone is SWAT officers can guesstimate the suspect's location in the residence by how much telephone line they allow into the house. Depending on the model, many of these throw phones can be customized with concealed microphones and cameras.

Additionally, the use of a designated 'throw phone' prevents the suspect from speaking with anyone other than the negotiator on the other end of the phone. The phone also allows other negotiators to monitor the conversation.

A third option to communicate with is through the use

of a robot. Using the robot allows others to use its cameras and zoom in on specific areas. One down side to the robot is most are equipped with speakers and microphones but very few have the ability to talk and hear at the same time. Most use systems similar to those at fast food drive-thrus, where only one person at a time can speak. This is manageable but the suspect just has to be told of the limitations when negotiations begin.

The reason I believe we continued to use the armored car's PA was it worked. We had explained the problems we were encountering but Eric was able to work through the challenges. It was not optimal, but it worked.

The big question. Why did SWAT Commander Burns allow the tactical intervention when it appeared we were making strong progress in the negotiation? Before I give the answer, I would like to provide a brief background.

I have known Commander Burns for over twenty years. He was a SWAT officer earlier in his career so was well versed as a tactician. What was impressive to the negotiators was that after being appointed as the SWAT Commander, he took the time to learn our trade. He attended our 40-hour negotiation school, training sessions, and even seminars we instructed. He came to know the art of negotiations as well as, and even better than, some of the negotiators on the team. Simply put, he was exceptionally knowledgeable.

Commander Burns also showed incredible restraint and put such a high regard for the sanctity of life. There were many events that I felt as negotiators we had done all we could and the event would require a tactical resolution. He would have us go back at it, making sure we did absolutely everything we could before he sent the tactical team in.

On this event, Commander Burns said he was considering many factors. Brian made it clear he was suicidal and intended to die that evening. He even further explained that he would make the officers shoot him and knew he just had to point his gun at them to get his wish. Brian's truck was disabled and he had no way out. The event had been going on for 5 ½ hours and Brian was in a busy intersection located 1/8th of a mile from the freeway. He had also fired a round into the air. As the day progressed, the area and freeway would only become more populated. If Brian fired another round, where would it impact and would even more people be in jeopardy?

SWAT Commander Burns considered all of these factors and called by cell phone for an update. He forgot that I had switched places, with the approval of the command post, and was talking with Brian. Even though my caller ID displayed the commander was calling me, I was in the middle of talking to Brian and could not answer. I handed my phone to Eric so he could talk to the commander.

Unbeknownst to me, when Eric answered the phone, Commander Burns believed he was talking to me. He asked, "Do you think we are making progress?", to which Eric, who was still relatively new at the time, answered, "No." I obviously had a different opinion. Commander Burns, considering what he was dealing with and then hearing from who he thought was his seasoned negotiator that we were not making progress, gave the order. To this day, it still bothers the three of us.

I am angry with myself for not just answering and putting the call on speaker phone. I knew the call would have been important. Eric felt guilty because he did not understand at the time why I felt we were making progress and should wait. It certainly was not his fault as he was simply giving his opinion.

Commander Burns felt the worst. He tried to be patient and allow the negotiators to defuse the situation. He began to consider all the factors and what would happen if Brian fired more rounds as the surrounding area became more populated. He listened to the progress of the negotiations over the radio but finally decided to call one of the senior negotiators for their opinion. How was he to know someone else would answer the phone?

To make matters even worse, it is ultimately the SWAT Commander who is forced to deal with the aftermath of his decision. There were so many lives which were forever changed. A wife lost her husband and a daughter lost her dad. A father lost his son and a man lost his life.

Brian was a good man who fell upon some tough times. Unfortunately, he was the sole person responsible for the chain of events which caused the SWAT officer to take his life. Brian's actions forever impacted many people, including the SWAT officer who was forced to protect himself and his team.

The events of January 17, 2008, are permanently etched into many of us, including Commander Burns and I. It is a night we will forever remember how we did all we could to try and save a man who could not see the goodness in himself.

This is a picture of SWAT Officer Peter Montesanti, the officer who shot Brian Ramirez. Photo taken at the Coroner's Inquest and the photo came from the Las Vegas Review Journal newspaper, who printed it and ran an article.

This is a still photo taken from the surveillance video footage from Sunset Station Casino. It shows Brian Ramirez as he stood in front of the armored vehicle, just seconds before he was shot. I was given the video by a homicide detective.

This is a work card photo of Brian Ramirez. It was taken by LVMPD and given to me by a homicide detective.

A picture of the scene where Brian Ramirez was shot. It shows his Dodge truck blocked by two SWAT armored vehicles.

CHAPTER 7

MOB NEGOTIATIONS

Christiano Decarlo was an interesting man. He was well educated, having obtained his college degree from Rutgers University. Although rather unassuming with a strong entrepreneurial spirit, he had connections with people which made him a force to be reckoned with. By his mid-20s, Christiano had entered the lucrative outcall services in Las Vegas as a business owner. Soon after, Christiano used these connections to try and further his business.

The outcall services, also known as escort services, are plentiful in Las Vegas. There are over 175 of these legal, licensed businesses in the Las Vegas area, many of which are owned by the same people. Escort services advertise they can send a male or female entertainer to a hotel, 24 hours a day, 7 days a week, for a flat fee. That is usually in the area of $200. This fee is often advertised as one hour of dancing and entertainment. More than 80% of that fee belongs to the business. The entertainers arrive and explain to customers that they work for tips, usually much more than the initial $200 fee. It is easy to see just how profitable these outcall businesses can be. And while many of the outcall businesses run a legitimate operation, others are merely fronts for prostitution. To further confuse the issue, prostitution is legal in several Nevada counties, but it remains illegal in Clark County, in which Las Vegas resides. Many tourists who visit Las Vegas are unaware that it is illegal, especially given the amount of advertising done for these outcall/escort services up and down the Las Vegas Strip.

Christiano contacted some of the people he had connections with, who coincidently happened to members of the Gambino crime family. This was the same crime family that, at that time, was allegedly still being controlled by Gambino crime boss John "The Teflon Don" Gotti, who was serving time in prison. Through Christiano's contacts and relationships, several members from this Mafia crime family traveled to Las Vegas to help dissuade other outcall service owners from competing with Christiano. One of the arriving 'associates' was Vincent Congiusti, who was an alleged hit man who bragged of using a cordless drill on peoples' skulls to help influence their cooperation. Unfortunately for Christiano, Congiusti, and others who assisted on this plan, but fortunately for the competing outcall service owners involved, the FBI was conducting an undercover operation and was able to stop Christiano and five others before anyone was hurt. During a search after the arrest, police recovered a cordless drill, weapons, and bulletproof vests proving those involved intended to follow through with their threats.

In Christiano's 2000 federal trial, the Assistant U.S. Attorney described Christiano as "The ultimate leader, the ultimate organizer" (according to an article printed in *the Las Vegas Review Journal* on 09/05/2009), and was described as the person who "set the ball in motion". For Christiano's role in the case, a federal judge sentenced him to five years in prison.

Prior to his arrest Christiano had done well for himself. In addition to owning the outcall service, he also claimed to own a jewelry store and was the partial owner of a sports book. He boasted that he made $750,000 a year through the businesses he owned. Although he served a five-year prison sentence, Christiano still claimed to have substantial assets upon his release. However what Christiano said he cherished most upon his release was the relationship he began with a woman he met; a beautiful 27-year-old Italian woman named Gianna Pamies.

Christiano was a handsome man. He wore fine clothes, drove luxurious cars, and easily won over Gianna. Their relationship began in 2004 and was full of love. They often showered each other with gifts. One gift from Gianna which Christiano adored was a $4,000 custom suit she purchased for him.

He decided he was at a point in his life that he needed to make some bold changes so he liquidated nearly all of his assets to purchase 260 acres of land in Sandy Valley, Nevada. Christiano believed this land, located 50 miles southwest of Las Vegas, near the California border, was going to be an incredible investment opportunity for him. Unfortunately, all that glimmers is not gold.

Christiano quickly found the land he purchased required a great deal of clean-up, demanding additional investment. Attorneys became involved and he had to pay them too. It did not take long before Christiano became cash-strapped and had to move in with Gianna, who still lived at home with her parents. Not only was the land investment causing stress, but soon the living arrangements and their relationship grew problematic. Gianna felt Christiano was becoming increasingly aggressive and although she suspected the land investment was largely to blame, felt it was now time for her to make her own bold life change. In early April, 2009, she ordered Christiano to move out.

Christiano did not take the news well. He felt betrayed by Gianna, someone he loved deeply and felt he had done so much for, including liquidating his assets for the land investment that he hoped would provide for their future together. He was also cash-strapped and had nowhere to go. Although hurt by the break-up, Christiano was bitter for how he felt mistreated by Gianna.

Christiano began bombarding Gianna's cell phone with text messages in attempts to reconcile their relationship and alluding that he planned to harm himself over the hurt he felt. The text messages became so incessant that she was forced to change her phone number. Unable to text her, Christiano began emailing her, upping the ante by threatening suicide and describing to her how he would do it.

While dealing with the change of phone number and trying to ignore the email messages, Gianna came out from the front door of her home one morning to find someone had poured a chemical onto the hood of her Mercedes Benz, damaging the paint. She believed the culprit to be Christiano and this, along with the constant messages, caused her to obtain a restraining order against him. After obtaining the order she told Christiano about its existence. In Las Vegas, restraining orders are only valid after they have been served on the affected party by a peace officer.

The house Gianna lived in with her parents was a relatively modest home; a newer single-story residence which sat on the corner lot of a nice neighborhood. The front yard was grass, enclosed by a small pony wall, topped with wrought-iron fencing. On the side of the yard were two large, decorative, terra-cotta vases, each aesthetically pleasing, lying in the dirt on their sides.

On April 23, 2009, at approximately 6:00 p.m., Gianna was at home and noticed movement at the side of her house. As she looked out the window, near the vases, she saw Christiano. She could see him sneaking around the outside of the house. He was wearing the $4,000 suit she had purchased for him but the suit was dirty and he was clearly disheveled. His appearance was out of character for him.

Christiano was unaware his presence had been detected. Gianna wondered why he was there as she had told him he was no longer welcome and about the restraining order. Not wanting to take a chance with a confrontation, she called the police.

At 6:16 p.m., Gianna called LVMPD and reported Christiano being outside of her home. She explained to the dispatcher how Christiano was the subject of a restraining order but that the order had not been officially served on him. She never mentioned Christiano's suicidal threats.

A patrol officer, Officer Casey Pirih, was in the area when the call for service at Gianna's home was dispatched.

Officer Pirih arrived minutes later, well ahead of his back-up unit. This was a routine call for service and no mention of violence or weapons was mentioned. Officer Pirih decided to make contact with Gianna prior to his back-up unit arriving.

Gianna saw the patrol car arrive and stepped out of the front door to greet the officer. Just as Officer Pirih walked up to meet her, Christiano suddenly appeared, emerging from the side of the house and only a few feet from the pair. He was holding a Colt .45 semi-automatic pistol, with the hammer cocked and his finger on the trigger. The gun was pressed firmly underneath his chin.

Officer Pirih immediately drew his pistol, pointed it at Christiano, and simultaneously stepped in front of Gianna to shield her. Officer Pirih gave Christiano verbal commands to drop his weapon and ordered Gianna to run to safety.

After Gianna ran away from the area, Officer Pirih moved to a better position of cover, still ordering Christiano to lower his pistol while also broadcasting emergency traffic to the dispatcher on what had occurred. He asked for additional officers to respond to his location and asked they expedite as he was by himself.

As Officer Pirih began talking with Christiano, arriving units began to block the area. Supervisors arrived and established a command post. Another officer was successful in locating Gianna and brought her back to the command post to be interviewed.

Officer Pirih's dialog with Christiano was superb. He allowed Christiano to explain all he had been through while remaining non-judgmental. Officer Pirih had several factors working against him. One was the physical location Christiano was in. After he initially emerged from the side of the yard to confront Gianna and Officer Pirih, he slowly retreated back to the side yard area, near the terra-cotta vases. This area provided very few areas where Officer Pirih could talk to Christiano while still providing sufficient cover should Christiano suddenly begin firing. This caused

Officer Pirih to shout which hindered the building of rapport with Christiano a bit. An even bigger issue, which became impossible for Officer Pirih to overcome, was trust.

During their conversation, Officer Pirih explained he understood the hurt Christiano was experiencing. He told Christiano if he would just put down the pistol they would get him the mental health help he was in need of.

Christiano told Officer Pirih of the extensive experience with the criminal justice system he possessed and knew since he was a convicted felon and in possession of a firearm, he would be sentenced to prison for a long time. Officer Pirih tried to convince Christiano that the courts would be willing to overlook the Ex-Felon in Possession of a Firearm charge. He said the courts would view the totality of the situation, that it stemmed from a domestic incident, and how Christiano was only threatening to harm to himself. Christiano said that while Officer Pirih was passionate about charges not being pressed, Christiano knew the decision would not be left to Officer Pirih. This caused the mistrust issue.

Patrol supervisors at the scene monitored the communications Officer Pirih was having with Christiano and realized after nearly 30 minutes of back and forth dialog, a peaceful resolution did not appear likely. SWAT and Crisis Negotiators were requested to respond.

From a negotiator's perspective:

SWAT and Crisis Negotiators arrived at 7:30 p.m., less than an hour after the incident first began and less than 30 minutes after they were requested. In fact, we all arrived so quickly that patrol officers were still in the process of evacuating nearby homes whose occupants could be in the line of fire. SWAT officers began were donning their equipment which allowed negotiators to brief and come up with a plan.

During our initial briefing, none of the above organized crime information was known. The only information we had at that time was Christiano's name and descriptors - that he was armed with a .45 pistol, and it was suspected this was over the breakup he had with Gianna. We were also told that he was a convicted felon for a federal charge of "Conspiracy To Interfere With Interstate Commerce Through Threats and Violence" but honestly, none of us had ever heard of that charge. We only knew his conviction meant he was a felon and unable to possess a firearm. We also had access to Gianna, who was at the patrol command post.

Based on the information that I had at the time, I selected Officer Janeen Walsh to be the primary negotiator. Although she was relatively new to the Crisis Negotiation Team, I picked her as she was from New York and we believed Christiano was too. She was also the only female negotiator present on this call and, while it was a crap shoot, I felt it may help. I say crap shoot because none of these incidents involving relationship issues are the same. Although a female was the target of Christiano's despair, we had enjoyed many successes using a female negotiator in similar relationship-based negotiations as the female officers often have a more soothing voice as well as can be reassuring when they talk to the man in crisis.

The other side to that same coin is that forcing the depressed man to speak to another female, albeit a police officer, could cause him only more grief. While we had certainly experienced that before, I felt this situation would be one where Officer Walsh could be successful. To further hedge my bets, I assigned Detective Joey Herring, a very seasoned negotiator, as Janeen's secondary. I knew not only would Joey use his experience to help coach and guide Janeen but should my assessment prove wrong, and Christiano had a hard time talking to a female, I could flip-flop their roles. If needed, Joey could assume the primary negotiator role as he would take over with the benefit of having been in place and heard everything already discussed.

I met with the SWAT Commander to learn what the

tactical plan was and discuss the plan on how we would communicate with Christiano. The SWAT officers were already dressed and loaded into two armored vehicles. They would move up to the front yard of the residence, parking on the outside of the pony-wall with a direct eye on Christiano. Once the two armored vehicles were in place and the SWAT officers in their respective positions, the SWAT officers would deploy a ballistic shield, next to one of the armored vehicle. The two negotiators would exit the armored vehicle and speak from behind the shield.

Realizing the negotiators were going to speak to Christiano in a quasi-face-to-face negotiation, and that those of us back at the command post would not be able to hear them, I had a body-bug transmitter placed on Joey. Placing the transmitter on Joey allowed Janeen to yell out to Christiano without being too loud over the microphone, yet we would still be able to monitor it. It also allowed Joey to covertly relay some of what Christiano was saying as the microphones are not usually strong enough to pick up what the suspect is saying. We have experimented with using other devices to hear what the suspects say, including parabolic microphones like those used by the National Football League on the sidelines at football games but it picked up too much ambient noise, including the engine noise from the armored cars running. We also had Joey wear an earpiece for his police radio so we could speak directly to him and relay new information received.

As the primary and secondary negotiators were moving into position with the SWAT officers, the Intelligence Coordinator, Scribe, and Tactical Liaison positions were all designated. The remaining unassigned negotiators would assist with gathering intelligence. We needed to learn more about Christiano's criminal background, where the gun came from, more on his relationship with Gianna, as well as learn what Christiano cared about.

The SWAT officers got into position and deployed the

portable shield for Janeen and Joey to speak from behind. Officer Pirih introduced Janeen to Christiano then returned to the command post where he could be debriefed by assisting negotiators. The transition from Officer Pirih to Janeen did not go as smooth as I had hoped for.

Officer Pirih met Christiano under a unique circumstance. Christiano approached him with the gun under his chin. To say those first few moments were tense would be an understatement. But one positive that did come from their meeting was Christiano saw true, raw emotion from Officer Pirih; both in what he said and through his body language.

Officer Pirih had his gun pointed at Christiano and plead with him to drop the pistol. He spent more than thirty minutes trying to convince Christiano that he was there to help him. As stated earlier, Officer Pirih did the best he knew how to. He even said the courts would not be concerned with his gun possession which Christiano knew would not be true. I am certain Officer Pirih was not intentionally lying to Christiano. I think he was trying to defuse the situation and probably wanted his statement to be true.

When Janeen took over she had only been verbally introduced by Officer Pirih. Her introduction occurred after 8:00 p.m., it was dark, and she was behind a shield. Even if she hadn't been behind a shield, both armored vehicles had the spotlights focused on Christiano which tactically prevented him from seeing behind the curtain of light. Christiano had the chance to see Officer Pirih's facial expressions. He was not even able to see Janeen.

Additionally, the location of the armored vehicle from which Janeen and Joey were located was a bit further than where Officer Pirih had been standing. Officer Pirih's location was arguably not the best but he also did not have the benefit of having an armored vehicle present. From Janeen's location behind the shield, she had to raise her voice quite a bit, almost yell, to be heard by Christiano. Unfortunately, this beautiful New York woman's voice, when yelling, sounded harsh. Almost like nails on a chalkboard. It certainly was not the soothing voice we were hoping for.

As Janeen did her best to establish a rapport with Christiano, negotiators debriefed Officer Pirih at the command post to learn what was said. Officer Pirih explained most of what we already had been told, that Christiano was devastated by Gianna's break-up with him. As we talked further, Officer Pirih did reveal a key piece of information to us that we did not previously have. When Officer Pirih was trying to convince Christiano to drop his gun, Christiano relayed that if his attorney, Greg Cortes, would respond and confirm he wouldn't be in trouble for having the gun, he would surrender. Christiano further explained how Greg had helped him in his previous federal case and their work also morphed into a friendship. This information provided us with another person we could contact for assistance.

We also interviewed Gianna. She was the person who helped shine a light onto Christiano's prior criminal history as well as his connections to people in organized crime. She explained the stress Christiano was under after putting all of his money into a land deal that proved to be a poor investment. She told us Christiano had kept the pistol at his property in Sandy Valley for protection.

Gianna explained how the stress increased when Christiano moved in with her and her parents and how she finally decided to end their five-year relationship. After doing that and forcing him to move out, she found her Mercedes damaged and suspected Christiano of committing the act. Gianna said she decided to obtain the restraining order against Christiano after that and the incessant text messages and emails.

Gianna showed us the text messages she had saved as well as the emails he sent. Christiano made it exceptionally clear in at least one of the email messages of his intent to kill himself. In the email, he attached a brief video which showed how he had rigged a pipe to a running vehicle's tailpipe and placed the other end into the vehicle to pump the noxious fumes inside.

Gianna said she did not know whose vehicle was in Christiano's video but his intentions were clear. In the video, Christiano verbalized his intent to die, explaining he could not live without her. He appeared very sincere.

When we begin a negotiation, it is important we seek out several facts. First, what caused this? Usually something has occurred within the last 24 hours, although this trigger can extend out 48 or even 72 hours' prior, which caused the person to act out. The triggering event typically exceeds the person's normal coping mechanism and they act out. For Christiano, his main trigger was the crumbling of his relationship with Gianna. The arrival of the police car just forced him to set his plan into motion.

Another important fact to seek is learning what is most important to the person in crisis. This will help the primary negotiator as they talk to the person, to help convince them how other people care. We learned from Gianna that Christiano was lacking in this area.

Gianna shared with us that Christiano had been previously married and had three young children, all of whom lived in Arizona. Christiano rarely spoke to them. She said she did not believe he had any real relationship with his children nor with his parents. Gianna explained he had no known hobbies. She said he sold his pawn store and jewelry store and put everything into the Sandy Valley land deal, so the land deal was the only thing important to him. Except, of course, for Gianna.

She said Christiano constantly explained how he could not live without her. She also added that Christiano was not a bad man but with everything that was going on, she simply could not take it anymore.

We took the information we had gleaned and gave it to Joey. Joey digested it and came up with themes for Janeen to use. Unfortunately, Janeen was still struggling to establish a rapport with Christiano. We also told Joey of the relationship Christiano had with his attorney, Greg Cortes, and that we were in the process of trying to contact him and have him respond to our location. I explained to Joey I was aware of the struggles Janeen was having and that I would continue to monitor their conversation over the transmitter to see if it warranted a change of negotiators.

When SWAT initially moved up in the armored vehicles, they also set-up several wireless cameras which transmitted their view back to the command post. We could see the area where Janeen was talking from and could hear how she had to yell to communicate with Christiano. Although the area was lit up with vehicles' spotlights, the dirt area between the two terra-cotta pots where Christiano was lying, was poorly lit.

We asked the SWAT Commander if it would be possible for his team to deploy a robot, which was equipped with lighting as well as audio and video capabilities. By moving the robot into place, it would allow us to have a better visual on Christiano as well enable us communicate without yelling to him. The SWAT Commander authorized the robot and SWAT officers began to prep it for deployment.

The time was approaching 9:00 p.m. and Janeen had been talking to Christiano for nearly an hour. Listening to the negotiations being transmitted back to the command post, it was clear that Christiano was frustrated with Janeen and there was no rapport. In fact, he was downright nasty with some of the things he said to her. A change was certainly in order and I flip-flopped Janeen and Joey's roles, with Joey taking over as the primary negotiator.

As we implemented the change, other team members had been successful in contacting Greg, Christiano's attorney and friend. As luck would have it, he was not far from our location and agreed to respond.

When Greg arrived, a negotiator debriefed him. I asked if they could obtain a TPI tape as I thought it would be best to have a 60-90 second reassuring tape from his friend and attorney. The tape would let Christiano hear that he was present at the scene and would be there to help him through the process. Greg was very gracious in not only providing the tape, but also gave us more of Christiano's history, nothing protected by attorney/client privilege. It was also clear that Greg was a true friend of his.

We had the tape sent forward and Joey played it. While Christiano appeared touched, he asked Joey to have Greg come forward and talk to him. We obviously could not allow this especially since Christiano had a cocked gun under his chin. Christiano became very agitated when he was told Greg could not come up. Joey offered numerous suggestions.

One suggestion was if Christiano put the gun down, Greg would not only come up and meet him but would also ensure he was treated fairly by the police and would not be questioned by the officers. Christiano refused. Although we could hear Joey had a much better rapport with Christiano, Christiano remained upset about the situation he was in and said the only way he was leaving the scene was in a pine box.

Joey continued to talk with Christiano, but Christiano said he felt as if he was being 'played' and believed the police would attack him. He assured us that if the police tried to rush him, he would pull the trigger and instantly kill himself.

Joey tried to reiterate we were only there to help. Christiano felt the police would assault him so he manipulated the two terra-cotta pots and climbed inside. With every move he made, Christiano kept the cocked pistol pressed under his chin and his finger on the trigger. Christiano pulled the second pot close to his head, making it difficult for us to see him. He shared with Joey he believed we were trying to "trick" him and knew the SWAT officers planned on rushing him.

As Joey did his best to calm and reassure Christiano down, I asked for negotiators to obtain a second TPI tape from Greg. I wanted a second tape which would again express Greg's friendship and desire to be there for him. At 10:00 p.m., nearly 3 ½ hours after the incident began and 45 minutes after Greg's first audio tape, we obtained the second tape and sent it forward. Joey played the second tape but Christiano remained agitated. Christiano not only complained about the situation he was in, but added that we now refused his only request to speak to his best friend, Greg. In my rush to get a peaceful resolution, I put too much stock in the repeated use of Greg's tape.

Christiano confided to Joey how much he missed Gianna. How that he longed to just be near her. He said four days before this incident, he got dressed in the suit she gave him and walked to her house. He knew she wouldn't invite him in so he concealed himself next to the terra-cotta pots on the side of the yard so he was not noticed. He said it felt so good to be that close to her, he could not leave. He had stayed there, lying on the ground and concealed by the terra-cotta pots for four full days. He never left. Not to eat or even use the restroom.

The SWAT Commander advised the robot was ready for deployment but I asked if it could wait for a few minutes. We were having a team discussion on how to handle the attorney conversation request and I wanted to have a plan before we likely made Christiano even more uncomfortable by rolling a robot next to him.

Everyone, with the exception of Joey and Janeen who were still talking with Christiano, were part of our discussion. We were fortunate as our volunteer team psychologist had also responded and was there to participate. We needed a plan to deal with Christiano's request to speak with Greg.

I discussed the reasons why we never put a third-party on the telephone. The situation is simply too hard to control. Often times, the person the subject in crisis wants to talk to is the cause of their frustration. Allowing them to talk on the phone affords the subject in crisis the ability to exact the ultimate guilt; exclaiming, "See what you've done to me!"

then killing themselves. It forces the person they cared about to hear it and live with it the rest of their life. We simply don't do this. Had Christiano asked to speak with Gianna, we would have assumed the same. But this scenario was different. He was asking to speak with really the only friend he had left in the world. The same man who had helped defend him during one of the darkest chapters of his life. A man he truly respected. In my mind, this made a difference.

As admirable of as a job as Joey was doing, Christiano remained agitated and refused any of Joey's help. I mulled it over and realized I could switch to a third negotiator but I believed we would be back in the same boat. I certainly didn't see a SWAT intervention, (gas, less lethal, K-9), being used as they would likely cause Christiano to kill himself or expose the SWAT officers and allow Christiano to take a shot at one of them. The only real risk with putting Greg on the phone is it would be it would allow Christiano to say his 'goodbye' and force Greg to listen if Christiano then chose to kill himself.

Listening to the negotiation broadcast and hearing Christiano curse Joey about the situation he was in, especially his loss of Gianna, I knew we had to do something. We were now nearly four hours into this event and Christiano remained steadfast about wanting to kill himself over what he perceived as 'no way out'. If Greg was willing to take a chance of speaking to Christiano over the phone, knowing what could occur, should we allow it? Given what we were up against, we all felt it was worth the risk. Our pysch doc concurred.

Several of the negotiators approached Greg with the proposition, explaining that Christiano was adamant about speaking with him. We were candid with him about our concerns, based on our collective experience, of the true risk of Christiano killing himself while he was on the phone with him. Greg, as a true friend, said he agreed with our assessment but that as his best friend, he knew he had to try.

We immediately sent word to Joey that we were going to allow Christiano to talk with Greg over the telephone. Joey was shocked by the news, as it's simply something not in our negotiator playbook. We told Joey we would prepare a 'throw phone" and have it delivered to Christiano via the robot. By using the robot we would be able to get the additional lights, cameras and communication capabilities on the robot under the guise of needing the robot to deliver the phone.

Christiano took the news well. He also seemed relieved. But give someone and inch and sometimes they will want to take a mile. After we broke our own cardinal rule and were making arrangements so he could talk to his friend, Christiano was so thankful that he also wanted us to deliver him a cigarette and soda. Well, at least he wanted something from us, allowing us the opportunity to barter.

It was approaching 10:45 p.m., more than four hours after the incident began. Greg was coached by fellow negotiators on what to say and the robot was moved into place, carrying the 'throw phone' in its claws. Greg was in the command post, waiting to ring the phone.

Joey spoke to Christiano over the speaker on the robot as the robot rolled closer to him. He reassured Christiano there were no tricks and that we were just delivering a telephone. Christiano grew visibly anxious as the robot neared him but Joey continued talking over the robot's speaker, explaining Greg was on the other end of the phone waiting to talk to him. I am sure from Christiano's perspective, having numerous spotlights focused on him and having a robot roll towards him with a human voice being broadcast from it must have felt like something from a sci-fi movie. It was the best plan we could come up with at the time.

The robot was guided remotely into place by one of the SWAT operators. It stopped directly next to where Christiano was lying. The images we received in the command post from the robot's camera, aided by the additional lighting it also provided, gave us a clear view of the terra-cotta pots he was lying in.

Joey spoke to Christiano over the robot's speaker as the throw phone was ringing, asking him to answer the phone. He explained it was Greg ringing the phone who was waiting to talk with him. Christiano must have believed it was a trick as he refused to exit the pot to grab the phone from the robot's claw. Christiano's beliefs may have been partially correct as I'm sure if he wiggled out of the pot and put the pistol on the ground to answer the throw phone, SWAT was certainly close enough to hit him with enough less lethal options that it would have ended the incident.

Christiano was stubborn. He refused to move out of the pot to answer the phone. He even stopped responding to the questions Joey asked him over the robot. So now what? We had broken our own protocol and placed the person Christiano described as his only real friend on the other end of a phone but he refused to answer it. To make matters worse, he had even stopped talking to the negotiator.

Christiano continued to keep the Colt .45 pistol pressed to either his chest or under his chin, moving it occasionally. As we watched him on the cameras, it appeared Christiano was physically comfortable with the location he was in. We had to find a way to make Christiano uncomfortable and want to talk to us.

The fire department was on-scene. It is typical for them to attend these types of incidents since there is a significant chance it could end with an injury. Seeing the firefighter/paramedics parked near the command post gave us an idea. Since the evening temperature was falling and it became chilly outside, maybe they could trickle one of their hoses and make the ground he was lying on wet. With the ground wet, Christiano would be uncomfortable and may be motivated to move. It sounded unconventional but it was approaching midnight, a full hour since the robot arrived with the throw phone and five hours since the incident began. We were simply attempting to motivate Christiano to talk to us.

As the firefighters were preparing their hose, Christiano unexpectedly shimmied out of the decorative pot and grabbed the throw phone from the robot's claw. He did so with one hand, using his other hand to keep the pistol pressed against his chest. He was even able to open the latches of the throw phone's pelican case in the same manner. Since he never put the gun down, he never gave the SWAT officers' an opportunity to deploy less lethal options on him and since he came out on his own, and unexpectedly, the firefighters did not have the chance to use their hose on the plan we created. At least Christiano finally took the phone.

When Christiano picked up the phone, Greg was on the other end of the line, as promised. This would be the moment of truth; with Greg's friendship, would Christiano listen to reason and put down the gun or would we witness him take his own life as we had feared? Neither.

Christiano discussed the same story with Greg that he had with the two previous negotiators; he was distraught over his break-up with Gianna. With his best friend on the phone, he was looking for a shoulder to cry on. Greg listened for a bit and, as coached, eventually asked Christiano to put the gun down. Christiano refused even his best friend's request.

Greg used his friendship to break through some barriers. He reminded Christiano of everything they had been through together, personally and professionally. Once reminded of their true friendship, it broke down a wall and Christiano started to cry. Unfortunately, the crying intensified as Christiano continued to dwell on the negatives. He continued to tell Greg how the love of his life left and that he was broke because of the poor land deal investment.

Christiano would vacillate between crying to yelling, then cursing. It wasn't directed at Greg, just about the position he had now put himself in. Even worse, despite all the positives we coached Greg to say, Christiano said he saw no way out. Christiano repeated his earlier demand for cigarettes and a drink. We had Greg explain if he put the gun down the police would deliver the items to him. Christiano again refused, admitting the gun was the only thing that gave him the power to keep the police at bay.

Our big time move, allowing his friend to talk to him over the phone, was a bust. After twenty minutes on the phone, Greg was no closer to resolving the issue than either of the previous negotiators. It wasn't Greg's fault. He did a fine job, selling every idea we gave him.

Christiano remained despondent. He told Greg since the police were now present while he was in possession of the firearm, he would be going to prison for a long time. He explained that losing his freedom on top of already losing his money and the love of his life was more than he could bear.

I decided we should pull Greg back off the phone but keep him in reserve as we might need to use him again. Greg appeared relieved when we told him we were going to have him take a break. I also thought since we were giving Greg a break, instead of returning to Joey, we could consider using a third negotiator.

Joey had done a good job talking with Christiano but no real rapport had developed. We had even tried Greg but to no avail. Since Christiano was again asking for cigarettes and a drink, maybe a new voice would be beneficial and could bargain with him. We were six hours into the event and I was hoping for bit of luck. I also felt that if Christiano resisted the third negotiator, I maintained the option of returning to either Joey or Greg.

Detective Eric Ravelo is a skilled negotiator with a tremendous amount of experience. To use a baseball analogy, he is also a great 'closer', someone who can come in and finish the event. Eric has a unique ability to take what's already been done and said then put his personal spin on it and get a peaceful resolution. And since Christiano also wanted something, the cigarette and drink, Eric would have something to work with.

As the clock passed midnight and after a short break, Eric

made contact with Christiano through the robot's speaker and introduced himself. We knew ahead of time he would not answer the throw phone again without more cajoling.

After his introduction, Eric explained that Greg was mentally drained from their conversation. Christiano showed compassion, saying he understood how hard it had to have been for Greg to see him in the position he was in. He also seemed to welcome the opportunity to speak with Eric. It was only a few minutes before Christiano repeated his request and asked again for a cigarette and a drink.

As Eric made small talk with Christiano, working on establishing a rapport, I approached the SWAT Commander to see if we could provide Christiano with his two desired items. I explained we could use the cigarette and drink to try and gain ground as we had yet to make any real progress. The delivery of items was authorized.

I relayed the news back to Eric and asked him to work his magic; to see what type of deal he could strike with Christiano for the delivery of the cigarette and drink. Eric took the information and, like a trained professional, waited for the right time to ask. Sure enough, at 12:20 a.m., less than twenty minutes into their conversation, Christiano again asked Eric for the items.

Eric already knew the items had been approved. Rather than the typical answer that he would have to go check, Eric was ready with a response. Eric replied, "If I can get you a cigarette and drink, and show you that I'm a man of my word, will you put the gun down and meet with me one-on-one so we can resolve this?" Christiano took the bait and agreed. And Christiano's answer was not, "Ummm, let me think about it. Yea I guess so." It was direct, almost relived that the event would end soon and positively.

Since we knew what Christiano wanted from his previous request, we had someone run to the store and purchase a bottle of Gatorade and a pack of cigarettes. We had the items waiting at the command post and only would need the SWAT officers to deliver them.

The SWAT officers were not as convinced as we were that Christiano would abide by his word. The officers put the bottle of Gatorade and the pack of cigarettes into a small plastic shopping bag and tied two knots at the opening. Their plan was since the bag would be difficult to open, if Christiano put the gun down to open the bag, they would hit him simultaneously with several less lethal options. The negotiators were unaware of their plan.

At 12:30 a.m., SWAT officers tossed the plastic bag to Christiano. With the gun still pressed against his chest, Christiano grabbed the bag with his free hand and like a hungry rat, used his teeth to tear open the bag and empty its contents. Talk about a team of frustrated SWAT guys!

As the SWAT guys were groaning about how Christiano had defeated their plan, we as negotiators began groaning as well. In his plastic bag, they gave him a large, full bottle of Gatorade, and Christiano promptly drank down the entire contents. Our groaning ensued when we watched on the camera that in the same bag they didn't include one cigarette instead they gave him a whole box of them! Christiano asked for a cigarette and we gave him twenty. You can imagine the problems this may cause.

Eric took the negative and spun it into a positive. He explained to Christiano how he empathized with the position he was in and knew Christiano would enjoy more than one cigarette. What else could he say since the damage was already done? Christiano was appreciative and he smoked the cigarette down in what appeared to be one long drag. As expected, he lit up a second cigarette then a third.

Eric reiterated to Christiano how we were there to help him. He reminded Christiano that we had Greg respond and even put him on the phone; something that is seldom done. Eric also reminded Christiano of his promise; that he would put the gun down and walk over and meet Eric after the cigarette and drink was delivered.

Christiano broke down. He began sobbing, claiming he could not put the gun down. He praised Eric for being a man of his word. He even commended the police in general for treating him well all evening. He said he just could not bring himself to put the pistol down and walk out.

All of this conversation with Christiano was still being done over the robot's speaker. Eric asked Christiano to pick-up the throw phone, as it would be easier to talk, but Christiano refused.

Eric began a 'full court press'. He explained all the positives Christiano still had to look forward towards. He included how his very best friend, Greg, was still on-scene and waiting to help him. Eric even offered to put Greg back on the phone but Christiano shook his head no and began to cry. As he cried, he continued to smoke cigarette after cigarette. He also never moved the gun which was still pressed to his chest, with the hammer cocked and his finger on the trigger. It was clear, however, that Christiano was at least listening to Eric.

It was nearly 1:00 a.m. and Christiano remained emotional. We were still only able to talk to him through the robot as he continued to refuse to answer the throw phone. As Eric continued to talk, I assembled another team meeting.

As a team, we felt we had covered nearly every base. We recited everything we had done but it seemed Christiano was only getting more emotional. He remained focused on the downward spiral his life had taken. Admittedly, it was a lot; he lost his businesses to get the cash he needed, his land investment had soured, his girlfriend left him, and he was now exposed to the felony charge. It was a lot to overcome.

The SWAT Commander attended the team meeting and commended everyone for the work they had already done. He explained that because of the location Christiano was in, it remained difficult for the SWAT officers to use any less lethal options and asked if there was any way Eric could convince Christiano to move the gun away from his chest.

The SWAT Commander felt if they had just a brief moment with the gun pointed away, they were going to hit Christiano with numerous less lethal options.

The less lethal plan called for SWAT to hit Christiano simultaneously with four different types of less lethal options; a flash-bang to disorient him, less-lethal wood baton rounds fired from a 37mm gas gun, a K-9 dog, and a fire hose. A fire hose? We had never heard of that option before.

The SWAT Commander said they had never used a fire hose on a suicidal subject but since the hose was there with the line charged and ready, the force of being hit with water from the high-pressure hose would help push the gun away and/or further disorient him. It would add to the less-lethal options they were already deploying and give the SWAT officers time as they were moving in from behind their ballistic shield.

Our team meeting came at the perfect time. As we were concluding the meeting we could see on the camera Christiano spiraling down even further. His breathing became more labored. He kept the gun pressed tightly into his chest and rocked slowly back and forth, crying even harder. We had seen this type of behavior before and it's usually when the person is working up the courage to pull the trigger. We had to disrupt his thought process as soon as possible. I told Eric to immediately engage Christiano over the robot's speaker.

Eric started calling out to Christiano, reminding him that Greg was still present and eager to see him. Eric reminded Christiano how far he had come after his prison release and could easily rebuild again. He told him to even think of the small things, like how good the cigarettes tasted. That statement caused Christiano to chuckle a bit, evoking a response that if we waited long enough, if the gun did not kill him, the cigarettes would.

Eric capitalized on that brief bit of humor and told Christiano he could imagine how difficult everything seemed but that it would all be ok. Eric encouraged Christiano to just take baby steps and he would be there to support him the entire way. He asked Christiano to just take the first baby step and try pointing the pistol at the ground to just see how it felt. And Christiano did.

In the blink of an eye, SWAT pounced. We watched the screen as a flash-bang deployed and we could see the wooden dowels, fired from the gas gun, as they struck Christiano. The police dog was already striking him as water from the fire hose was as well. Although it all happened in seconds, it also suddenly seemed to move in slow motion.

The SWAT officers were moving up as the dog was still attached to Christiano. He was pinned to the ground by the force of the water when we suddenly saw his hand come up and a bright light flashed. Christiano fired a .45 pistol round into his chest.

SWAT officers reached Christiano immediately after the gun discharged. His pistol fell to the ground. The powerful round had torn through Christiano's chest, blew through his lung, and made a large hole in his back. Luckily, the SWAT Team's tactical physician was present at the scene.

Officers who had just rushed to disarm Christiano were now trying to help close the life-threatening wound he self-inflicted. Officers assisted with applying a field dressing to the large sucking chest wound over his lung. They did their best to stabilize Christiano's condition and he was rushed to a hospital. After three days in the intensive care unit, Christiano miraculously survived.

Two weeks after the incident, I went to the hospital to check on Christiano. To my surprise, he was alert and doing rather well. He had been through several surgeries but was expected to make a full recovery.

Christiano and I spent six hours together, talking about life and everything that occurred that evening. He was exceptionally apologetic and expressed his thanks for everything that everyone did for him that night. His memory of the incident was spot on; he remembered Officer Pirih by name, as well as Janeen, Joey and finally Eric.

Christiano shared his life story with me. He told me about his relationships with friends belonging to the Gambino crime family as well as the federal crime he had been convicted of. He further detailed his busted land deal and the loss of his girlfriend. He said he would have never imagined that a guy like him, with all he had been through and achieved, would ever camp out on the side of a girl's house, just to be near her. I asked him if he even contemplated hurting Gianna, as that was the impression we had and wondered if that was why he brought the gun with him.

Christiano sat back and paused. He took a deep breath and said he brought the gun because he knew Gianna would only listen to him if he had the pistol. When pushed further, Christiano said he didn't think he would hurt her, but upon further inflection, said he wasn't sure. He then began to cry.

We spent more time talking and Christiano calmed down. When it came time to say goodbye, he again asked me to share his thanks with everyone involved. As I walked out of his hospital room, Christiano laughed a little bit and said he promised he would call me if he ever got into this type of situation again. He explained it hurt too damn much to do the same thing again, pointing to the dressing covering the bullet wound in his chest. Hopefully, after all he's been through, he never makes that call.

Lessons Learned:

Officer Pirih did an incredible job as the first responder. He was surprised by an armed gunman yet had the presence of mind to not only shield the victim but provide lethal coverage. After ensuring Gianna was in a safe location and finding adequate cover for himself, he transitioned into meaningful dialog.

Christiano said in his later interview he did not believe Officer Pirih after he tried to convince him he would not be charged. I believe Christiano made that statement with the benefit of hindsight. In fact, the bond Officer Pirih formed with Christiano was so strong that I question our decision of replacing him with Janeen.

As previously mentioned, when we witness good communication and rapport between the suspect and the first responder, we have left the first responder in place and provided him with our support. I do not think I understood, or paid attention, to how well Officer Pirih had done as this would have been a situation where we could have provided a supporting role and evaluate as we went along. Oftentimes we - specifically I - were too quick to arrive on scene and take over communications. Had I taken a little more time, I would have seen the value of leaving Officer Pirih in place. Besides, Christiano was in no hurry to go anywhere.

Another area for improvement was my selection of the primary negotiator. I stand by my earlier thoughts of it being a relative crap shoot on the effectiveness of a female versus a male primary negotiator, for the reasons already stated. What I should have taken into consideration was the location from which she would be operating from.

If I would have given more thought that the position Janeen would negotiate from, I would have realized she would be required to yell. Janeen has a beautiful voice. She is soft spoken and her words are soothing. Unfortunately, when she had to yell, her voice screeched, which was comforting to no one. I should have either considered a different means of communication for her or had someone else assume the primary negotiator role.

We have discussed the issues we created when we gave Christiano an entire pack of cigarettes. I believe Eric did an admirable job at setting up the deal; having Christiano's commitment of surrender for delivery of the cigarette and drink. By delivering these two items, what did we really stand to lose? If Christiano went back at his word, we were in the same position as we were just in. Actually, better.

Eric would demonstrate he was a man of his word as well showing compassion. But we over-delivered. Not only with the cigarettes but also by providing a huge drink. A smaller sized Gatorade would have been sufficient.

I make the over-delivery statement with a word of caution. We do not want to deliver items that will ultimately be upsetting. Let me explain. Some old thoughts on negotiations believe we should make the suspect work for everything they get. You wanted a cigarette? That is exactly what we delivered. Oh, I'm sorry, you needed a match to light it? What will we get in exchange for the match? It happens. We need to be reasonable.

It was obviously a huge error to deliver an entire pack of cigarettes. Even a heavy smoker would need ample time to finish twenty cigarettes. Same with the oversized bottle of Gatorade. Although Christiano was clearly parched and slammed down the entire bottle, we should have given him a more reasonable sized bottle. It would have pleased him to receive the drink and showed we were true to our word yet kept the door open for him to ask for another drink. The same was true for the cigarette.

As demonstrated in other chapters, we can sometimes suggest items to the suspect without ever doing so verbally. It would be easy to assume Christiano's need for a beverage since he had gone without while sitting for days on the side of house. By nonchalantly drinking a cold beverage in front of him, it's amazing how fast they realize how badly they also want a drink. It can help open the lines of communication. The same holds true for cigarettes.

I am not, nor have I ever been a smoker. During an event when our intelligence folks learn the suspect is a smoker, I have gotten a cigarette and fired it up in front of them and smoked it. It made me put on my best poker face and trying by hardest not to turn blue from smoking it but those who are smokers understand the craving initiated when they smell that smoke. Especially under times of stress. Again, it can open negotiations up when the suspect suddenly asks for one of the smokes.

Finally, the topic of the fire hose. While it had never been previously used on one of our suicidal subjects, I certainly could see the value in it. Especially when its use was combined with the other less lethal options they were deploying. I think the real issue was the timing of the tactical intervention.

We had been dealing with Christiano for over six hours prior to the assault. I think we all, myself included, were anxious to reach a conclusion. Knowing he had many more cigarettes available to smoke did not help our anxiety levels. Unfortunately, we can fall victim to "action imperative".

Would Eric have continued successfully and been able to have Christiano surrender peacefully or would Christiano have digressed and would we have been back at square one? On this event, I believe Eric was beginning to influence Christiano. He developed a bond with him and in a short amount of time was able to convince Christiano to move the pistol away for his chest. But since we do not have a crystal ball, everyone has their own opinion.

We begin to look at how long we have been on an incident. We consider the police resources being used and the innocent citizens we have displaced. We come up with a plan and wait for our window of opportunity; progress be damned.

It takes strong leadership to look at the entire situation and determine if that first opportunity is the one to be taken. If we fail to take action when the window of opportunity first presented itself, will we get another? It is also much easier to apply this thinking on lone barricaded subject or suicidal individuals since the only person likely to be harmed is them. The stakes are much higher on a hostage situation which makes that first decision to act much shorter. I certainly understand why the role of SWAT Commander or incident commander, the person who makes this decision, can be a lonely role.

It takes time to influence human behavior. To find the right match of negotiator versus suspect, who communicate well together, can be difficult and time consuming. But at the price of what? Do we put a time limit on these things? It's like the old question, "How long is a rope?" It depends. We know during a tactical intervention there is the possibility for the loss of life. What about the aftermath? What about what the tactical officer will be forced to endure for doing his job or the criticism the police agency will take for the decision they made? Leadership is lonely.

What we do know is this. Christiano's actions brought together experts in their field who shared a common goal of saving a stranger's life. Each discipline did their very best to reach a peaceful resolution. Ultimately it was Christiano who hurt himself. He also happened to be fortunate that our SWAT Commander had the forethought to add a tactical physician to the team as the doctor's work, aided by SWAT officers on the scene, saved Christiano's life. That cannot be argued.

I took this photo from the video as it was being transmitted to the SWAT command post during the event. It shows Chris Decarlo, dressed in a suit and sitting in the dirt while pointing a .45 pistol to his chest.

I took this photo from the video as it was being transmitted to the SWAT command post during the event. It shows Chris Decarlo as he was trying to conceal himself inside a pot with the .45 pistol pressed into his chest.

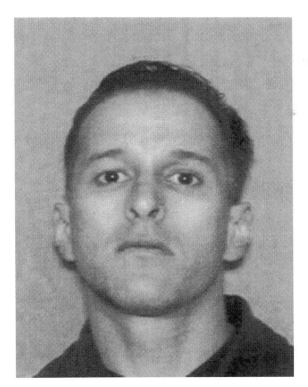

LVMPD's booking photo of Chris Decarlo.

I took this photo from the video as it was being transmitted to the SWAT command post during the event. It shows the pots Chris Decarlo was hiding in.

*I took this photo from the video as it was being transmitted to the
SWAT command post during the event. It shows Chris Decarlo
coming out of the pot while the robot moved up to deliver him a throw
phone. Chris's other hand has the .45 pushed against his neck.*

CHAPTER 8

CHRISTMAS BABY NEGOTIATIONS

The city of Las Vegas is surrounded by various mountain ranges creating almost a bowl-type setting. One of the main historical streets, Las Vegas Boulevard, runs north and south, through the heart of town. Nellis Air Force Base is located on the northeast end of the valley, just off of Las Vegas Boulevard North. The amount of personnel assigned to the air base exceeds the housing available on the government installation. Many years ago, a substantial amount of affordable housing was added to the area. Unfortunately a large portion of the housing is now run down and the area is frequented by non-military personnel. The abundance of affordable housing has caused unscrupulous people to flock to that area.

Less than two miles west of Nellis Air Force Base, just several streets away from Las Vegas Boulevard North lies a series of multi-unit complexes which fall into the above description. One in particular is located in the 4300 block of Paramount Street and was the scene of a prolonged hostage negotiation.

In the late 1990s, Sonia Rodriguez, a 26 years old woman, had moved from Mexico to Las Vegas. After arriving in town, she met Jose Ponce, also a 26-year-old from Mexico. They began dating and while they never married, they stayed together for ten years and share four children in common.

During mid-2007, Sonia and Jose had their fourth child, Ivan, and were in need of a place to stay. Sonia's parents allowed the couple and their four children to move into their home, located in the 4300 block of Paramount Street. It was a well-kept, single story, three bedroom residence.

Although they had a place to stay, Sonia and Jose's

relationship was crumbling. According to Sonia, Jose had just lost his landscaping job and did not appear eager to look for new work. She also said he had begun using methamphetamine which, in addition to the added expense, was causing additional problems in their relationship.

Sonia said she tried to work through her problems with Jose but it was difficult. She said Jose had no one else to turn to and she felt sorry for him. She explained that Jose had a strained relationship with his own family, not having talked to his mother, father, or one of his sisters in many years. The only family member that he did talk to was another sister, Hilda. They spoke on a weekly basis.

In addition to relationship problems Jose also had immigration issues. Sonia said he was in the United States illegally and had been deported back to Mexico. In 2005 he again snuck across the border, reuniting with his Sonia and his children. In 2007, Jose battered Sonia during an argument and she called the police. Police arrived and learned Jose was again in the United States illegally. He was deported a second time but returned a few months, just prior to the birth of his fourth child, Ivan.

As much pity as Sonia had for Jose, his methamphetamine use and behavior became more than she and the family could handle. In early 2008, she insisted Jose move out of the residence but agreed he could still come back to see his children. Sonia explained his children were the most important thing in Jose's life. While she did allow him to come see the children, it did not stop his criminal and sometimes violent behavior.

Living on his own, Jose had been arrested for stealing a vehicle and for possession of narcotics. In May, 2008, Jose was arrested for Battery - Domestic Violence, again for beating Sonia, this time so severely that he nearly knocked her teeth completely through her lip.

Why Jose, who after each incident was booked into the county jail, was not deported or at least held for the immigration violation is a mystery. Jail records would have displayed he had been previously deported twice. It can only be surmised that the jail was waiting for deportation order to come through when Jose went for trial. Unfortunately, Jose never attended any of his court proceedings, causing arrest warrants to be issued for his offenses. Jose likely understood that he would be deported if he went to court.

Sonia had called the police on Jose in early December, 2008 but he was gone when the officers arrived. The patrol officers did tell her that Jose never went to court on his previous criminal cases and had active warrants out for his arrest. They explained all she had to do was call the police when he returned and they would respond and arrest him. She kept this information as the "ace up her sleeve" as she knew she would likely need to call the officers when Jose was causing problems.

Due to the family issues, Christmas, 2008 was a difficult time for Sonia and the children but they were determined to make the best of it. She understood Jose loved his kids and wanted to include him in the Christmas celebration. She had spoken to Jose and they agreed he would come over to the house on Christmas Eve to celebrate. Sonia told the children about their father's attendance and they were excited. Unfortunately, Jose was a "no-show", not even calling to explain why. His broken commitment disappointed the children and infuriated Sonia for what it did to them.

On Christmas Day Sonia took the kids to see a movie in the afternoon. When they returned home, she found Jose sitting inside the house. He knew better. He knew he was not allowed in the house when she was not home. Besides, she was extremely upset that he missed the Christmas Eve celebration and did not even have the decency to call. The two got into a heated argument. Sonia knew it was time to play the "ace in her sleeve."

On Christmas evening, at 7:14 p.m., Sonia dialed 911 to report Jose and have him arrested for his outstanding warrants. She gave the police dispatcher her residence location as well as Jose's information and his arrest warrant data. As she was providing the information Jose came into the room discovered her talking to the police on her cell phone. Sonia's cell phone was the only phone in the entire house. Enraged at Sonia for turning him in, he took and smashed her cell phone, making it inoperable.

Patrol officers were dispatched to the residence and had Jose's arrest warrant information along with his physical description. The officers were also notified of the reported struggle on the phone line before it was abruptly disconnected.

The two patrol officers arrived and began walking towards the front of the residence. Sonia saw them approach and ran from the front door with three of her children, explaining to the officers that Jose was inside with their baby, Ivan. As the officers approached the front door, they could see Jose carrying Ivan in his arms and running towards the back door. One of the officers ran to the back door, leaving the other officer at the front, preventing Jose's escape. Sonia did say that no one other than Jose and 18-month-old Ivan were in the residence. The officers effectively had Jose contained.

Other additional officers began to arrive to assist. As the officers were formulating their plan they could see Jose through the open window blinds. He was carrying Ivan in one arm and holding a blue steel semi-auto pistol in the other. A routine family disturbance and arrest warrant service suddenly morphed into a potential hostage situation.

Officers pulled back. They used the PA system on a patrol car and tried to convince Jose to exit the residence but he refused. Since he had smashed Sonia's cell phone and with no hard line into the residence, the officers were unable to call him. Even more problematic, Sonia told the officers Jose was not a violent man, which ran completely counter to his criminal background including the two domestic violence calls with her as a victim. She also said she had never seen

Jose with a pistol, something the officers were witnessing for themselves. At approximately 9:00 p.m., with the situation the officers were facing, SWAT and Crisis Negotiators were requested.

From a negotiator's perspective:

During my time as a negotiator, I had been called out on nearly every major holiday. We've gone out on Mother's Day, Father's Day, Thanksgiving, Valentine's Day, and even New Years. For some reason it seems holidays cause either too much stress on people or there's just something in the air that makes people act out. Whatever the case, I was now adding Christmas Day to this list and my family, while understanding, was not very happy. Although inconvenient, we all understood it was part of the deal. To add insult to injury, it was also exceptionally cold outside, making working conditions that much more frustrating.

After being briefed on all the above details, we began to determine how we would approach this scenario. We were told that while Jose spoke fluent Spanish he also conversed in English. This was important intelligence as it would help determine who would be selected as the primary negotiator. Of the negotiators present, one negotiator spoke Spanish fluently and another spoke conversational Spanish fairly well.

Since Jose had destroyed Sonia's cell phone I asked the SWAT Commander, Lieutenant Larry Burns, if he wanted us to have the "throw phone" readied for deployment. Not only did Commander Burns want to throw phone prepared, he wanted it done expeditiously. The commander advised us that as the SWAT officers arrived and took over containment positions from the patrol officers, they could hear Jose yelling from inside that he wanted a telephone. This is usually a good sign, indicating his willingness to communicate.

On most incidents, negotiators talk to the person in crisis

by either calling them on their residential landline or cell phone. If neither of those exist, we can use a "throw phone", as previously discussed. Since the dedicated "throw phone" allows for other negotiators to monitor the phone calls and contains covert listening capabilities, we opted to use this type phone over the cell throw phone.

As the throw phone was being prepared, I had the chance to make the negotiator assignments. I selected Sergeant Andy McDermott, the negotiator who spoke conversational Spanish fairly well, to serve as the primary negotiator. I did ask that if he was successful in making contact with Jose, to attempt to keep the negotiation in English, if possible, so the rest of the team could monitor the negotiation. If Jose preferred to speak Spanish, I had several Spanish interpreters present who could monitor the call and advise us of what was being said.

I chose Detective Eric Ravelo, the fluent Spanish speaker, to go forward with the SWAT officers in the armored vehicle and speak to Jose over the PA system. While it may seem these negotiator assignments were backwards because of their language skills, I felt there was a good reason for this decision.

Because Jose had destroyed Sonia's cell phone, I knew the only way we would be able to talk to him was if he accepted a phone from us. Up until that point, the only communication Jose participated in was yelling back and forth. Thankfully, he yelled in English so we understood what he was yelling. I also knew through experience that when we deploy the throw phone, the subjects are sometimes fearful of some sort of police trick, and refuse to open the case.

Even if the subject never communicated over the throw phone, we know they will likely hear what is broadcast over the PA system. Anyone in the area could hear what we were saying and that we were doing it in both English and Spanish. People in the area hearing our amplified pleas is a good thing, especially if the event turns sour.

Finally, if Jose was to answer the throw phone and insist on speaking only in Spanish, I had Andy to talk to him. If Jose's Spanish was too fast and Andy was unable to keep up with him, I could always switch Andy out and replace him with Officer Eric Ravelo, since he would no longer be needed on the PA.

At 10:00 p.m., Eric went forward in the armored vehicle with the SWAT officers. SWAT snipers had been deployed and they verified what we had been told in briefing. They could see Jose walking inside of the residence carrying Ivan in one hand and a blue steel semi-automatic pistol in the other.

I told SWAT Commander Burns the throw phone was still being prepared for deployment but asked if we could begin trying to contact Jose over the PA system. Permission was granted.

Eric began speaking over the PA to Jose, encouraging him in both English and Spanish to come outside and promised him he would not be hurt. While it was not likely Jose would follow these instructions, it was important to broadcast our pleas to him in a compassionate tone, so citizens in the area could verify our attempts.

As Eric spoke over the PA, we prepared and tested the throw phone. We had used the throw phone enough on previous incidents to know it must be tested prior to each deployment. It is an electronic piece of equipment and Murphy's Law dictates something will go wrong when it is most needed. After testing, the phone was brought forward to the SWAT officers for its delivery.

At 10:30 p.m. the throw phone was brought forward and Eric announced its presence numerous times to Jose. Eric broadcast that he was aware Jose had requested a phone and explained officers were going to put the phone through his window. He told Jose which window the phone would be placed into, to not be alarmed, and that no officers would enter his house.

While understanding that telegraphing the officers plan is dangerous to the SWAT officers involved, the SWAT officers had trained and planned for phone insertions like this. We wanted to make sure Jose knew this was just a phone being delivered so he did not panic and shoot at the SWAT officers.

After the phone was delivered through the window, Andy began ringing the phone but Jose would not approach the case. We had Eric broadcast numerous times over the PA system, trying to convince Jose the case just contained a phone and there was someone on the other end of the line that wanted to help him with the situation he was in.

We continued to ring the throw phone for over an hour but Jose refused to answer. We could hear the phone ringing so knew it was functioning; he just would not answer it. SWAT snipers radioed the command post and reported they could see Jose pacing through the house. He was still carrying Ivan and the pistol.

We knew if SWAT officers entered the house there was obviously a tremendous likelihood Jose could either harm himself, the baby, or shoot at the SWAT officers. And although SWAT officers train incessantly for situations like this, we wanted to explore other options. If Jose did something to force the SWAT entry, that was a different story.

While we understood Jose was estranged from most of his family, we had been told he had a strong relationship with his sister Hilda. Other negotiators had already contacted Hilda, transported her to the command post and interviewed her. Since Jose refused to answer the telephone for us, we thought possibly hearing Hilda's voice would motivate him to answer.

We had one of the negotiators obtain a sixty second tape recording from Hilda. Over the tape, she explained she was present at the scene and would meet with him as soon as he came outside. She was very reassuring, explaining he would not be hurt and for him to answer the ringing telephone. Hilda explained she had met with the officers and were convinced they were there to help him. She provided her message in both English and Spanish, for our benefit as well as those in the nearby area which by then included the media.

We reviewed her audio recording and it sounded wonderful. We had a Spanish-speaking officer review the Spanish portion of the tape to ensure it matched the English version then sent the tape recording forward. Commander Burns authorized it and we had Eric broadcast Hilda's recording over the PA for Jose to hear.

While we were obtaining the tape recording, Commander Burns also authorized several audio and video devices to be covertly installed by specialists around the residence. This not only helped narrowed down Jose's location in the residence, but also help provide additional intelligence for Commander Burns and the team as well.

At nearly 11:45 p.m., over an hour after the throw phone was inserted but only shortly after playing Hilda's audio recording, Jose approached the throw phone case. He kicked the case a few times, probably to see if it was some sort of trick. He finally answered the ringing phone and was greeted by Andy.

Andy had a warm introduction with Jose, speaking in English. Thankfully, Jose responded in English which allowed myself and other team members to monitor the conversation without requiring an interpreter.

When the conversation started, Jose was very calm, explaining he had not heard the phone ringing because he had been asleep. Although he knew Jose's statement was untrue, Andy did not challenge it. Andy said he understood and explained he just wanted to make sure he and the baby were both okay.

Andy spoke like the true seasoned negotiator he was. He asked open ended questions encouraging Jose to talk. Jose provided his side of the story. He explained Sonia had thrown a telephone at him and always made up stories to get him in trouble. Andy praised him, agreeing he was a good man and agreeing the situation was likely nothing more than a big misunderstanding.

Jose seemed receptive to Andy's suggestions but also made it very clear of his fear of being deported. Andy tried to reassure Jose that is not why the police were there, but Jose began to cry, indicating he knew the gravity of the situation.

Within fifteen minutes, Andy had done such a stellar job talking with Jose, that Jose said he was tired of what was going on and wanted to turn himself in. Jose also explained that Ivan was asleep in the crib. Unbeknownst to Jose, the covert camera which the SWAT Commander had deployed, had already provided us with this intelligence.

Andy discussed the surrender ritual to Jose. Jose was to walk out the front door with his hands in the air and listen to the verbal commands from the officers out front. He was instructed to leave Ivan in the crib.

Andy continued to reassure Jose. He explained that after the officers took him into custody, Andy would walk up and meet him and they would get the situation resolved. Andy also thanked Jose, explaining that he was doing the right thing.

Although Jose was still sobbing, he seemed receptive to everything Andy told him. He said he wanted a few minutes to make sure Ivan was okay and then he would come out. Any time someone is emotional, we do not want to let the person off the telephone as we lose our ability to talk and influence them. Quite candidly, we were worried that Jose was emotional about being arrested and/or deported and worried he may hurt himself or the baby.

While Andy made his best attempts to keep Jose on the telephone, Jose was adamant that he was going to hang up and take a short break. Andy tried to have Jose just put the telephone down, not hang up, but Jose insisted he needed a short break. Realizing Jose's stubbornness, and not wanting to hurt the rapport already established, Andy asked Jose to promise that after a five-minute break that Jose would come outside. Jose agreed to this promise and hung up the phone.

Commander Burns was monitoring this part of the negotiation and also was aware of the risks if Jose hung up the phone. He briefed the SWAT officers on this situation. While Jose was offline, SWAT snipers and the covert camera could see Jose still crying and walking in and out of the room his son was in. Ivan was still sleeping in the crib.

After five long minutes, Jose never exited the front door. He broke his promise.

Andy began ringing the throw phone, but Jose refused to answer it. After twenty minutes of ringing the phone, he finally answered. He was still crying but his demeanor had changed.

Through his tears, Jose confessed he knew when he exited the house, he would be deported and he would never see his children again. Jose remarked, "I just can't do this". Even more alarming, SWAT snipers reported Jose had the pistol in his hand and his finger on the trigger.

Andy attempted to calm Jose down as well as reassure him. He explained that we had no plans of deporting him but even if that was to happen he had already come back twice. What was to stop him from a third time?

In the command post we were examining the camera views and trying to see the type of pistol Jose was carrying. As we were doing so Jose brought up the pistol, admitting to Andy it was a .45 semi-automatic. As Jose continued to talk Andy knew his mission; he had to keep Jose on the phone, downplay the situation, as well as try to calm him. Much easier said than done.

Andy continued to reassure Jose, explaining that the issue with immigration could be worked out and how much his family needed him. Andy also tried to use the Christmas theme, explaining if he did anything to himself, it would forever ruin Christmas for his children. The verbiage Andy used was a masterful way of broaching the topic of suicide without actually bringing it up. Unfortunately, the conversation seemed to continue in circles and I was looking for something that may tip the scale.

As Andy continued talking with Jose, I asked the team members their opinion of having Andy replay the audio tape from Hilda. Hearing her voice over the PA system 45 minutes earlier encouraged Jose to answer the phone. I asked the team's opinions if hearing Hilda's message more clearly over the telephone would help, especially since Jose was saying that no one in his family cared about him. As a team, we all felt playing the tape could only help, not hurt our position. We needed to build Jose's self-esteem up and also get his mind off of immigration. The SWAT Commander agreed with playing the tape as he also felt like Jose was digressing, not because of what Andy was saying, but because of the bad position he had put himself in.

Just after 12:30 am, Andy played Hilda's audio recording over the phone. Immediately after, Andy used its content to try and convince Jose how much his sister cared about him. Andy explained Hilda was waiting for him at our command post and that she would be allowed to meet with him as soon as he came out.

Jose thanked Andy for letting him hear his sister's voice. He confided that as happy as he was to know his sister cared about him so much, he remained frightened as he knew from his previous experiences that his deportation was a certainty. Andy repeated his earlier unorthodox approach, explaining how Jose could just come back again if he was deported but Jose refused to consider the options.

Andy tried a more direct route. He bluntly asked Jose to meet him outside the house and promised he would help him resolve the immigration issue. Jose refused. He said he was not going to come out, and then even more ominously, warned Andy he wanted to "take his chances", and hung up the phone.

Jose's statement sounded like a challenge. We reached that conclusion as the only alternative to surrendering was to fight us. And Jose was not crying when he made this last statement. What was he planning? Andy continued to ring back into the telephone but Jose would not answer. For the next thirty minutes, Andy would periodically ring the phone but Jose would ignore it. Jose could be seen by SWAT snipers and on the covert camera, walking throughout the residence, still holding the pistol in his hand.

Although I was concentrated on the negotiation, I was aware that SWAT was making tactical preparations should the incident take a sudden violent detour. Their plan included an explosive breach on the front door should they need to make an emergency entry. The SWAT officers had already received permission and covertly deployed the explosive breaching device on the door. Jose was unaware of its presence.

At 1:10 am, Jose finally answered the throw phone. Unfortunately, Murphy's Law had entered the picture. When Andy tried to talk to Jose, a loud buzzing sound could be heard on the phone line. Everyone in the command post monitoring the negotiation could also hear the buzzing sound. It was so loud, it made it difficult to hear what either Andy or Jose were saying.

Andy apologized to Jose for the loud buzzing sound and asked him to please stay on the telephone with him and talk through it. Assisting negotiators and I attempted to diagnose the problem to see if it could be corrected. All the equipment on our end checked out fine. The problem likely resided inside the throw phone unit itself. Even if we pulled the throw phone back, we had no way to repair it as it would have to be sent back to the manufacture.

The buzzing sound grew louder. Not only was it distracting, but it was one more issue Jose would be forced to deal with instead of concentrating solely on the issue at hand. After twenty minutes of trying to talk through the buzzing sound, Jose became as frustrated as we were and slammed down the telephone. We rang the phone but he refused to answer. Who could blame him? On the covert cameras, we could see Jose was so upset at the ringing throw phone, he even covered the device with a blanket and pillow to mute the ringing.

We had reached a stalemate. Jose was so focused on being deported he would not listen to anything else. As good of a job as Andy did in speaking with Jose, the constant buzzing on the phone prevented him from influencing Jose. We needed a fresh idea.

Our team uses TPI tapes on a very frequent basis. They are typically used as they were in this incident; playing a tape-recorded message from someone close to the suspect after the tapes content has been reviewed.

As mentioned in the previous chapter, there are several reasons why we do not put a TPI on the phone with the suspect. Among other reasons, it is hard to control what the person says on a live phone call. But just as in the previous case, there are exceptions.

Reviewing the incident, it appeared that Jose's position was deteriorating. We were concerned that Jose truly felt he would never see his children again and since he saw little hope in his life, that he could kill Ivan and then himself.

We began to consider our options. I witnessed the positive effects Hilda's voice recordings had both times we played them for Jose. She was the only family he talked to. It seemed like another time to deviate from our playbook and allow Hilda to talk directly to Jose, although heavily coached.

I pitched the idea to the Commander Burns and giving the gravity of the situation, he approved. Andy and other negotiators met with Hilda and began coached her on what to say and what to avoid. We would still be forced to deal with the buzzing sound on the phone but felt Hilda could overcome it due to her relationship with her brother.

Hilda proved very coachable and was ready. Ready to implement the communication plan, we had Eric, who was still forward in the armored vehicle, begin to speak to Jose over the PA again. Eric explained we were ringing the phone because Hilda wanted to talk to him. At 2:00 a.m., as soon as Eric broadcast it, Jose answered the phone.

Hilda did a wonderful job. She spoke lovingly to Jose in such a sweet voice. Just as she had been coached, she explained to Jose that they could get through the situation together and now he was not alone. Although the buzzing continued on the phone, Jose seemed to listen to every word, tuning out the distracting buzz. Hilda continued, explaining to Jose how much he was loved by his family and pled with him to come outside.

Jose began his conversation with Hilda very stoic, telling her he just wanted the police to come inside the house and get him. It seemed that the seriousness of the situation began to set in with Jose and he again began to cry. He told Hilda he was going to go away for a very long time. She pleaded with him to not put his children, especially Ivan, through this. It appeared Jose was prepared for an armed confrontation.

Hearing her brother cry proved too much for Hilda. Once Jose started crying, Hilda followed suit, only making the situation worse. This of course was compounded with the loud buzzing that made it difficult to hear either person. We tried to coach Hilda back but she became too emotional. To make matters even worse, Ivan could be heard screaming in the background. The cameras verified he was still in his crib, crying, but the screaming was just one more issue to contend with. With Hilda unable to continue, Andy jumped back on the phone line but Jose became disgusted and hung up.

Unfortunately, just as in our previous case, breaking our protocol and putting the TPI directly on the phone failed. I still believe it was a good idea with low risk and high gain. I believe the constant buzz and the sound of his sister crying were too much to bear. Even Jose must have been equally disgusted with the throw phone. The covert cameras showed he had thrown it into a side room, indicating he would no longer talk on it.

The cameras showed us Jose had retrieved the crying Ivan from his crib and was attempting to comfort him. He could be seen walking throughout the house carrying the pistol and the baby. We had to come up with other ways to communicate.

If the constant buzzing sound heard over the throw phone was not bad enough, the phone system began to malfunction even more. With no action from our end, the throw phone started suddenly beeping. Loudly. It appeared we were doing something to make the phone keep beeping. It was easy to see how irritated Jose became. Irritating an armed man with the life circumstances Jose was dealing with is certainly not beneficial.

We again checked all of our connections in the command post but it was a malfunction in the throw phone itself. It was obvious by viewing the covert cameras the beeping noise was irritating Jose. He finally became so frustrated that he took a knife and completely cut the phone line cord, which successfully stopped the beeping. In hindsight, I wish I would've had thought of asking the SWAT officers to pull the cord back and remove the phone, relieving a source of irritation to Jose.

During this downtime, I met with Commander Burns to discuss the situation and what options we had available. Thankfully, Commander Burns had already come up with an idea that would be beneficial to not only negotiators but to the tactical side as well. His plan was to move a robot inside the residence.

The robot used during this time was untethered and controlled by remote. It was small enough to be deploy through a front door and was equipped with cameras and microphones. The robot would allow us to see additional views into the residence as well as communicate back and forth with Jose.

While the robot was being prepared for deployment, I again met with the negotiation team to discuss our strategies.

I felt Andy had established a good rapport with Jose and was communicating well. I wondered how Jose would react when the robot was moved into the house. He was uncomfortable when they put the throw phone in the window. What would he do when a large robot came in?

I felt that when the robot was moved into the residence we should introduce a different negotiator to speak to Jose through the robot and judge his response. When the robot entered the house, Jose would be scared. Who would not be? Having someone other than Andy speak to Jose would allow the introduction of the robot yet save Andy and the rapport he had established. We would be able to save Andy as the "good cop" and reuse him after Jose calmed down. Additionally, maybe a new voice could help. A new negotiator would not wear the blame Andy unfairly received from Jose for all of the phone problems.

Eric Ravelo had already spoken to Jose over the PA so his voice was familiar. I knew Eric would be the best suited to take over as the primary negotiator over the robot.

As the robot was being prepped, Eric was brought back from the armored vehicle and briefed. The robot would be controlled by a SWAT officer from the rear of the armored vehicle. We decided this would be the same location Eric would negotiate from as we would be able to hear both sides of the negotiation through the robot, which feeds audio and video back to the command post. A secondary negotiator would also accompany Eric to provide assistance.

One downside to our negotiation plan meant the negotiators would have to stand outside in the twenty-something degree weather and speak from behind the armored vehicle. As trivial as it does sound, most of the negotiators come to the incident dressed to operate from the warmth of the command post so would likely be ill-prepared for the cold. It also does not usually get as cold in Las Vegas as it was that evening.

It took time to have the robot unloaded, prepped, tested,

and deployed. During that timeframe, Jose could be seen by SWAT snipers and the covert camera still walking through the residence holding the handgun with his finger on the trigger and carrying Ivan in the other arm.

At 4:25 a.m., more than two hours after we had last spoken to Jose, the robot was moved up to the front of the residence. It took that long for the robot to be prepared. During those two hours, we had Eric speak to Jose over the PA, trying to calm and reassure him. SWAT continued to monitor his movements, remaining ready to make an emergency entry if necessary.

The robot was moved to the front door. Although an explosive charge was placed earlier on the same door, SWAT officers went up with the robot and found the front door to be unlocked. They removed the explosive charge, pushed the front door open, and the robot was driven inside.

Eric began immediately began speaking to Jose through the robot as it rolled inside. As predicted, Jose was petrified of the robot's presence. He was so scared that he even pointed his gun at the robot. SWAT Commander Burns was monitoring the robot and was prepared to give the SWAT entry order if things went bad.

Jose initially had a hard time understanding that a live human being was speaking to him through the robot but Eric was eventually able to calm Jose down. Jose also finally realized he was speaking to Eric but remained a bit agitated.

Eric did a remarkable job assuming the role of the primary negotiator. Eric was cognizant about the tone of his voice, intentionally speaking soft and slow to Jose. The phrase we use on our team is "slow and low" when talking to a suspect. Eric was applying that phrase perfectly.

Eric used a soft tone and was very reassuring as he spoke to Jose. This paid off as Jose continued to listen to what was being said. As Eric continued to speak, it was clear a rapport was developing. In fact, just ten minutes into their negotiation, Eric had Jose agreeing to come outside.

Unfortunately, Jose had made the same promise to Andy. It was also a promise that he broke.

Eric and Jose continued to talk and Jose continued to voice his fear of being deported. Eric explained he would work on getting Jose an attorney who specialized in immigration issues but Jose seemed distracted. He seemed distracted because Ivan continued to cry, even as he held him.

Jose's thoughts were also scattered. In the middle of their conversation, Jose would ask several times if the police were hiding in the house. Eric always did his best to defuse Jose's concerns and each time tried to bring Jose back to the main issue at hand. Eric promised Jose that if he came outside, that he would work with him and immigration officials. Most importantly he assured him that neither he nor his child would not be hurt.

The rapport we witnessed between Eric and Jose was just as strong as what Andy had shared. It did not seem beneficial to put Andy back in as the primary negotiator as Eric was saying all of the right things. Jose just seemed scattered. His body movements were much more animated and he was easily agitated. I think the presence of the robot had a great deal to do with this, but at that point in time, communicating with him through the robot was the best option.

Unfortunately Jose's antics were not helping the situation. While carrying Ivan and the pistol, Jose would often move from room to room, appearing convinced someone was in the house with him. In addition to the situation he was in, his prior methamphetamine most likely added to his paranoia.

At one point, Jose opened the front door and stood in the open doorway, still carrying the pistol in one hand and Ivan in the other. We could see Jose's actions over the camera feed and the SWAT snipers were broadcasting it over the radio as well. Eric tried to capitalize on Jose being in the doorway, praising him for being a man of his word about exiting and reminding him to put the pistol down and continue coming outside. After a few minutes, Jose retreated back inside with Ivan, closing the door behind him. Eric made a valiant effort.

Eric continued his reassuring dialog to Jose but Jose's paranoia seemed to increase. He continued his animated movements and darting from room to room while carrying Ivan. Eric continued to remind Jose that his family was outside waiting for him. Jose yelled back that he knew he was going to be taken to jail and screamed how he would rather die than go back to jail. This was the first time Jose mentioned death. It seemed like we were digressing.

It was 4:45 a.m. and Jose was continuing his bizarre behavior. He continued to run across the hallway and into different rooms while holding Ivan and the pistol. As Eric spoke to Jose, reassuring him that he would assist him with his immigration issues, Jose became more liberal with where he pointed the pistol. In one of the camera feeds, it appeared that Jose brought the pistol up towards Ivan's head. We had the tape replayed several times, reexamining where Jose was pointing the pistol.

Intentional or not, Commander Burns told me in not so unspecific terms that he would not permit Jose from repeating any type of perceived threatening gesture towards the baby. Jose's life was a distant second to Ivan's. The commander made sure I understood if Jose moved that pistol towards the baby, it would have grave consequences. The commander's message was crystal clear.

Patrol officers had been dealing with this incident since 7:14 p.m., meaning we were now nearly ten hours into it. Negotiators began our communication with Jose at 10 p.m., meaning we had been talking with him for nearly six hours. While I believe both of the negotiators did an outstanding job, both of Jose's promises to exit the house were lies. Jose's behavior was getting worse. His behavior was the most threatening we had witnessed since arriving at the scene. Because of Jose's actions it was easy to read a SWAT intervention appeared imminent.

My suspicions were correct. SWAT Commander Burns told me because of Jose's actions, a plan was in place for SWAT officers to intervene should Jose continue his threatening acts. Commander Burns did convey he believed both Andy and Eric did admirable jobs in speaking with Jose but wondered before a tactical intervention was ordered, if I could try to speak to Jose.

Although I knew I could not say anything to Jose that either Andy or Eric had not already conveyed. I believe Commander Burns wanted his own reassurance that we, as a team, did everything possible to solve this incident peacefully.

I knew from watching Jose on the camera that if he kept up his antics, it would force the SWAT Commander to order an intervention which likely would get Jose hurt or killed. I further understood this decision would be solely based on Jose's threatening actions, but more than anything, I did not want to see Jose get so agitated that he hurt the baby. I agreed to take the opportunity to speak to Jose, and I knew if I could not change his behavior immediately, that my time was limited.

At 5:45 a.m., I left the command post and met Eric at the rear of the armored vehicle. I also appointed a senior negotiator to assume the Team Leader position and give updates and input to Commander Burns.

I briefed Eric on the plan and also accepted any suggestions he could offer. Just prior to taking the microphone from Eric and talking to Jose, I made sure to tell Eric what an incredibly good job he did. Eric also understood the reason for this change.

I introduced myself to Jose and just as with Andy and Eric previously, the handoff went well. I was able to transition into the primary negotiator role with relative ease. Not because of anything I did or said but because Jose had been through the same changes twice before. Unfortunately, many of the things that I was about to tell Jose had already been conveyed to him by both Andy and Eric.

One rule our negotiation team tries to abide by is never lying to the subject. One of the main reasons we try to follow this rule is it is not uncommon for our team to deal with the same subject more than once. If we lied to them to get them into custody on the first incident, it would be exceptionally difficult to establish any trust on a second incident. Secondly, many of the subjects we deal with have been through the criminal justice system before. They know what typically happens, and tend to be able to tell call your bluff when they are being lied to.

This was one incident I was willing to break the rule on. I had to get Jose to come outside. At nearly any cost. I remembered his earlier threat that he would rather die than go to jail. He told us he feared losing his children and his behavior became even more threatening. I believed if SWAT officers attempted an intervention, Jose would either kill Ivan or simply point his pistol at the SWAT officers, either of which would cause the officers to shoot him.

I knew I was repeating topics which had already been covered. At 6:00 a.m., I tried pushing the envelope a bit. I told Jose that if he would just come to the front door, I could talk to him personally rather than over the robot. That seemed to intrigue him as the command post reported he exited a bedroom and walked towards the front of the house, but he was still carrying the gun and Ivan. Believing this was some indication of progress, I continued the same theme of being able to personally talk with him outside versus over the robot.

After less than five minutes, Jose opened the front door. Rather than speaking to him over the robot, I began to yell out phrases to him from behind the armored vehicle. I began by praising him for doing the right thing and coming to the door. So far, so good. I also kept to my word, I was talking to him and not speaking over the robot.

Since he came to the door, I figured I would continue

pushing the envelope. I yelled to Jose that this entire event was nothing but a huge misunderstanding. I then began my "fudging". I told Jose I would have Sonia write down on an official affidavit that the incident was just the result of a misunderstanding. Jose seemed to like what he was hearing as he began to respond positively back to me. I was pulling these claims out of thin air and praying Jose would not ask to hear Sonia say them herself.

I was desperate and took a bigger chance by increasing the lies I was willing to tell Jose. I wanted to tell him what I thought he wanted to hear but it had to be something that would also be believable.

I yelled to Jose that I was aware of his immigration issue and that Eric had told me to try and find an attorney that could help. I took it a step further, falsely telling him the immigration attorney had arrived and was waiting at the command post to help him. While I realized this was a big risk of him calling my bluff, the reward of him coming out and us ending this peacefully seemed worth it. I also knew what would likely occur if he did not come out.

At 6:10 a.m., Jose continued to closely listen to what I was telling him and my sincere offers to help him. I told him all he had to do was leave the gun inside and he could even come outside holding Ivan in his arms. Before I said this, I knew the SWAT officers wanted Ivan left inside so they could deal with Jose by himself. I just did not feel Jose would agree to leave his son inside given everything he had said throughout the evening.

Several more minutes passed by and I continued the same themes. I repeated how Sonia was going to claim this was a misunderstanding and that the immigration attorney was going to help him with the deportation issue. This must have finally sunk in as Jose walked out into the front yard carrying Ivan with both hands. No pistol could be seen.

I began to praise Jose for what he was doing, ensuring him this was all going to work out. With the SWAT team leader's permission, I even stepped away from behind the armored vehicle to make visual contact with Jose as he was walking towards my direction.

Jose had walked through the front yard, towards the armored vehicles and was approximately 25 feet from me. I was heaping on the praises like I had never had done before. Jose enjoyed the praise, likely thankful the whole ordeal was about to be over. Just before he reached me, two SWAT officers flanked out which startled Jose.

I could immediately see by the look in his eyes and the body language that followed, Jose was scared. I tried to reassure him, telling him that it was going to be okay. To just keep walking towards me. It was too late.

Jose was carrying Ivan in one arm. He suddenly turned around and began to sprint back towards the front of his house. As he was doing this, he used his free hand to dig his hand into his waistband area. Seeing their opportunity and addressing the threat presented, several SWAT officers were already right on Jose's heels. They tackled him to the ground while simultaneously pinning his hand to prevent him from accessing whatever was in his waistband. Ivan was knocked to the ground as well. Additionally, just as they're trained, one of the SWAT officers scooped up Ivan and ran with him to cover behind the armored vehicle.

Within seconds, the SWAT officers had Jose in custody. He had nothing in his waistband; he too tried to bluff. When the officers entered the residence to clear it, they found the pistol Jose had. It too was a fake; a metal replica pistol.

It was finally over. Eight hours of negotiations and three changes in primary negotiators. Witnessing what had transpired throughout the evening, the change in Jose's behavior, and his threatening movements with the pistol, I honestly did not believe this incident would end peacefully. Considering this incident began on Christmas day, one would have to wonder if this was a gift we received. While the SWAT officers' tactics ultimately saved Jose's life, you have to wonder if a little divine intervention was also involved, especially considering the day this started.

Lessons Learned:

I believe our arrival, briefing, assignments, and deployments went as well as could have been expected. It took us much longer than it should have to have our throw phone ready for deployment. Although throw phones are cumbersome because of the telephone lines which need to be run, they are a great option because of the added features available with their use; microphones and cameras. Since this incident, the team has practiced the delivery of the throw phone and had reduced its deployment time dramatically.

We did make a mistake when we sent the throw phone forward. We forgot to mark off distances on the phone line so the SWAT officers would know how far Jose was from them. By making small marks on the phone line, in ten foot intervals, and limiting how much phone line the suspect pulls inside, SWAT officers would have a general idea of how far the suspect could be from them.

Before we deployed the phone, we tested it on both the suspect and negotiator end to make sure everything was working. To this day, we still do not know what caused the mysterious buzzing over the line. Once we did our basic trouble shooting and realized the problem was likely in the throw phone itself, we should have explained this to Jose and pulled back the phone. I guess we were hoping it would get better on its own.

Another problem we had was we limited ourselves on a back-up plan should the throw phone become inoperable. Having a second throw phone is not a practical option as they are expensive. We were fortunate since we had the robot to use which offered the audio/video features we needed.

I had left out the use of the portable cell phone option. This option was not considered because embarrassingly, when we arrived on the scene, we found the three batteries we had for it had not been charged for a long time and they were all dead. To make it worse, no one thought of plugging them in at the start of the event so they could charge! We were all disappointed to find them dead and moved to the next option. To help rectify preventing this from occurring in the future, we developed a CNT equipment checklist. The checklist details which equipment needs to be fully charged weekly and routine maintenance that needs done. It's the simplest things, like not having batteries for the tape recorder or bodybug that will cause huge problems if not paid attention to.

This event allowed us to discuss callout protocol for CNT events. Specifically, clothing. While it is a luxury to have a large tactical operations center, TOC, the truth is, it is not realistic for everyone to be inside of it. Especially when the mission is on-going. As this incident demonstrated, we have to be prepared to be outside for extended periods of time, in all types of environments. This taught many of us, including myself, of the importance the proper clothing. The job is hard enough. It is even harder when you're cold or wet.

This image was taken from a video shot by Lane Swainston, who was at the scene and filmed the incident. It shows suspect Jose Ponce, as he holds his baby, Ivan Ponce, taken as he began to exit the house.

This is a photo of the front of the house of the incident.

I took this photo from the video as it was being transmitted to the SWAT command post from the robot during the event. It shows Jose Ponce as he walks down the hallway, towards the front door and towards the robot, carrying the gun in his right hand and his son, Ivan, in his left hand.

This image was taken from a video shot by Lane Swainston, who was at the scene and filmed the incident. It shows Jose Ponce, after he was taken into custody by SWAT, being lead away from the scene.

This image was taken from a video shot by Lane Swainston, who was at the scene and filmed the incident. It shows negotiator Eric Ravelo as he negotiates with Jose Ponce, thru the robot.

I took this photo from the video as it was being transmitted to the SWAT command post from the robot during the event. It shows Jose in the living room, with a pistol in his right hand, pointed toward his baby, Ivan, in his right hand.

This is a photo I took which shows a closeup of what the robot looks like.

This is a photo I took which shows a closeup of what the robot control panel and monitor looks like.

This image was taken from a video shot by Lane Swainston, who was at the scene and filmed the incident. It shows the moment the robot pushed open the door to the residence Jose was barricaded in.

This image was taken from a video shot by Lane Swainston, who was at the scene and filmed the incident. It shows when SWAT officers pinned Jose Ponce to the ground and took him into custody.

CHAPTER 9

MICHAEL O'CALLAGHAN - PAT TILLMAN MEMORIAL BRIDGE JUMPER

The Hoover Dam opened in 1935 and holds the title for both the largest reservoir and largest hydroelectric station in the United States. It is located in the furthest southeast corner of Nevada, perched 800 feet above the Colorado River. The dam connects Nevada to Arizona, with US93 running along top of it. While it is located 30 miles east of Las Vegas and contained within Clark County, it is within the Federal Bureau of Reclamation boundaries and policed by that agency. Some comically refer to them as the Dam Police.

When the dam opened, no one could have predicted the amount of traffic that would cross it. Many drivers slowed down while crossing to admire its size, causing tremendous traffic congestions. Sadly, the dam has also been the location used by numerous people to jump to their death.

To help ease traffic congestion and to help alleviate some of the security concerns after 9/11, a bypass bridge was constructed to allow vehicle traffic to cross the Nevada/ Arizona border and avoid the dam. This bypass bridge opened in 2010 and was named the Michael O'Callaghan – Pat Tillman Memorial Bridge in memory of former Nevada governor Michael O'Callaghan and to honor Patrick Tillman, the former Arizona Cardinals football player who left his lucrative career to join the Army but was tragically killed while deployed in Afghanistan. The bridge stands 900 feet above the Colorado River, making it the second highest bridge in the nation. The Michael O'Callaghan – Pat Tillman Memorial Bridge is not under the jurisdiction of the Bureau of Reclamation. It is within the boundaries of Clark County, making it the Las Vegas Metropolitan Police Department's responsibility.

On July 12, 2012 at 10:24 a.m., a male subject who only identified himself as "Jacob" called 911. Jacob said he was depressed and planned to jump from the Michael O'Callaghan – Pat Tillman Memorial Bridge. Following protocol, the LVMPD dispatcher transferred the call to the Hoover Dam Police, as they have the closest officers to respond. Upon receiving the call, Interagency Dispatch placed Jacob on hold, frustrating him and causing him to hang up. Jacob then called one of the Las Vegas news agencies and repeated his threat and hung up again, prompting the news agency to again notify LVMPD. Although Jacob had disconnected from them, Hoover Dam Police received the details from LVMPD and dispatched officers to the bridge.

Eleven minutes after Jacob's initial 911 call, Interagency Dispatch called back to LVMPD. They explained that three of their officers had located Jacob, but due to his position on the bridge and the threats he was making to jump, they asked for LVMPD Crisis Negotiators to respond. In addition to the three Hoover Dam police officers, their police chief, was also enroute and said since he would be arriving long before LVMPD resources, he would act as the incident commander.

LVMPD crisis negotiators seldom respond to incidents without tactical support. When negotiators are requested and activated, they fall under the supervision of the tactical commander. At 10:41 a.m., six minutes after the Hoover Dam police located Jacob, the LVMPD SWAT Commander was notified. The SWAT Commander approved the request and initiated a callout for SWAT, crisis negotiators, and other assets to be enroute to the Michael O'Callaghan – Pat Tillman Memorial Bridge, providing basic details about the call.

Unbeknownst to responding units, the Hoover Dam police chief had requested arriving LVMPD units to cross the bridge and park on the Arizona side, in a staging area he had established. Due to problems with the LVMPD radio system, the chief's information was not received by responding units.

We started this event from behind the eight ball. When we receive a request to respond to an incident, we are given an exact address or intersection. On this event, we were told to respond to the Michael O'Callaghan – Pat Tillman Memorial Bridge. This bridge is nearly ½ mile long and located in two states with numerous observation points. A specific location should have been given as it would have prevented vehicles from driving past Jacob with the sirens on, increasing his anxiety.

At 11:11 a.m., SWAT and crisis negotiators began arriving, parking at various locations on both the Nevada and Arizona side of the bridge. Several units were unaware Jacob had positioned himself near the center area of the bridge and had driven past him with their red lights and sirens activated. Their very conspicuous arrival visibly made Jacob even more frightened while the three Hoover Dam police officers tried to talk him out of his plan to jump.

The LVMPD SWAT Commander and Crisis Negotiator Team Leader arrived at the same time and both parked on the Nevada side of the bridge, in the visitor parking area. This parking area was large enough to accommodate the arriving vehicles as well as provided cover and concealment to the bridge area. The bridge was accessed from the parking lot by climbing several flights of stairs. The top of the stairs opened to a large reception area which is where the SWAT Commander and CNT Leader met with the Hoover Dam police chief. This reception area later was designated as the ad-hoc command post. The area would also serve as the location from which the negotiators were briefed and deployed from.

The bridge is four lanes wide and over 1,900 feet long. Each side has a pedestrian walkway. The two north and southbound travel lanes are separated by a concrete barrier.

The pedestrian walkway has a four-foot-tall concrete barrier separating it from vehicular traffic and a four foot high iron slotted fence on the opposite side to contain pedestrians.

Jacob had climbed over the metal fencing on the northbound side of the pedestrian walkway. He was using his hands and arms to hang on to the metal railing to prevent from falling. The three Hoover Dam police officers were talking to him from the pedestrian walkway area.

From a negotiator's perspective:

I received the negotiator callout at 10:45 a.m., for a male jumper on the Michael O'Callaghan – Pat Tillman Memorial Bridge. I responded to the scene as the CNT Team Leader. We had not received any information on where they wanted us to park but I assumed we would obtain this during our thirty-minute drive. We knew receiving arrival information would be important since there were multiple access points to this bridge.

Unfortunately, the police radio system we were operating with at that time was problematic and due to the tall canyon walls, made it even more difficult to receive any radio reception. Driving to the bridge, we were fortunate as many of us responding to the incident happened to catch up with one another and we caravanned to the area.

As luck would have it, the SWAT Commander was the lead car in the caravan. He pulled into the rest area on the Nevada side of the bridge, arriving within 30 minutes of the call. However, not everyone had caught up to the caravan which caused many of the responding units to drive beyond our staging location, across the bridge, and into Arizona.

We grabbed the gear we believed necessary and ascended the stairs. When we reached the top of the stairs I could see three uniformed Hoover Dam police officers talking to Jacob in the center area of the bridge. I could see Jacob was a white male who appeared to be 40 years of age. He was dressed in a black T-shirt and gray shorts.

This male, later identified as Jacob Foreman, was standing on the outside of the northbound metal fencing of the pedestrian walkway. He had his back to the river and was facing the police officer on the roadway. He was holding on to the metal railing using his hands and arms. The three police officers spoke to him from the pedestrian walkway area, separated from him by a four-foot-tall concrete wall.

Although it was just after 11 a.m., it was mid-July in Las Vegas and the temperature had already surpassed 100 degrees. One of my initial concerns was that Jacob would become sweaty and lose his grip.

It was decided that the area at the top of the stairs had a large enough gathering space which would serve as the ad-hoc command post. It would also be the area crisis negotiators would brief and deploy from.

As the Hoover Dam police chief was about to brief the SWAT Commander and I on the details of the call, I noticed vehicle traffic on the bridge was continuing. The only traffic restriction imposed was to close one of the two northbound lanes. Although the lane closest to Jacob was shut down, the northbound lane next to it was allowed to continue. Since the one lane had been shut down, it caused a bottleneck as well as a tremendous traffic jam for Arizona drivers approaching the bridge.

If the traffic problem was not bad enough, to complicate matters even worse, passing drivers frustrated from sitting in traffic yelled cruel remarks to Jacob. As negotiators tried to convince Jacob that people cared about him, passersby's yelled "Jump!" Whether this is their attempt at humor or they are yelling out of frustration from the traffic, it is exceptionally problematic for a negotiator who is trying to establish rapport with the jumper and convince them of their self-worth.

Another issued caused by the single lane closure was there was no room for the tactical team to stage and prepare should a tactical intervention become necessary. Although it would infuriate those trying to cross the bridge into Nevada, we needed all northbound traffic stopped. Not only would it prevent people from being close enough to yell their suggestions to Jacob but it would also allow an operational area for the SWAT officers to work from.

We attempted to have the police dispatcher contact the units who had yet to arrive and direct them to our staging area. Unfortunately because of problems mentioned with the radio system we were unable to reach them. Through coordinated use with our cell phones, were finally able to contact those who had not arrived and guide them to the correct location.

The SWAT Commander I worked with during this and subsequent events was different from the one mentioned in previous chapters. The former SWAT Commander was selected for another assignment. This new SWAT Commander was a seasoned lieutenant with the agency. Prior to his hiring as a police officer, he had spent many years in the military and had a great deal of experience. Although he did not have the same SWAT or negotiator experience as the previous commander, the SWAT Team Leaders he had in place were exceptional tacticians and leaders.

After the briefing, the SWAT Commander ordered all northbound traffic from Arizona stopped. He assigned the SWAT officers, including the large armored vehicle which arrived on scene, to park on the bridge to begin putting together their tactical plan.

The stopping of all vehicle traffic and SWAT officers working from the bridge was a source of contention for the Hoover Dam police chief. When he voiced his concerns to the SWAT Commander, an argument ensued. The Hoover Dam police chief explained his officers had been talking to the subject for over an hour and it was only now with the large contingent of vehicles arriving that the suspect suddenly became so animated and anxious.

In front of the group of negotiators and other supervisors present, the SWAT Commander asked, "Who's in charge here?". The police chief answered "Well, I have no jurisdiction on the bridge", prompting the SWAT Commander to declare, "Well, once you call me, I'm in charge, so I really don't care what you want." This set the tone for how the two agencies would interact. From that point forward, the police chief was reluctant to offer any advice.

The SWAT Commander took charge of the event and ordered the Hoover Dam police chief to finish handling the vehicle traffic to the bridge, adding he wanted traffic stopped in both directions. The Hoover Dam police chief explained he did not have enough resources to accomplish the task and had to request additional assistance from the Nevada Highway Patrol. This further delayed the shutting down of vehicle traffic.

As the heated discussion was taking place between the SWAT Commander and Hoover Dam police chief, I used this time to assemble the arriving negotiators, brief them with what little information I had, and make assignments.

After their discussion ended, I met with the police chief to obtain any information he had on the suspect or incident. He explained that due to his late arrival he knew little about the event. He said since he had three of his officers talking with Jacob, he would have one of them leave and meet with us. I told him if he was able to do it and if it would not cause any issues with Jacob, it would be tremendously helpful for the negotiators to hear from someone firsthand what had occurred.

A few moments later, a Hoover Dam police officer, who had been one of the trio talking with Jacob, moved away from the group and walked over to meet us at the command post. The Hoover Dam officers relayed they had limited intelligence on the suspect and that he only gave his first name was Jacob. He said they had been speaking to Jacob for over an hour.

Jacob told the officers he was depressed and had driven to the dam from Las Vegas. He said he had taken a handful of pills before walking out onto the bridge, but could not remember what type of pills they were. The officer indicated Jacob was speaking freely with them but became increasingly more agitated as he saw the volume of LVMPD personnel arriving.

With the limited information we had, we also made another observation. Jacob was a white male adult who appeared to be in his early 40s. Given his current behavior and his demographics, I believed Jacob to be a high risk for suicide. While it is arguably easy to make that assumption with the location Jacob was in, as a team we consider as many factors as possible. One factor, proven through research is middle-aged white males are one of the highest groups to commit suicide.

I made the negotiator assignments: primary negotiator, secondary negotiator, intelligence coordinator, and scribe for the event. I selected Officer Michele Iacullo as the primary negotiator. Although she was relatively new to the team, she had strong negotiation skills. In case the use of a female primary negotiator became an issue with Jacob, I picked Detective Jarrod Grimmett as Michele's secondary negotiator. He was a very seasoned negotiator and a great coach. He could also assume the primary role if a problem developed with Michele. I added a third person to assist them, Detective Joey Herring. His role will be discussed later.

As SWAT officers were getting their position ready, it afforded Michele and Jarrod a few moments to discuss their negotiation plan. They would need to find a way to positively transition away from the Hoover dam officers talking with Jacob as well as come up with themes Michele would use during the negotiation.

While Michele and Jarrod were discussing their strategy, it was a priority for the assisting negotiators to identify who Jacob actually was. We needed to obtain as much background information on his as possible so we could feed the information to Michele. We also needed to learn why Jacob wanted to die.

Within a matter of minutes, the primary and secondary negotiators had concluded their strategy discussion and were ready for deployment. Traffic had not been fully stopped and the tactical assets were still getting into position so the commander asked them to wait a little more. Having more time for the negotiators assisting with developing intelligence on Jacob was helpful.

From dealing with jumpers on other face-to-face negotiations, we learned through experience that communicating updated information to the forward negotiators is always a challenge. To help address this issue, one of the procedures implemented was to equip the secondary negotiator with a concealed earpiece on a radio channel dedicated to negotiators on scene. The earpiece allows the crisis negotiations team leader to provide updated critical information to the secondary negotiator without disturbing the primary negotiator who is speaking to the subject. When there is a lull in the conversation, the secondary negotiator can whisper the information received to the primary negotiator, who can use it as they see fit.

We had previously tried placing the bodybug transmitter on the primary negotiator, hoping it would provide us with better sound, but we were wrong. On face-to-face negotiations, it is usually easy to hear what the primary negotiator is saying. The difficult part is always hearing what the suspect says. Placing the bodybug on the primary does little to pick up the suspect's voice as they are often too far away due to safety concerns.

We have tried several other deployment options for relaying information but have not found any in particular which allow us to hear both sides of the negotiation as well as pass along critical information.

The technique which has worked best for our team is, when manpower permits, to add a third negotiator to go forward with the primary and secondary. This third negotiator is equipped with an earpiece on a dedicated radio channel and usually stays in the background. In addition to what we hear from the secondary negotiator's bodybug, this third negotiator can relay important updates on what is said. This third negotiator is also in a better position to receive intelligence updates and walk forward at the appropriate time to deliver it to the secondary negotiator. Although these updates can be given to the secondary negotiator over an earpiece, the secondary should be concentrating on the negotiation and coaching the primary.

We have used this third negotiator on several of these face to face negotiations and it has worked well. The positives of using this third negotiator are often brought up after the event by several of the negotiators during the event debriefing.

The three negotiators were ready to go forward and several negotiators were working on developing intelligence. Another obvious task that needed to be completed is debriefing the Hoover Dam officer that spoke to Jacob once relieved by the tactical officers. We had already received some information from the third Hoover Dam officer but a thorough debrief with the first responder is a must.

At 12:05 a.m., nearly an hour after SWAT and negotiators had arrived, the three negotiators loaded into the armored vehicle with several SWAT officers and moved forward. Other tactical assets were already in place. It took time for the traffic to be shut down and allow the SWAT officers to get into position.

During any face-to-face negotiation, our negotiators are trained to discuss with the SWAT Sergeant where the tactical team would like them to stand and what is the area they cannot walk past. It is critical the negotiators are placed in an area which is advantageous to the tactical team but also allows them to remain safe.

Another mandate for negotiators who work from an elevated position being forward on a jumper is the requirement for them to wear a rappel harness and be "tied off," a lesson we'd learned the hard way. To be tied off means each of the negotiators' rappel harnesses are affixed to a rope and the rope is anchored on the opposite end. Although a negotiator should never get close enough to allow a subject to grab them, this safety practice was enacted as an extra layer of precaution, as we know sometimes the unpredictable can occur.

One of the concerns for any negotiation we responded to is the transition from the first responding officer to the negotiators. If the initial officer has developed a rapport with the subject and is communicating well with them, it is not uncommon for the negotiators to assume the role of secondary negotiator, allowing the initial officer to continue the communication. When transitioning on a jumper, this practice does not happen as often since it is difficult for us to monitor any conversations between the initial officer and the subject.

Another concern when arriving on jumpers is the arrival of additional personnel and vehicles, such as armored vehicles and armed SWAT officers. On this particular case, just watching Jacob's demeanor it was easy to see he was extremely agitated with our arrival. We made a very large footprint when we arrived on scene.

Due to Jacob's obvious anxiety issues with our arrival, which was confirmed during our debrief with the Hoover Dam officer, I asked the SWAT Commander if we could keep the armored vehicle back as possible to help keep Jacob calm.

The SWAT Commander had already informed us of his plan. He directed the large armored vehicle to pull up and face towards Jacob. The heavy vehicle would provide a location for the safety ropes to be anchored to as well as provide an area behind it which the SWAT officers could stage. Additionally, the vehicle would provide some shade for the officers due to the extreme temperatures. Given the concerns I expressed, the SWAT Commander agreed to keep the vehicle back as far as they could.

At 12:12 p.m., the armored vehicle containing the negotiators arrived on the bridge. SWAT officers parked the vehicle on the furthest northbound travel lane away from Jacob. Negotiators exited the vehicle, moved forward, and made contact with Jacob. The two Hoover Dam police officers walked back to the command post and were debriefed. The handoff went as well as could have been expected.

Michele did a great job talking with Jacob. She kept her voice low and it was soothing. Jacob expressed his concern about the sudden presence of the armored vehicle and the SWAT officers. Michele handled the inquiry like a professional. She explained they were part of the team but reassured Jacob they would not approach him or do anything to him. Despite her explanation, Jacob remained cautious. He believed the SWAT officers were present to assault him and take him into custody. He yelled out loud enough for everyone present to hear that he would jump if anybody approached him.

As Michele did her best to calm Jacob down, assisting negotiators were scouring the area for any clues to help identify Jacob. Negotiators ran registration requests on every vehicle in the area and were able to locate Jacob's. They used his vehicle information to obtain background information on him.

Negotiators also searched the nearby walkways. On a path leading to the bridge, they found an empty pill bottle with Jacob's name on it. The prescription pill bottle was for anti-anxiety medication. We researched the medication and learned that if taken in large doses, the person could become lethargic and pass out. This was a huge concern.

The empty pill bottle lead credence to Jacob's earlier

claim of taking the pills before moving on to the bridge. In addition to his demographics, it also showed the seriousness of Jacob's suicidal intent.

We conducted a criminal background check on Jacob which revealed only one prior arrest for battery domestic violence. It was a crime that occurred ten years prior. He was hardly the hardened criminal type. Further research into Jacob's background revealed he was reportedly married to a woman named Leah and they lived in a home in North Las Vegas.

Eleven minutes into the negotiation, the SWAT Sergeant reported back to the command post that they forgot to tie off the negotiators. Since this was a safety concern, it needed to be accomplished. I also realized that when Jacob saw armed SWAT officers approaching the rear of the two negotiators, he would become fearful an assault had begun and would jump from the bridge.

Michele and Jarrod were wearing their required rappel harness. The SWAT officers had just forgot to attach the safety rope to it. Instead of having the SWAT officers walk up and attach their ropes, each one could take turns walking back to the armored vehicles to have the ropes attached.

The ropes needed to be attached as a precaution but Michele and Jarrod were in a safe location. Jacob remained on the outside of the bridge while Michele and Jarrod had the four-foot concrete wall separating them. While they were safe, we wanted to follow protocol and have the negotiators attached to safety lines in case a "what if" scenario occurred.

After we learned the ropes had to be attached, the SWAT Commander added that he also wanted the armored vehicle to move closer to Jacob. He told us it would limit the amount of safety rope they would have to use. The armored vehicle also had a wireless camera mounted on its roof so moving it closer and repositioning it would provide a better view at the command post.

The command post was not far from where Jacob and

SWAT/negotiators were. We could see everything that was occurring. There was also no way the armored vehicle could be moved closer to Jacob without it being incredibly obvious. Even for someone not in crisis, firing up the vehicle's large diesel engine and maneuvering it closer would cause anyone in its vicinity to be distracted by the movement.

Jacob was already anxious about the presence of the SWAT officers and the large vehicle. He voiced his concern, believing they had moved to the bridge to assault him. He also warned us that if anyone approached him, he would jump to his death.

I believe negotiating with jumpers is one of the more difficult negotiations. They have the ability to jump at any time and can verbally keep people at bay. Negotiators have to work even harder to develop trust and rapport as there are limited tactical options available. We certainly want to avoid doing anything that causes undue stress. The person in crisis sees the tactical team and crisis negotiators as one element so anything negative either disciple does can hurt the other.

I asked the SWAT Commander if he would reconsider his order of moving the armored vehicle closer. I gently explained unless there was a true safety reason, moving the armored vehicle closer to Jacob could be the catalyst to make this already frightened and agitated man jump from the bridge.

The Hoover Dam police chief, who was still standing in the command post area, overheard our conversation and echoed my same concerns. He took it up a notch, pleading with the SWAT Commander not to move the vehicle closer. The SWAT Commander answered that it was his decision and it would be implemented.

Realizing the deadly ramifications possible from this decision, I asked the SWAT Commander if we could have a few minutes to explain to Jacob what was going to transpire. We would use Michele to inform Jacob how the vehicle was only going to be moved up for safety and reassure him that it was not any sort of trick or assault.

We quickly developed a plan on how we could communicate the move so there were no surprises. I told the SWAT Commander I would telephone the third negotiator who was seated in the armored vehicle and explain the plan. The third officer would then get out of the armored vehicle and meet the secondary negotiator and again explain everything so it could be related to the primary negotiator. The communication plan does sound a bit like the "telephone game", but it was the best we threw together on the fly.

To ensure the armored vehicle did not move until we knew Jacob was aware, our plan required that after the secondary negotiator had explained everything to the primary negotiator, the secondary negotiator would give me a verbal signal to confirm Jacob was aware of the plan and ready. It required Jarrod to listen to Michele as she explained the plan to Jacob. If Jarrod believed Jacob understood and would not be adversely affected, Jarrod would raise his thumb, giving a "thumbs up" to indicate to me Jacob understood. The command post was close enough for me to easily see his verbal signal.

At 12:23 p.m., just one minute after the agreed-upon plan and without warning, the SWAT officers moved up behind the two negotiators with ropes and secured them to their safety harness. Understandably, Jacob felt as if the officers were going to assault him and became extremely fearful, squatting down and threatening to jump.

Obviously, there was a huge miscommunication issue. Michele tried to explain to Jacob that the officer was just securing a rope to her for safety but Jacob felt she was lying to him. She spent the next few minutes trying to regain Jacob's confidence. Because of the sudden SWAT movements and Jacob's agitated state, Michele had yet to explain the pending movement of the armored vehicle.

Michele took ten full minutes, talking to Jacob and trying to calm him down. He remained untrusting after witnessing the SWAT officers' movement behind her with the rope. He questioned why else she would need a rope attached to her if the SWAT officers were not planning an attack.

Michele was working from a position of disadvantage. She was trying to gain Jacob's trust and the simple act of the SWAT officers coming up behind her, unannounced, made Jacob feel he was being lied to. But this was a lone, suicidal male. Although Jacob's location was fouling traffic, the truth is, he had only been on the bridge for less than two hours. Michele had also only been talking to him for fifteen minutes. What negotiators learn and preach to others is, "Time is on our side".

At 12:33 p.m., Michele was successful in calming Jacob down but was still working on gaining his trust. Jarrod had told her of the SWAT plan to move the armored vehicle closer but she had yet to deliver the news.

Michele had yet to finish explaining to Jacob the reason they needed the armored vehicle to move closer. I could tell she was doing a fine job with her explanation as I was monitoring her communications through the bodybug at the command post. Jacob was guarded with what Michele was telling him. I had my eyes on Jarrod and he gave no signal; no thumb up.

Without reason or explanation, the armored vehicle suddenly started moving. What was happening? I knew Michele had not finished explaining the plan. Jacob saw the large vehicle moving closer towards him and began to panic. To make it worse, and a deal we had never been told, several SWAT officers were walking closely behind the armored vehicle. Jacob could see them as they approached.

They continued to slowly approach and Jacob squatted down. He nervously uttered, "Oh no. No. No. What are they doing?"

I was mortified. I asked the SWAT Commander why they were moving and he began talking to the SWAT officers over the radio. To be honest, I could not remember what he said.

All I could hear was Michele doing her very best to calm Jacob down. The damage had been done. The secondary negotiator was just as startled as I and began looking around. He knew he had not given the prearranged signal.

The armored vehicle and officers inched forward. I was not sure what he had already said into this radio but I pleaded with the SWAT Commander to have them stop. We could all see the damage their movement was doing to Jacob. He was frantic.

Briefly after my pleas I heard Jacob yelled out, "I'm gonna jump. If they come any closer, I'll jump!"

Before we could get the officers in the armored vehicle to stop, Jacob had witnessed enough. Jacob jumped.

We all watched in horror as Jacob fell nearly 1000 feet to his death. We witnessed him fall into the rocks along the Colorado River and there was nothing we could do about it. A slew of emotions flooded in. Anger and sadness were the chief ones. And I was not alone.

None of the negotiators could believe what just took place. Michele and Jarrod felt betrayed as they knew what the plan was but someone began too soon. Animosity against the SWAT Commander was beginning to form.

We conducted a short debriefing at the scene. Unfortunately, the SWAT Commander further angered many of the negotiators when he said it was opinion that Jacob simply let go from being fatigued and due to the medication he had taken. The Hoover Dam police chief attended the debriefing and was also equally upset with the commander's comments. Why did they have to move the armored vehicle? What was the urgency?

The Bureau Commander who oversaw the SWAT section during that time frame called for a formal inquiry of this incident. Interviews were scheduled with all the key people who were present.

It would take several weeks before those interviews were conducted and many weeks more before an official report was produced on this incident. In that time, a horrible twist had occurred.

The evening of Jacob's death, the Clark County Coroner's Office went to make the death notification to Jacob's wife, Leah. When he went to their residence, there was no response. Fearing something bad had precipitated Jacob's death at the bridge, officers were requested to force entry into the house.

After making entry inside the residence, officers found Leah deceased. The story quickly reached media outlets. Many believed Jacob had done something nefarious to his wife then went to the bridge and jumped to his death out of guilt. At the time of the story, the manner of death had not yet been determined.

All of the details from this incident were discussed during the interviews with the officers involved. Interestingly, the SWAT Commander reported that he had asked one of the negotiators in the command post area if the message of the armored vehicle moving had been delivered to "Jacob" and understood. He said he was told yes. I was there the entire time and stood next to the SWAT Commander. I never heard him ask.

The investigation concluded there was simply a "miscommunication" between the SWAT Commander and the Crisis Negotiation Team Leader. I never accepted that conclusion. I guess while it was possible the commander asked a different negotiator about the message delivery, I never heard it and none of the CNT members said they were asked.

It is my belief that not as much attention was given to this formal inquiry because most believed that Jacob had murdered his wife then jumped to his death. Many felt it was one less murderer the world had to live with or be forced to care for in prison.

Many months later, long after this incident had been forgotten about, the Clark County Coroner's Office ruled Leah's death as being accidental. During their investigation, they learned she had been very ill. An autopsy revealed she had suffered from chronic bronchitis and evidence the coroner discovered suggested she overdosed on an antihistamine. It is my belief that Jacob struggled with his wife's continual illness. His world completely fell apart when he found that she had died from an apparent accidental death. Being despondent, he drove to the Michael O'Callaghan – Pat Tillman Memorial Bridge and called 911, hoping someone could ease his pain. Sadly, those of us charged with helping Jacob in his time of need did not perform at our best. Jacob not only died from the fall but also died from a broken heart.

Lessons Learned:

We started this event from behind the eight ball. When we receive a request to respond to an incident, we are given an exact address or intersection. On this event, we were told to respond to the Michael O'Callaghan – Pat Tillman Memorial Bridge. This bridge is nearly ½ mile long and located in two states with numerous observation points. A specific location should have been given as it would have prevented vehicles from driving past Jacob with the sirens on, increasing his anxiety.

The radio system we were operating from at the time of this event was plagued with problems. The issues we experienced on this incident were added to the list of repairs needed. Thankfully, radio coverage for this area had been improved.

The command post was established at the top of the stairs, above a rest stop area. The area at the top of the stairs provided ample room to operate from but it was too close. It was convenient to work from this location as we could see everything as it was occurring. We could see the cars vehicles move into place and deployment of the officers. We could even see Jacob. We did not need to be that close.

The rest area at the bottom of the stairs would have

served as a better command post location. We would have been close enough to the incident but far away to remain out of the suspect's view. With the camera equipment and audio transmitters present on scene, we could have had the audio and video sent to us and remained out of the operational area. Sometimes, leaders get too close to the action which can hinder the operational effectiveness of the team.

The difference in leadership we experienced with the SWAT Commander on this incident versus the previous commander was noticed by many of the people present. It was especially felt by the Hoover Dam police chief. While it is true that only one person should be in charge during incidents like this, maintaining a cooperative relationship bears tremendous fruit. Everyone present was working towards the same goal; to save Jacob's life.

It was a mistake to not shut down traffic prior to our arrival. Whether it was a lack of manpower or a noble gesture to shut down only one lane and allow traffic to continue to flow, having cars pass close to Jacob was problematic. The three Hoover Dam officers were doing their level best to peacefully resolve the situation yet they had to contend with motorists driving by and yelling for Jacob to jump. While shutting down the traffic causes a nightmare for motorists, it is the right thing to do. In this situation, motorists had the ability to turn around and cross into Nevada, using Hoover Dam, just a few miles from their location.

We also made a mistake by deploying the two negotiators from the armored vehicle without ensuring they had safety ropes attached. I believe this was simply an oversight since we had not dealt with many jumpers. While not a viable excuse and thankfully the safety lines were not needed, upon discovering our mistake we attached the lines as our policy mandated. Unfortunately, our execution for attaching the safety lines was subpar. This was most likely due to a lack of communication. Although air time is important during a critical incident, we witnessed during this event the problems lack of communication can cause.

Without question, the biggest problem encountered during this event was the placement and subsequent movement of the armored vehicle. The Hoover Dam police chief witnessed Jacob's behavior prior to our arrival and knew bringing the large contingent of officers/vehicles was only going to exasperate the problem. Since three Hoover Dam officers were already talking to Jacob, we could have taken more time and considered the deployment of our resources. We had plenty of time to ensure we placed our assets in locations which were advantageous to the mission but considerate of the burden it would have placed on Jacob.

I understand that suspects do not control police tactics. It is the suspect's behavior we are trying to influence and if we can accomplish the same task by putting a piece of equipment in a position that is least offensive to the suspect, should we not attempt to do so?

Lastly, each team member, from each of the disciplines utilized, brings their own experiences with them. As the leader, we do not have to be the most knowledgeable in every area. We just need to be smart enough to surround ourselves with people who have knowledge in areas we lack. It was easy to see from a negotiator's point of view, and even the Hoover Dam's police chief's point of view, that the movement of officers up next to Jacob was going to have a negative effect.

This is not about questioning authority or not having respect for rank. In a paramilitary organization, we understand who makes the ultimate decisions. It is simply about considering the totality of the situation and listening to the opinions of those around you. Everyone understands leaders must take action if the suspect puts someone's life in jeopardy. Barring that, time is usually on our side.

If we take time and slow the momentum, it usually proves advantageous for a peaceful resolution.

This is a picture of the Pat Tillman Bridge, taken from the command post area, at the observation area. It shows where he jumped from.

This is a photo of the Pat Tillman Bridge. It is the center area where he jumped from.

CHAPTER 10

ALONE IN LAS VEGAS

Southaly Ketmany, a Laotian male, lived in the Sacramento, California area and had been married to Kim Reroma for nine years. They dated for six years prior to their marriage, giving them fifteen years together as a couple. Together they share two beautiful children, a boy and girl, ages nine and thirteen. Southaly is the average American male. He drank on occasion and did not use illicit narcotics. He had no real criminal history to speak of other than a few traffic violations. He also had no known mental health issues. Kim certainly did not believe he was a violent person. Unfortunately, as happens with many couples, problems developed and in 2009, the couple divorced but remained friends.

Kim believed that Southaly still had feelings for her and wanted to rekindle their relationship. She had already moved on and was dating someone else. Southaly had also been unemployed for nearly two years and was experiencing financial difficulties. All of this was likely the start of Southaly's downward spiral.

Samantha Phomphachanh said she is one of Southaly's closest friends. She said she had known him since junior high school and the two talk nearly every day. She echoed the description given of Southaly, an average man going through a difficult time in his life. She added Southaly travelled to Las Vegas four to five times per year to play poker and said she had witnessed a drastic change in Southaly in mid-June, 2013.

She explained that at that time Kim went to court and won full custody of both children and her understanding was that Kim planned on relocating with the children to Georgia and that plan had sent Southaly into a deep depressive state.

It was also when she first began noticing him act out of character. Despite Kim winning full custody of the children, Samantha said Kim and Southaly still remained friendly.

In early July 2013, Samantha said Southaly had met several friends in Las Vegas to celebrate a bachelor party. She happened to be in Las Vegas at the same time and managed to meet them at one of the famous Las Vegas nightclubs. Samantha explained that when she saw Southaly in the club, his eyes were rolling into the back of his head and when she asked him what was wrong, he admitted to her that he had taken "Molly", an illegal synthetic narcotic.

People who take "Molly", equate it to being very similar to the drug Ecstasy. That similarity is what helped make it so popular. The shocking truth is that no one knows what is contained in each "Molly" pill.

Manufacturers of "Molly" are not pharmacists. They are street dealers trying to make money. They fill the capsules with what they believe makes their supply the best so each dealer is different.

Many of the manufacturers fill the capsules with a powder form of Ecstasy, which gives the user a euphoric, almost out of body experience. The drug causes people to feel a warm, relaxing sensation, becoming friendly with those around them. Unfortunately, some street manufacturers add methamphetamine to their "Molly" mix, which can cause mixed experiences for users. What most "Molly" users agree upon is that each dealer's mix can vary.

Southaly likely found himself experimenting with "Molly" to overcome the depression he faced. Sadly, the experience he had at the bachelor party which caused his eyes to roll back in his head would not be his last experience with the drug.

On Wednesday, July 17, 2013, Southaly and several friends drove from their home in Sacramento, California and arrived in Las Vegas, staying at one of the famous resorts. On Friday, July 19, Southaly set into motion a chain of events that would forever change his life.

After checking into their hotel, Southaly and his friends visited a Vegas nightclub and stayed until the early morning hours. During their nightclub stay, Southaly allegedly took four "Molly" pills and began acting strangely; that included falling to the floor and hallucinating that he was being stabbed, yet no one was near him.

At 4:20 a.m., hotel security came into contact with Southaly and attempted to calm him down but he became combative and had to be brought into the security office. His strange behavior continued with Southaly telling the security officers, "Kill me now. Just stab me". Because of his behavior, physical condition, and admissions of taking narcotics, hotel security summoned medical help. An ambulance arrived and transported Southaly to a local area hospital. He was treated and released from the hospital that same Saturday at 11:53 a.m..

Later Saturday evening, the Henderson Police Department, in a city located just south of Las Vegas, came into contact with Southaly. They responded to a complaint of an Asian male, dressed only in his underwear, running through an apartment complex in the area of Warm Springs and Green Valley Parkway, taking off his clothes. When Henderson police officers arrived they found Southaly to be the man people called to complain about.

The Henderson officers described Southaly as appearing to be under the influence of narcotics. He was complaining of being chased by people who wanted to kill him. Southaly told the officers he was taking his off his clothes because his attackers had placed a tracker on him. The officers attempted to get Southaly medical attention but he threatened he would fight anyone who attempted to do so.

The officers conducted a routine record check on Southaly. It showed Southaly had an outstanding bench warrant for a minor offense of Basic Speed. To solve the issue they were dealing with, they arrested Southaly for the outstanding bench warrant which removed him from being a problem in the area.

Jail records were a bit unclear but it is believed Southaly was released from jail for his outstanding bench warrant sometime during the early evening hours of Sunday, July 21. Unfortunately, it would not be his last dealing with the police.

On Sunday, July 21, at approximately 10:20 p.m., Southaly again began his bizarre behavior. This time neighbors called police after witnessing Southaly knock on random doors in the residential area near Las Vegas Boulevard and Blue Diamond Road, on the south side of town. A patrol officer contacted him and issued him a warning about his actions.

Ninety minutes later, Las Vegas police received another call complaining about Southaly. Another citizen saw him stumbling down the center of Las Vegas Boulevard, the same general area he been previously contacted by police. This time he was carrying a large rock.

Patrol officers were again dispatched and located Southaly. Likely due to the volume of calls he continued to generate, as well as to help protect him from getting hurt, LVMPD officers arrested him. He was booked into the county jail for the offense of being a Pedestrian in the Roadway. Southaly spent nearly a day and a half in jail before being released on Tuesday, July 23, at 4:00 a.m..

During the morning hours of July 23, beginning at 7:30 a.m., it is believed Southaly was responsible for several additional police calls. Each of them described an Asian male matching Southaly's description and acting suspiciously. These calls for service were in the same general area where Southaly had been located and arrested on Monday evening.

On Monday, July 22, several of Southaly's friends, including Samantha, Southaly's brother Tony, and even Southaly's ex-wife, Kim, became concerned for his well-being. The trio had been told that Southaly's friends had witnessed him fall onto the floor in the nightclub. Those friends had returned home to California and left Southaly in Las Vegas.

Samantha, Tony, and Kim were worried. They were the ones closest to Southaly but he had not contacted any of them. It was not like him. They tried to call his cell phone but their calls went unanswered.

Samantha reached out to one of the friends Southaly had traveled to Las Vegas with. When asked about Southaly's last whereabouts, the friend informed Samantha he last saw him in the residential area of Las Vegas Boulevard and Blue Diamond Road. The friend said he witnessed Southaly armed with a knife and hiding behind a row of bushes. He told the friend he was being chased by people.

Samantha asked the friend why they did not call the police. The friend replied that due to Southaly's disoriented state as well as him being armed with a knife, they were afraid he might be shot if police contacted him. They assumed he would be better off if they left him on his own.

After learning about his bizarre behavior and concerned for his safety, the trio got into a vehicle and drove from Sacramento to Las Vegas. As they made the long drive the trio could not comprehend why Southaly would not contact any of them, especially if he believed his life was in danger. They arrived in Las Vegas during the morning hours of Tuesday, July 23.

After arriving in Las Vegas, Kim, Southaly's ex-wife, contacted Las Vegas police and explained the details she had. She filed a report with the police, listing him as a missing person

While filling out the police report, Kim heard a broadcast over a nearby police officer's radio. The broadcast gave information on a suspicious person who matched Southaly's physical description. Kim inquired with the police officer about the radio broadcast she heard. The officer explained the police call for service was located in the residential area of Las Vegas Boulevard and Blue Diamond. She recognized this location as the same place Southaly's friend had last seen him the previous morning.

Kim finished filing the missing person report. She also knew in her heart the suspicious person police call she overheard involved her ex-husband. Although unfamiliar with that particular area of town, Kim drove to the residential area near Las Vegas Boulevard and Blue Diamond to attempt to locate Southaly herself.

Police arrived in the residential area and began their search. Kim also arrived in the same area and conducted her own search. Neither group was able to find the man who citizens called to report on. Kim stayed in the area. She knew Southaly had to be nearby.

At 5:00 p.m., a few hours after the suspicious person call, homeowner Patrick Jordan returned to his residence located in the 9000 block of Crystal Rock Circle. His home is located in the same general residential area of Las Vegas Boulevard and Blue Diamond Road, on the south end of Las Vegas. When Patrick entered his house, he made a shocking discovery. A strange man, dressed only in underwear and socks was in, watching television.

Patrick confronted this man, a person he had never seen before. He yelled to the stranger, "Get out of my house!" The uninvited guest, later identified as Southaly responded to Patrick's request by screaming back, "Kill me!" Frightened by the encounter, Patrick fled from his own home and called 911.

Several patrol officers, including a patrol sergeant, responded to the call. Patrick explained to the arriving officers that no one except the stranger was in his home. He said he had no idea who the man was but knew when he left the house earlier in the morning, the home was locked and secured. The man certainly did not have his permission to be in the house.

The front door was standing open but was covered by a metal, mesh-screened security gate. The plan was to approach the front door to see if they could still see the suspect inside. If he was still inside, they would make entry and take the man into custody.

The group of officers arrived at the front door. Through the security gate, they saw Southaly inside. Just as the homeowner had described he was dressed only in his underwear. The officers' entry plan changed when they also noticed Southaly was carrying a large butcher's knife.

The officers immediately realized they were dealing with an armed suspect but at least had the metal gate separating them. They attempted to talk with Southaly but he refused to answer them. They established containment on the residence should Southaly try and flee and the sergeant made sure the officers were properly prepared should that happen. Officers were prepared with less-lethal devices as well as having designated officers to provide lethal coverage should the less-lethal devices fail.

Southaly was armed with the large butcher's knife but was contained inside the house. The sergeant knew the dangers posed if he authorized his officers to make entry. As long as Southaly remained inside, he was not an immediate threat to the officers. It was a classic barricaded situation.

At 5:36 p.m., the patrol sergeant contacted the LVMPD SWAT Commander and requested assistance. The SWAT Commander explained that SWAT and Crisis Negotiators were just finishing a separate callout and asked for the patrol officers to make a few additional attempts to contact Southaly. The commander instructed the sergeant to call him back if the incident could not be resolved.

Sometime after 5:30 p.m., Kim said she received a telephone call from a person who identified himself as a police sergeant. The sergeant asked her questions about Southaly including if he had any mental health issues and confirmed that he spoke English. Kim asked the sergeant why he was asking all of these questions of her. The sergeant explained he obtained her cell telephone number from

Southaly's missing person's police report. He told her he believed the barricaded person they were dealing with inside the homeowner's residence was Southaly.

Kim said she was still in the same residential area from the previous call. She had not left as she believed Southaly would still be in the area. She said after answering the sergeant's questions she drove through the neighborhoods and simply followed the trail of police cars. Through her own investigation she was able to arrive at the scene and met with the sergeant she had spoken to on the phone.

When Kim arrived she positively identified a photo of Southaly. She was also able to let the police know that while Southaly and she had been divorced for two years, he was still on her cell phone account. She told the officers that she had checked his cell phone records and confirmed he had not made any calls since Friday evening.

Police at the residence continued their attempts to contact him. He refused to speak with them. An officer asked Kim if she would be willing to assist them and speak to Southaly over the PA system in the patrol car. The officer felt that if he heard Kim's voice, he may be motivated to come out or at least enter in to a conversation with them.

Kim agreed and accompanied the officer to the front of the residence in the patrol car. She said she spoke over the PA, broadcasting to Southaly that she was present and to come outside. She reassured him she would be waiting outside for her and that he would not be hurt. There was no reply.

At 6:17 p.m., forty-five minutes after his previous call to the SWAT Commander, the sergeant again called back. The patrol sergeant explained they had made numerous attempts to contact Southaly but were unsuccessful. The sergeant again made his request for SWAT and negotiators. The SWAT Commander advised him they would be enroute.

While waiting for SWAT and negotiators to arrive, the sergeant allowed his officers to stay at the front door of the residence and continue to contact Southaly. Their plan remained intact, ensuring both lethal and less-lethal options in case Southaly exited the house and was noncompliant.

The sergeant established a command post away from the house. He moved Kim to the command post area so she could be interviewed by arriving negotiators and began to conduct the necessary evacuations.

From a negotiator's perspective:

When this call came, our team had just finished a callout in another area of town so simply caravanned to this new one. We arrived at the command post together, which seldom occurs.

While SWAT officers were assuming inner perimeter locations, we received a briefing about what had taken place. Very few details on Southaly listed above were known at the time of the briefing. That was information developed by negotiators who had conducted research at the scene.

During the briefing we were told Southaly was inside a residence which did not belong to him. The officers said he appeared delusional and dressed only in his underwear but was armed with a large butcher's knife. The officers also said he refused to speak.

As we continued our briefing, we learned Kim had reported Southaly as a missing person. Officers explained they had used Kim to try and contact Southaly over the PA system but he did not respond. She told the officers that she believed his current mental state was caused from someone possibly "spiking" his drink with an unknown narcotic. The officers told us that Kim remained at the command post and was willing to assist us.

I selected Detective Joe Pannullo as the primary negotiator. He had over fifteen years of experience as a police officer and had been a negotiator for one year. Although relatively new I believed his easy-going personality and communication skills would work well in this situation.

I assigned Sergeant Jose Hernandez as Joe's secondary negotiator. Jose had nearly seven years of negotiator experience and is also a strong coach with a proven track record of helping newer negotiators, which made him an ideal selection as the secondary. Joe and Jose are both great men who also work well together.

Additional negotiator assignments, including the intelligence coordinator, the scribe position, and the tactical liaison were also made.

Listening to what had already transpired, it was easy to ascertain that Southaly was extremely paranoid. Having the uniform police officers at the front door was likely exasperating his paranoia. We had to consider the best means of communicating with him which would offer the best opportunity to succeed.

Kim had told us that Southaly's cellphone had not made any calls since Friday and current calls to the phone went directly to voicemail. We did not believe contact with Southaly on his cell phone would be an option. Our belief was later confirmed. Southaly had discarded his cell phone during the Henderson PD incident for fear people were tracking him.

I felt the best option for initiating contact with Southaly was through the delivery of a throw phone. The SWAT officers could deliver the phone to the door then back away to perimeter locations. It would alleviate the large police presence at the front door, something not conducive to a person experiencing a mental crisis.

I did consider how the delivery of the throw phone would appear to Southaly. If he was already paranoid, a team of armed SWAT officers placing an object at the front door then backing away would certainly be uncomfortable. Although we were making an educated guess, I felt that at least trying this option was worth it. Besides, even if Southaly refused to take the throw phone, we would at least know we made the effort.

My secondary plan should Southaly refuse to accept the throw phone was to use a cell phone. We keep one in the negotiator command post which can only call one phone number, 911. All other outgoing calls are blocked. The cell phone can receive incoming calls but we are the only ones who have the phone number to it. It prevents outside people from calling in and interrupting our negotiations.

Should Southaly not accept either phone, the next option would be to use a remote PA system. The remote PA consists of a speaker which is placed near the doorway, with a bodybug attached to it so we can hear replies. The remote option allows us to speak into a microphone located several residences away so it is not as threatening.

Finally, should none of these options work, my last resort would be to ask the SWAT Commander if we could use the robot and move it to the front door. One of the positives to using the robot include the robot's camera allows the images to be transmitted back to the command post for real-time viewing. The robot is also equipped with audio and video capabilities so we can have a conversation with the suspect through it. Additionally, if necessary, the robot can be used by the tactical team to set an explosive charge for an immediate entry.

There are drawbacks to using the robot. The biggest issue with using the robot on this event would be dealing with Southaly's extreme paranoia. Even a person not in crisis would feel uneasy witnessing a robot drive remotely to their door and hearing someone speak from it. Southaly had already expressed his belief that people were after him and trying to kill him. I felt using the robot would only add to problem and wanted to reserve its use as a last resort.

I wanted to discuss the various communication ideas with the SWAT Commander. It was the same commander I dealt with previously on Michael O'Callaghan – Pat Tillman Memorial Bridge incident. Since that event our relationship had become strained but we remained professional.

After presenting the ideas, the SWAT Commander said it was his desire to have the primary and secondary negotiators speak to Southaly from behind a shield. He shared with me his tactical plan.

The tactical plan called for the SWAT officers to load into the armored vehicle with the two negotiators accompanying them. They were to drive to the front of the residence dressed in their normal tactical gear. It would also require the two negotiators to also don tactical vests and helmets, the same worn by the SWAT officers.

When they arrived at the front of the home the team would dismount. Two SWAT officers would lead the group and each carry a large ballistic shield. The remaining SWAT officers would tuck behind them. All of the SWAT officers carried pistols and several carried .223 rifles. Two of the officers each carried a single-shot 40mm shoulder fired gas gun loaded with an eXact-iMpact round for less lethal options in addition to the Tasers the officers carried. The two negotiators were to trail behind the SWAT officers.

As the group approached the front door, they were to relieve the uniformed patrol officers who were still present and trying to talk to Southaly. From behind both the shield and the team of SWAT officers, the negotiators were to yell out and attempt to make contact with Southaly. To a guy like Southaly who was paranoid and believed people were after him the communication plan would likely not be the most successful approach.

I shared my concerns with the SWAT Commander who had control of the scene. He wanted his plan implemented. His belief was that since patrol officers were already at the front door and had established a quasi-foothold, it was logical not to give up ground already gained and move back to a further position. In any paramilitary organization, the only correct response was "Yes sir", and his plan was briefed.

Joe, our primary negotiator, met with Jose, the designated

secondary negotiator and they discussed their plan to initiate contact with Southaly. Jose was outfitted with a bodybug so we could monitor the negotiation from the command post. He was also equipped with a concealed earpiece on a dedicated radio channel so pertinent information could be immediately transmitted to him which he could share with the primary negotiator.

The scribe position was filled immediately and they began documenting the event, beginning with the negotiator briefing. The intelligence coordinator prioritized and assigned duties to the team. Those who were assisting with developing intelligence learned many of the details listed above as the negotiation was progressing.

At 7:01 p.m., the plan was set into motion. The armored vehicle, with those listed in the plan, loaded up and drove to the front of the house. As discussed, the SWAT officers moved to the front of the residence behind the cover provided by the two officers carrying ballistic shields. They relieved the patrol officers at the door. Prior to leaving the command post the homeowner provided the SWAT officers with the key to the front metal screen door as well as the remote control to open the garage door.

The SWAT officers opened the garage door giving them an interior door to use as a possible entry point if needed. Eleven minutes after their arrival at the front door and creating a safe position, they had Joe and Jose exit the armored vehicle and move to the rear of their position. Once the negotiators were in position, the SWAT Commander authorized them to initiate contact.

For seven minutes, Joe began yelling out to Southaly, trying to make contact. I claim "yell" since Joe stood to the rear of SWAT team, much further from the door than the patrol officers were. He had to significantly amplify his voice to be heard. Southaly did not respond.

The manner in which Joe was attempting to make contact likely frightened Southaly. Joe and Jose were dressed in the same ballistic vests and helmets as the SWAT officers. They walked up and joined the rear of the SWAT stack, standing behind the SWAT officers carrying shields and assault rifles. In other words, they looked just like them.

The SWAT team has, and always will, have my utmost respect. They do a job that few others are capable of doing. To be effective, and safe, while doing their job, they need a great deal of equipment. The equipment, or tools, protect them and others while completing their mission.

Everything they have or wear has a purpose. Their uniforms not only show solidarity and team but project professionalism. The shields they carry and the weapons they possess are needed to protect themselves and others as well as to address specific threats.

The job of a negotiator is different. While we are on the same team and trying to accomplish the same mission, to end the incident peacefully, it usually is advantageous for the suspect to see the difference between SWAT and negotiators. I try to convince the suspect they want to talk to me, as I am there to help them. If they refuse to talk to me, they will be forced to deal with my friends. Seeing that difference helps motivate them to talk to negotiators.

As mentioned in previous chapters, it takes time to influence human behavior. It can take longer when the suspect is under the influence of narcotics or has mental health challenges.

After seven minutes of negotiations, the SWAT Commander authorized the SWAT officers at the front of the residence to use the homeowner's key and open the security gate. As a safety precaution, the two negotiators were brought back to the armored vehicle while the officers attempted to open the door.

As I heard their plan to open the gate, I was mystified. If they wanted to open the gate, why not do it before bringing the negotiators forward? If we brought the negotiators forward to talk, did anyone really believe they would be able to reach a peaceful resolution in seven minutes?

The opening of the gate proved more problematic than anticipated. Each time the SWAT officers approached the metal screen door, Southaly came out from behind an opened interior door and simply held the lock, preventing the officers from turning it. The SWAT officers could see that Southaly was still armed with the butcher knife but he never spoke a word to them while at the doorway.

Each time they put the key in the lock, Southaly would emerge, hold the lock and prevent the officers from turning it. As they were trying to open the door, SWAT officers asked Joe to speak over the armored vehicles PA system to try and reassure Southaly the officers were only there to help him.

Joe did an admirable job. He spoke in a reassuring voice, trying his best to convince Southaly to come outside and that he would be okay. As Joe spoke, the SWAT officers tried opening the metal screen door five different times. Southaly's presence of mind could be debated but the SWAT officer's actions of trying to unlock the door only hurt the negotiator's efforts of persuasion. After the fifth attempt the gate opening tactic was abandoned.

As stated, the SWAT Commander is in charge of SWAT tactics and negotiator efforts. While he does not need anyone's approval prior to making decisions, had he asked myself, anyone on the Crisis Negotiation Team, or even the team psychiatrist who was present at this event, we would have both advised him that using the key to attempt to open the gate would only fuel Southaly's paranoia. The attempt would also the hurt the trust the negotiators were hoping to instill.

At 7:29 p.m., just minutes after the officers stopped trying to open the gate, Joe and Jose were brought out from the armored vehicle and placed back to the rear of the SWAT stack again. I felt bad for them both.

Joe was again asked to yell out to Southaly and try to engage him in dialog. Joe and Jose both understood how difficult the request would be. Southaly was exceptionally paranoid and there was a SWAT team at the metal screen door. As a voice was yelling to remain calm and claiming that everything will be okay, a group of armed men were trying to get into the house. Not the most ideal situation. Joe and Jose never questioned their assignment and went right to work, attempting to make contact with Southaly.

As Joe was attempting to contact Southaly, we looked at what we could provide him to assist Joe in his efforts. I asked one of the negotiators to contact Kim and attempt to obtain a TPI tape recorded message from her. The patrol officers explained to us during the briefing that they had used her to speak over the PA. Since we were not present when this happened we did not know what she had said. I felt a message from someone whose voice he recognized and cared for, one which would convey love, hope, and reassurance, could help Joe establish contact with Southaly.

Obtaining a TPI tape recording is not as easy as it sounds and can sometimes be time-consuming. The person often needs to be coached on what to say. Left to their own accord, people have a tendency to make statements they think are helpful but can actually be counterproductive to the negotiating process.

We first interview the TPI subject and learn what is important to the subject in crisis. Using the information gleaned, we often draft a script the person can simply read.

After interviewing Kim we learned that Southaly's children were one of the most important things to him in his life. Kim also again explained her closeness with Southaly and her willingness to help him. The negotiators prepared a script for Kim to read into a tape recorder. In my opinion, they applied just the right amount of finesse. The following is their draft:

"Southaly it's Kim. I just wanted to let you know that I'm out here and that I'm worried about you. Please come out. The police will not hurt you. They just want to make sure that

you get the help that you need. I'm begging you, (Southaly's son's name) needs you. (Southaly's daughter's name) needs you home to take her out for pedicures and the kids miss your drive-in dates. I'll be out here waiting for you and will be by your side through this whole thing. Please come out and talk to me. You will not be arrested. Again they are just going to take you to the hospital make sure you get the help you need. The kids love you. I love you. I'm here. Please come out."

The portion of the TPI about Southaly not going to jail and only transported to the hospital was a subject that I discussed with the incident commander prior to the negotiators moving forward. The incident commander has the ultimate decision as to what happens with the suspect after the incident is resolved. On this event, if we were able to get Southaly to walk out on his own accord, the commander was okay with allowing him to receive mental health treatment. This does not preclude them from seeking criminal charges at a later date.

It is a good practice for the Crisis Negotiation Team Leader to meet with the incident commanders on these events to learn their intent and how much "wiggle room" we have. If they are adamant the suspect will go to jail, so be it. That is information we need to know so we can work it into the conversation. If the incident commander is open to allowing the suspect to be transported to mental health in lieu of being immediately arrested, that opens up additional avenues for us during our negotiations.

On this particular incident, although Southaly had caused several police calls for service, and by legal definition he committed a burglary at the homeowner's residence, the core issue was his mental health, although likely induced from narcotic abuse. While some may disagree, if convincing Southaly that he would not be arrested and only be seen at a hospital allows this incident to be resolved without any use of force, it is certainly a "win". In Las Vegas, it still allows us to file criminal charges on him when he is released after his seventy two hour mandated hold and evaluation by a physician. The incident commander for this event authorized a mental health evaluation resolution.

After the negotiators were moved back up to again attempt to contact Southaly, I assessed the work they had done and if there were any improvements we could make as a team. Joe was doing a great job, he just needed to be afforded the time necessary to make a difference. Jose was also providing tremendous assistance to him as his secondary. I also believed Kim's TPI tape would help Joe with opening the lines of communication. In short, I thought the negotiators were doing exactly what they were supposed to be. Not only were two of them forward making their best attempt at establishing contact, but the rest of the negotiators were developing additional information which would help the team effort.

Communicating with Southaly was not going to be an easy task. In negotiator speak, Southaly was known as a "non-responder." This category implies exactly what the name indicates - that the subject refuses to respond back. The vast majority of the time, while they might not respond back verbally, the subject in question hears what is being said. The objective is to find a "hook" or "trigger" that will pique their interests and cause them to enter into dialogue. From past experience, we found that those in mental crisis will take longer to respond as we have to gain their trust. Using Kim's TPI was one way we were going to try and establish Southaly's trust.

At 7:45 p.m., the SWAT Commander wanted to know how much longer it was going to take to obtain the TPI tape. The negotiators were working as fast as they could. Before they could get the tape, they had to work to calm Kim down who was rightfully worried about a man she still cared about.

The commander also voiced he did not feel that Joe was making a difference and wanted to know what my plan was.

I responded that Joe had been speaking for less than thirty minutes and was still trying to gain Southaly's trust. I said I would find out the status of the TPI tape and as soon as it was completed, I would make sure it was delivered to us quickly for our review of it.

The SWAT Commander said that since this person was not responding, there was no time for us to review the TPI tape. He wanted the tape sent directly forward to negotiators. I respectfully reminded him that our protocol was for all TPI tapes to be returned to the command post and reviewed prior to deployment.

All TPI tapes are reviewed so that the Crisis Negotiations Team Leader and SWAT Commander, who have been monitoring conversations occurring with the subject, can listen to ensure the tape covers the points needing to be conveyed. It is not uncommon for the tape to be reviewed, suggestions made, and have the tape sent back for revisions.

The SWAT Commander overruled the procedure. That is his prerogative. He ordered the tape be delivered directly to Joe and played for Southaly to hear. It became very clear to me that the SWAT Commander was growing impatient and wanted more progress to be made.

My attempts to reason and explain other negotiator options to him were in vain. I ensured his orders were carried out but internally, I questioned why the rush. Joe had only been talking for thirty minutes, not to mention the gate opening tactic he was forced to contend with.

I made sure the negotiators knew the tape was to be sent directly forward. After doing so, the SWAT Commander again questioned the effectiveness Joe was having as the primary negotiator. While I agreed there was room for improvement, as there always is, I felt that he was doing an admirable job. He also had a fantastic coach helping him. I conveyed my opinion to the commander.

After giving my opinion, the SWAT Commander took a cell phone call from one of the SWAT sergeants who was with the team at the front of the house. At the conclusion of the phone call, the commander told me he said he wanted to see Joe make more progress. I told him as soon as the TPI tape was delivered, Joe would play it and see if this elicited a response from Southaly. We could reevaluate Joe's progress after the tape playing.

With the time constraints that had been placed on us, neither Joe nor Jose would be given the opportunity to listen to Kim's TPI tape prior to playing it. They were being asked to play it blindly, without knowing its message. They would be forced to create themes on the fly after they heard it played aloud for its first time. It was unfair and did not set Joe up to be successful.

Before the tape was even delivered, the SWAT Commander informed me he wanted a change of negotiators. The change was to occur as soon as the TPI tape was played. Why? This negotiation was moving along just like hundreds before it.

Truth is, at the thirty-minute mark, we usually have not even begun to influence the suspect's behavior. The SWAT Commander knew this.

I felt like the commander was projecting animosity towards me. I knew he had not been happy about comments I made during the formal inquiry of the earlier Michael O'Callaghan – Pat Tillman Memorial Bridge incident. During the inquiry, I was asked my opinions and I gave them. Some were not very favorable. I also believed we were two professionals. We should be able to give our opinions, even if conflicting, yet still work together and accomplish the mission.

After hearing my plan, to play the TPI tape and evaluate Joe's progress as he moved forward, the commander made his decision. He said he felt like we were "spinning our wheels", and wanted the change. Immediately after the tape was played, Jose was to assume the role of the primary negotiator. Although I disagreed with his decision, I ensured it was implemented.

Just prior to 8:00 p.m., the TPI tape was completed and sent forward to the negotiators. I contacted Jose and explained the plan to him. He knew as soon as the tape was played that he was immediately to take over as the primary negotiator.

Prior to the playing of the tape, I asked the SWAT Commander if we could send the remote PA forward and use it amplify the playing of the TPI message. We have used the remote PA on previous calls to play taped messages and had good success. It would help ensure Southaly heard the message.

The commander said that due to the additional time it would take to set up the remote PA, he wanted the message played over a hand-held megaphone. He believed it would achieve the same amplification. Unfortunately, we had never used this technique before. Jose would not know how far back to hold the tape recorder from the megaphone to ensure a clear message was broadcasted. The SWAT Commander wanted the message played in this manner and it was implemented.

At 8:01 p.m., Jose took over as the primary negotiator and Joe rotated into the secondary position. As instructed, Jose played Kim's TPI tape over the hand-help megaphone. When he first played it, he held the recorder too close and the message was muffled. Jose played the message a second time which was clearer.

In the command post, we could hear the taped message being played over the bodybug. I listened to its message and the negotiators did a stellar job in obtaining it.

At 8:04 p.m., less than two minutes after Kim's message was played the second time, an order was suddenly given which ended our negotiation. Without warning, the SWAT Commander ordered over radio for the tactical team to make an emergency entry into the house. All the negotiators present, including myself, were stunned. There had been no change from the residence and no reports from the SWAT officers to indicate a threat. Why did he order the entry?

We were all glued to the radio. We listened for an update, hoping it would explain what had just occurred. Less than a minute after the entry was initiated, a broadcast was transmitted over the tactical channel. The officers said shots had been fired and the suspect was down.

I was not the only confused person at the command post. As I looked around, other negotiators, support personnel, and even the team psychiatrist had puzzled looks on their faces. We all knew Jose was appointed as the new primary negotiator and was to begin making contact after the TPI was played. As soon as Jose had started talking, the SWAT Commander called for the emergency entry. We all were stunned as it appeared the entry order was given without any basis. Surely, something must have happened that were unaware of, which caused the emergency entry order.

Inside the house, SWAT officers had begun attending to Southaly, who had been struck by the officer's gunfire. Emergency medical personnel were also brought into the house to attend to Southaly's injuries. They stabilized him and he was transported to the hospital with life-threatening injuries.

After Southaly was transported to the hospital, I met with Joe and Jose. They were still at the front of the house. They both looked completely dejected.

Jose took a deep breath and asked me what happened. I did not have an answer for him. I had no idea what caused the SWAT entry. Jose said he was confused. He said he was told he would have a chance to try and talk with Southaly but as soon as the tape finished, the officers made entry. I tried to reassure him but he was obviously disappointed. I knew we would gather and conduct a debrief so I hoped the answers to his and all of our questions would be answered.

The SWAT Commander first met with the tactical team to make sure they were okay. Anyone who has been through a critical incident and the use of deadly force knows the array of emotions that can come with it. He was extremely supportive of his team and his presence helped put them at ease.

After spending some much-needed time with the SWAT officers, the commander had the negotiators assembled where we would learn what took place. It would be our condensed form of a debriefing.

During the quasi-debriefing, we learned that a SWAT sergeant was one of the officers positioned near the front of the residence. He witnessed what took place each time the officers attempted to unlock the door and how easy it was for Southaly to defeat their entry plan.

Based on what he saw, the SWAT sergeant called the SWAT Commander on the phone and discussed an alternative entry plan. This was the telephone call I witnessed the commander receive while we were in the command post.

The tactical plan called for an entry through the rear sliding glass door of the residence. They would initiate the plan while they had Southaly at the front door. After the second playing of Kim's TPI tape, Southaly was at the front door, and the plan was implemented.

When the commander was told over the tactical radio that Southaly was at the front door, he used that window of opportunity and gave the command to enter. SWAT officers positioned in the backyard of the residence used a blank fired from a shotgun round to shatter the sliding glass door. As soon as the glass began to fall, officers made entry.

As the SWAT officers moved inside the house, they also deployed a K-9 in front of them. It was their hopes the dog would bite and hold onto Southaly, who was carrying a hammer in one hand and the large butcher knife in the other. It is believed that since Southaly stood still, the dog did not bite him.

SWAT officers approached Southaly and issued him verbal commands to drop his weapons. He ignored the verbal commands and was shot one time in the rib area with a 40mm eXact iMpact less lethal round. The round did not incapacitate him. Another SWAT officer fired a Taser round at Southaly but it apparently missed.

After being hit with the less lethal round, Southaly began to charge the SWAT officers, swinging the knife and hammer towards them as the officers backpedaled. Southaly got to within three feet of one of the SWAT officers, who ran out of room to backpedal.

The officer who had missed with the Taser shot saw the threat Southaly posed, transitioned to his handgun, and fired several rounds at Southaly. A second SWAT officer, who also identified the threat and was armed with a .223 rifle, fired several rounds. The gunshots hit Southaly and he fell to the ground.

SWAT officers immediately summoned for medical assistance. A tactical paramedic, who was embedded with the team, immediately began providing lifesaving care.

Southaly yelled out the officers' present, "Let me die. You guys are too late." An additional paramedic came up to assist and Southaly began fighting the paramedics. The tactical paramedic asked for assistance, saying Southaly needed to be subdued with a Taser. Several SWAT officers used their Taser and Southaly stop fighting. The paramedics finally stabilized Southaly and he was transported to the hospital.

Soon after our debriefing, we learned Southaly succumbed to his injures at the hospital.

Because deadly force was used, and this incident ended in the death of the subject caused by officers from our agency, two different investigations were initiated. The first investigation would examine if the use of deadly force was justified. The second internal investigation would examine the entire incident to see if proper procedures were adhered during the event and if best case practices were followed.

Investigators completing the use of force investigation

easily determined the two SWAT officers were justified in shooting Southaly. He was attacking them with both a knife and a hammer and other attempts to stop him had failed. The district attorney also agreed with this finding.

The internal review was much more contentious.

Many of the questions raised during the review centered around the SWAT Commander's decision making. He felt he had exercised due diligence. It was pointed out that the negotiators were given less than an hour to persuade Southaly to exit the residence. The commander believed Southaly's presence at the front door gave him the window of opportunity they needed for the rear entry tactical intervention

The SWAT Commander explained another large part of his entry decision relied on the information he received from his telephone call from the SWAT sergeant. The SWAT sergeant told him, and reiterated during the internal review, that "negotiations had completely failed". While certainly entitled to his opinion, this was something that should have been discussed amongst the leaders present, especially since there was ample time.

In my opinion, expecting a significant change in behavior from a person who is either under the influence of narcotics or is experiencing a mental crisis in less than an hour is extremely unreasonable.

Prior to this weekend, Southaly had never committed any criminal violations other than minor traffic offenses. As a team, with input from the CNT psychiatrist, we had assessed him as having an extremely low propensity for violence. It was clear Southaly was experiencing extreme paranoia and was not in a clear presence of mind. His recent drug use and life stressors exasperated his condition.

Although Southaly was armed with a butcher knife and a hammer, he was alone inside a residence. He was not hurting anyone, was not destroying any property, and had not made any threats since the uniform patrol officers first arrived. In fact, he never uttered a word. This was simply a lone barricade and time was on our side.

There is little doubt that once SWAT and negotiators arrived on scene, the event was rushed. While there were no guarantees that we would be able to successful in persuading Southaly to leave the residence peacefully, being given less than an hour to accomplish the task was exceptionally unreasonable.

Prior to the events which that occurred that weekend, Southaly was known to be a fun-loving, law-abiding father who had recently come upon some tough times. He had lost his job, was divorced from the woman that he loved, then lost custody of his children. Given enough stressors, any strong person can reach their breaking point.

Southaly's life had hit its lowest point. He needed professional help. His choice to use mind-altering narcotics undoubtedly exasperated the problems. But in his time of need, he needed a team of professionals to help him walk through his missteps and bring him to some semblance of normalcy. To accomplish that task would take time.

When SWAT and crisis negotiators arrive on an event, they work together as a team. They have a common goal of resolving the incident peacefully. They succeed and fail as a team.

In this event, the team members from each discipline performed admirably, demonstrating their true professionalism. Unfortunately, the same cannot be said for of the leadership components of both the tactical and negotiation teams.

Lessons Learned:

Anytime SWAT and crisis negotiators are sent to an event life has usually turned chaotic for someone. The person in crisis has exceeded their normal coping mechanisms. A team approach, using both trained tactical and crisis negotiators, has proven highly effective at peacefully resolving most incidents. To be successful, reliable communication has to be established and the point of view of the suspect has to be considered.

The many challenges Southaly experienced have been discussed. Because of his drug use and mental statement, it is questionable he even knew where he was. It was easy to see Southaly was in crisis. He was the subject of several incidents prior to this event. He was inside a stranger's residence armed with a knife and dressed only in his underwear. He refused to communicate with anyone, except for his initial statement of "Kill me" to the homeowner. How we tried to communicate with Southaly would be key to our success.

Several communication ideas were presented. Having two negotiators attempt to contact him by yelling from behind a group of SWAT officers is not the most ideal. It is hard to establish trust when yelling from behind a group of armed men, dressed in their same attire. That same group of armed men who are standing at the threshold of the residence, constantly trying to unlock the door as negotiators cry out to trust them and remain calm. They are certainly conflicting messages. One of the other communication ideas should have been explored.

There are many times a tactical team is able to take a suspect into custody without the assistance of crisis negotiators. They are well trained and very effective. If negotiators are included into the equation, barring an emergency, they should be given a reasonable amount of time to be effective.

When the negotiator began speaking, he was given less than seven minutes before the order was given to use the key and open the door. It violated any type of trust Joe was trying to establish with Southaly. The negotiators have to be given ample time to influence the person in crisis. Southaly was not doing anything to warrant an entry. He was not hurting himself, others, or even damaging the residence. Time was certainly on our side.

Even with the benefit of hindsight, I believe Kim's tape was an effective way of encouraging Southaly to begin talking with us. How the tape was delivered and played could have been improved upon.

The idea of obtaining a TPI is only one part of the equation. Who provides the tape, what they say, how they say it, and when it is played are all equally important. We have a procedure for the use of the tapes. The tapes are always reviewed in the command post before they are sent forward to ensure the message they contain is consistent with what is being said to the suspect by negotiators.

After the tape is reviewed, approved, and sent forward, the negotiators have the opportunity to review its contents so they know how to best introduce it. These tapes are never longer than ninety seconds so the review process is not time consuming.

In this event, neither review was done. It was speculated the review was skipped in the interest of time. That is a dangerous precedent. The person providing the TPI could have the best of intentions but if they say something counter intuitive to what is being discussed, it could set the negotiation process backwards. The person in crisis is more apt to listen to and believe the person they know on the tape versus the newly introduced negotiator. That is why it is imperative the message is consistent.

The order given for the change in negotiators is still baffling. Jose had much more experience than Joe but that was a moot point. I listened to what Joe said. What he said and how he said it was spot on. Unfortunately, according to the formal interviews, the SWAT sergeant did not have the same opinion and he shared his opinion with the SWAT Commander. This began the breakdown at the leadership level.

The SWAT Commander, SWAT sergeant, CNT leader, and CNT psychiatrist present all have years of leadership experience. Barring an emergency, the team has the benefit of time to discuss various plans. The beauty is, no one person has to be all knowing on all subjects. That is the strength of the team. We have the expertise of others to draw from. I think it would be easy to conclude that making the entry decision on this event, without the input from others present, especially a mental health professional, was a mistake. It was predictable the type of reaction Southaly would give. If asked, the professionals would have provided their opinions, which could have assisted in the decision-making process.

Making entry into a residence of a known armed suspect, who is believed to have a diminished mental health capacity, is dangerous. Southaly had already vocalized he felt people were trying to kill him. A group of armed men flooding into the house likely reinforcement his views. It was very predictable, given Southaly's behavior, that he would fight back if he felt threatened.

Although Southaly alone put himself into this position, as a team, we could have made a better effort to resolve the situation peacefully. Southaly's actions cost him his life. Unfortunately, his actions also caused several SWAT officers into a deadly force confrontation. That is something those good men will have to live with for the rest of their lives.

I obtained this picture from a report on the internet titled "Das Report Southaly Ketmany 081914". It was posted by the Clark County District Attorney's Office in regards to the officer involved shooting and the DA's Office ruling on it. The picture shows the front of the residence and where negotiators spoke from.

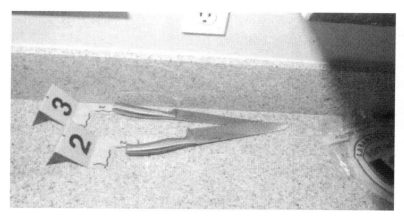

I obtained this picture from a report on the internet titled "Das Report Southaly Ketmany 081914". It was posted by the Clark County District Attorney's Office in regards to the officer involved shooting and the DA's Office ruling on it. The picture shows the two knives Southaly was armed with.

I obtained this picture from a report on the internet titled "Das Report Southaly Ketmany 081914". It was posted by the Clark County District Attorney's Office in regards to the officer involved shooting and the DA's Office ruling on it. The picture shows one of the Xact Impact rounds SWAT officers fired at Southaly.

CHAPTER 11

CNT CONCLUSION

So many people have used the following statement that it almost sounds cliché but it is one of the truest I can make; it was a privilege and honor to be a member of the Crisis Negotiation Team for 18 of my 30-year career, with the opportunity to lead the team for ten of those years. The only reason I left was due to my retirement.

During my 18 years, I responded to just over 1,000 barricade, suicidal, or hostage situations. We were successful at the vast majority of them but we did experience some losses. The losses will forever stay with those of us who gave our best effort to save their life. Although the losses were due to the person's own decision to end their life, it meant a family would never see that loved one again. Those of us tasked with trying to find a peaceful resolution share in the loved ones' pain.

To work with a group of men and women who hold dear the value of another's life that they are willing to give up so much of their own is something few people may ever understand. While they volunteer to be part of the CNT and are paid when they respond to an incident when they are off-duty, no one on the team does it for the money. And what money they do earn for responding to events never makes up for all they miss out on. They get out of a warm bed at 0300 hours on a cold winter night or respond to an event in the middle of a Las Vegas summer day at 120 degrees. Money cannot be a motivator to do this type of job.

During my time as a negotiator, I have been called out on nearly every holiday imaginable. From literally cutting into the Thanksgiving turkey to opening gifts with my children on Christmas, I have left my family during some of the most joyous moments. I have left them at movie theaters, restaurants, and at school events, forcing them to find a way home, all to help a stranger. I could have never taken the assignment had I not had the love and support from my wife and three sons. While they supported me, I did miss a great deal of important events that I can never get back. I wish I could say this was something only I experienced but sadly it holds true for every negotiator, SWAT officers, and others who respond to support these missions.

The men and women who make up the Crisis Negotiation Team have saved countless lives. For those who have done it, there is no better feeling. But we can never rest on our laurels.

It seems the amount of people who need help through a crisis situation is increasing. This of course is only magnified by the number of military veterans who are in dire need of help without the adequate amount of resources to assist them. To add to this problem, criminals appear more violent than ever. This means that Crisis Negotiation Teams, SWAT/ Tactical teams, and other supporting units have to train to ensure they have the very best skills to accomplish whatever is thrown their way. We must reach the level of preparation that should it be our own family member in distress or held hostage, that we feel confident that no team other than our own is more capable of handling the incident.

The people who make up the Crisis Negotiation Team will always have my utmost admiration and respect for the incredible job they do. They epitomize the Latin motto, "Servitas Vitate"; To Save Lives.

This picture was taken by Lane Swainston and given to me. It is a picture of the LMVPD Crisis Negotiation Team.

A friend took this photo. It was of me and my squad at a Shop With A Cop Xmas event.

This was a picture of me, taken by an unknown LVMPD photographer and placed on a LVMPD calendar and distributed throughout the police department. It shows me as I speak on the phone during an actual hostage negotiation. Also shown is Rod Jett, the then SWAT Commander.

AFTERWORD

FOREST THROUGH THE TREES

There was one topic I had considered including in the book but, as I sat down to write it, the wounds were too fresh, so I left it out. Since it has been just over a year and a half, and the wounds have slowly begun to heal I wanted to discuss it in hopes that it will allow someone to get the help they need. The topic is that of Post Traumatic Stress Disorder (PTSD).

PTSD is a condition many relate to military personnel but it also affects police officers, firefighters, medical personnel, and a litany of other people. In its simplest definition, people forced to see or deal with certain traumatic events can be scarred from their exposure. I have been to some of the most horrific crime scenes and exposed to police use of deadly force incidents which have had a profound effect on myself and those around me.

Living in Las Vegas, home to Nellis Air Force, we have witnessed countless airman, soldiers, marines, and other servicemen who have come back from deployments significantly different than when they left. We have responded as negotiators to deal with servicemen who have barricaded themselves or were threatening suicide after facing the myriad of difficulties associated with those suffering from PTSD. Having responded to countless events like these, I felt I was pretty good at recognizing the signs and symptoms of PTSD as well as being able to help those suffering from it. Unfortunately, when it is closest to you, you sometimes fail to see the forest through the trees.

My son Nathan is a Marine. When we watched him leave for his first overseas deployment in 2009 from 29 Palms Marine Corps base, he was full of vigor. We were so proud of him and his service to his country. When Nathan came back though, he was different. It was hard for me to put my finger on it, but he was just different.

In 2012, Nathan left for his second deployment. We again watched him depart but for some reason I could not help but think about the mild changes and wonder if they would continue. My worries were right. He returned unharmed, or so we thought. We were just thankful to have him home as unfortunately many families did not have the chance to experience our same joy.

Nathan returned to the civilian world, got a job, and life moved on. Days turned to weeks and weeks to months. I noticed Nathan could become irritable much more easily. He lost his job but explained it was management's fault. This happened again at his second job. He started drinking more. Stronger drinks and more of them.

Nathan bought a café-style motorcycle and rode fast. He went rock climbing at the nearby Red Rock Canyon without using safety gear. It was all right there in front of my face but I was too blind to see it. He was purposefully engaging in dangerous behavior. He was crying out for help but I didn't listen. All I saw was the poor behavior and was constantly on him about improving himself. Obviously, it was simply his bad-boy ways. There couldn't be anything wrong with my kid. I couldn't have been more wrong.

On August 23, 2015, just ten days after his 26th birthday and a night of binge drinking, my son took his own life. We were in shock. Nathan was a strong spirited man. I never thought someone as strong as he would ever find himself in the situation he was. Why didn't he tell me he had these issues? Two weeks later, I retired from the police department.

My retirement brought many quiet moments. Time to reflect upon the past. It was during these quiet times I realized Nathan had been crying out for help the whole time. I was likely too judgmental, preoccupied, or foolish to see. My quiet moments can be tortuous, playing the awful game of, "If I would have only…"

I spoke privately and separately with several very close friends of mine and confided my struggles. As close friends often do, they listened intently, non-judgmentally, and allowed me to cry. All things I wish I would have done more for my own son. But they also helped me understand I cannot change the past.

Our loss of Nathan has caused a tremendous open wound for me and my family. My wife, Shalene, along with our boys, Patrick, Devin, and Tyler, have all been devastated. The best advice I have received is to not be so quick to close the wound. To allow the wound time to air out and heal. I have tried to follow that advice and it is the main reason I chose to write this. I have also vowed to never make the same mistake twice; to constantly pay close attention to my family and friends and always remind them how much I love them.

There are countless people currently dealing with PTSD and the demons it can bring. I implore each of you to watch out for your friends and loved ones. Take time to learn the signs and symptoms of PTSD and be there to support those in need. Those suffering need us more than they can ever explain. Lastly, never miss an opportunity to hug your loved ones. We'll never know when it may be our last.

I love and miss you Nathan.

*Photos taken with my late son, Nathan, which includes
my other boys, Patrick, Devin and Tyler, with me.*

READ THE STORY BEHIND O.J. SIMPSON'S LAS VEGAS CONVICTION!

ROOM 1203 is the true story of the convoluted and bizarre events surrounding a violent armed robbery of a sports memorabilia collector in a Vegas hotel. On that night, O.J. Simpson put an exclamation mark on his spectacular fall from the height of Hollywood's glamour and glitz to a shadowy world of scams and schemers in Sin City. Written by the lead detective assigned to the case, the book provides details, insights and facts not previously reported, as well as the investigation that pieced the crime together and landed an arrogant man who believed he was above the law in a Nevada prison.

Read More: **http://wbp.bz/Rm1203**

Another Great Historical True Crime Read From WildBlue Press

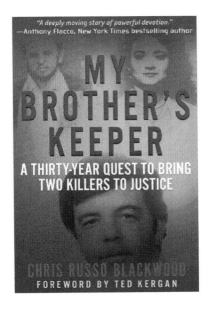

The moment he found out his brother was missing, Ted Kergan launched a relentless effort to bring two suspected killers—a teenaged-prostitute and her much older grifter boyfriend—to justice and find Gary Kergan's remains. Little did he know his quest would consume a fortune and take thirty years to reach a dramatic conclusion. MY BROTHER'S KEEPER is "a tremendous story of love and murder, faith and tenacity." (Steve Jackson, New York Times bestselling author of No Stone Unturned)

Read More: **http://wbp.bz/mbk**

Another Great True Crime
Read From WildBlue Press

For four years in the 1980s, a killer, or killers, stalked Virginia's Tidewater region, carefully selecting victims, sending waves of terror into the local community. Now, father-daughter true crime authors Blaine Pardoe and Victoria Hester blow the dust off of these cases. Interviewing members of the families, friends, and members of law enforcement, they provide the first and most complete in-depth look at this string of horrific murders and disappearances. The author-investigators peel back the rumors and myths surrounding these crimes and provide new information never before revealed about the investigations.

Read More: **http://wbp.bz/aspecialkindofevil**

More True Crime You'll Love From WildBlue Press

RAW DEAL by Gil Valle

RAW DEAL: The Untold Story of the NYPD's "Cannibal Cop" is the memoir of Gil Valle, written with co-author Brian Whitney. It is part the controversial saga of a man who was imprisoned for "thought crimes," and a look into an online world of dark sexuality and violence that most people don't know exists, except maybe in their nightmares.

wbp.bz/rawdeal

BETRAYAL IN BLUE by Burl Barer & Frank C. Girardot Jr.

Adapted from Ken Eurell's shocking personal memoir, plus hundreds of hours of exclusive interviews with the major players, including former international drug lord, Adam Diaz, and Dori Eurell, revealing the truth behind what you won't see in the hit documentary THE SEVEN FIVE.

wbp.bz/bib

THE POLITICS OF MURDER by Margo Nash

"*A chilling story about corruption, political power and a stacked judicial system in Massachusetts.*"–John Ferak, bestselling author of FAILURE OF JUSTICE.

wbp.bz/pom

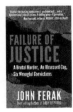

FAILURE OF JUSTICE by John Ferak

If the dubious efforts of law enforcement that led to the case behind MAKING A MURDERER made you cringe, your skin will crawl at the injustice portrayed in FAILURE OF JUSTICE: A Brutal Murder, An Obsessed Cop, Six Wrongful Convictions. Award-winning journalist and bestselling author John Ferak pursued the story of the Beatrice 6 who were wrongfully accused of the brutal, ritualistic rape and murder of an elderly widow in Beatrice, Nebraska, and then railroaded by law enforcement into prison for a crime they did not commit.

wbp.bz/foj